THE OBSERVER
GOOD GARDENING GUIDE

Water plants make an attractive setting for an old stone balustrade.

Previous page: A flourishing water garden with irises and decorative rushes.

THE OBSERVER
GOOD GARDENING GUIDE

Joy Larkcom, Arthur Hellyer, Peter Dodd

Introduction by Christopher Lloyd

CONTENTS

First published in Great Britain in 1983 by
Webb & Bower (Publishers) Limited

This edition published in 1984 by
Octopus Books Limited
59 Grosvenor Street, London W1

Designed by Vic Giolitto

Picture research by Liz Strauli

ISBN 0 7064 2083 7

Printed in Italy by A. Mondadori, Verona

The information given in this book applies to the
United Kingdom and countries in the northern
hemisphere. However, all the information can be
applied to the southern hemisphere provided that
the sowing times are advanced by six months. Thus,
if in the text you are advised to sow seeds in April,
you must sow them in October in the southern
hemisphere. Many parts of South Africa and
Australia have much higher temperatures than
those experienced in the UK and in these areas
plants described as half-hardy or even as cool
greenhouse specimens may prove to be hardy out of
doors. On the other hand, parts of the tropics and
sub-tropics may be too hot for some of the plants
mentioned to grow satisfactorily. Delphiniums, for
example, rarely germinate in hot conditions, unless,
like the Californian and Persian species, they are
native to warm parts of the world.

PREFACE

The Observer Good Gardening Guide began life as a major series in the *Observer Magazine* which ran over twelve weeks in the spring and summer of 1981. The British passion for gardening was our starting point. The series was conceived as a guide for both beginners and more experienced gardeners to provide a sound understanding of flowers, vegetables and fruit over the gardening year. What we tried to emphasize was that what counts, above all, in gardening is a sympathetic response to the living material.

We asked Arthur Hellyer, who has written countless articles and books on all aspects of gardening, to write the flower section; Joy Larkcom, a lively writer on the more unusual vegetables, to lure readers into growing their own; and Peter Dodd, a lecturer at Wye College in Kent, to provide the inspiration for fruit. Christopher Lloyd, the Magazine's distinguished gardening writer, was consultant editor of the series and contributed stimulating introductions each week. These have been put together at the beginning of the book to make a fascinating personal preview of the wide range of subjects covered by the authors. Many of the photographs were also especially commissioned, taken by Pamla Toler, whose imaginative eye invokes some striking and unexpected images.

It is this expertise and enthusiasm, so successful in magazine form, which are now brought together in this book.

Polly Pattullo
OBSERVER MAGAZINE

A spectacular laburnum walk in full flower.

INTRODUCTION

THE ART OF GREEN FINGERS

Care and understanding is what creates a display like this: antirrhinum 'Madame Butterfly' (top) and salvia 'Scorpio' (below).

Never was the saying 'well begun, half done' more truly applied than to the craft of planting. This is where those mysterious digits, green fingers, come in. Green fingers belong to people who have an understanding of living material.

Even a seedling annual with a total life expectancy of only six or eight months needs sympathetic consideration from the start if you are to be proud of it in its prime. The secret of success is to raise it from seed so that it never receives a check, either from lack of water and nutrients or from competition with neighbours; and then to move it to its flowering site so that it doesn't notice what has happened. That is to say, you shift it with enough soil adhering to its roots to avoid disturbing or breaking any but the smallest of them, and then bed it down with plenty of water.

Some annuals are generally designated as non-transplantable. They have no fibrous roots, only a single, fleshy tap-root that is easily broken. Most members of the poppy family fall into this category. With plants like this you can sow the seeds direct where they are to flower so that they never have to be transplanted. Alternatively, sow two or three seeds in each of a number of small pots, reduce them to one when the seedlings have germinated and finally turn out each survivor so that the root-ball remains absolutely intact and there is no disturbance whatsoever; then transfer to the flowering site.

The latter is a very simple form of containeriza-tion, and the method used for raising plants up to the size of young trees so that they can be loaded onto your vehicle from a garden centre and installed in your garden at any time of the year. If the ground that is to receive them is suitably fertile and in a good physical condition – nice and crumbly, and neither sticky-wet nor dust-dry – such plants stand the brightest chances of succeed-ing. But if, in a haze of good but woolly intentions, you poke a plant into a dry hole not large enough to receive it and spatter it with a dribble of water that hasn't a chance to reach its roots, then, talk to it kindly, croon lullabies to it as ever you may, it will die and serve you right. Your fingers are brown; go live in a sea-view flat at Bournemouth.

Container-grown plants are comparatively expensive, and although their numbers increase from year to year, by far the largest quantity of trees, shrubs and herbaceous plants are still lifted at the correct season and distributed for sale from the nursery with bare (or moderately bare) roots. The two best seasons for doing this are March-April and October-November. The spring rush is particularly frantic because a few warm days will bring everything into leaf, and once there are young leaves about demanding extra moisture, plants become more prone to drying out and less easy to establish.

So when you receive a new bare-root tree, shrub, rose bush or herbaceous perennial, your first concern should be to keep its roots moist right up to the moment of interring them. Never, for instance (and I've seen professional gardeners who should know better doing this over and over again) lay a plant on the ground by your side as you make its hole ready, leaving its roots to be dried by sun and wind. Keep them in a plastic sack till the last moment or cover them with a piece of dripping-wet hessian.

If you know your soil is liable to flooding arrange for adequate drainage in advance. If, on the other hand, you are planting near a wall, remember that this is the driest spot. So plant a little way – say 30–40cm (12–15in) – in front of the wall rather than hard up against it and work an extra-large quantity of water-retentive humus into the soil before planting. Peat, garden compost, farmyard manure, leafmould and many other bulky organic materials are suitable. If the subsoil, more than a spade's depth below the surface, is clayey or in some other way unpleasant, remove it and replace with good topsoil.

Thorough preparation of the ground before planting makes all the difference, especially where a tree with a long expectancy of life is in question. Nurseries usually sell trees with their full quota of unpruned branches because these look impressive. Roots are less so and get chopped back pretty mercilessly for ease of handling. You should prune the branches back so that their bulk matches what's left of the roots, otherwise the latter will be unable adequately to supply the former with water and nutrients. Any broken roots need trimming to give a cleanly cut surface that will heal quickly.

Make sure the soil is worked in around the roots when planting, and then tread firmly on them. If staking is necessary, don't tie too closely against the stake as a certain amount of stem movement will allow the trunk to develop a taper (like an upturned carrot) which gives it strength to withstand stormy winds when eventually it has to stand unaided.

Perhaps the most important point in aftercare, apart from an adequate water supply, is to keep competitive grass turf well back from any tree or bush that is not being grown in cultivated ground. All weeds are greedy but turf is worst of all.

Annuals provide a welcome opportunity for a yearly change in the border. Here annuals are used formally at Hampton Court.

GREENHOUSES FOR WORK AND PLAY

Whatever may be in flower at the time, the basic smell of growing plants, assailing you as you push open the greenhouse door, is peculiarly satisfying. It sets your nose twitching in appreciation. Here is a place to dally. There may be no heat on – just a little sun and a tang of freshness from an open ventilator. You feel relaxed and can work happily at a bench that doesn't make you stoop. Tidying plants, removing encroaching weeds (don't let that wretched little trifoliate oxalis with the yellow flowers take a hold), top-dressing and rearranging pots – these and the more basic tasks of sowing and pricking-out all go forward harmoniously in the greenhouse's pleasant ambience.

To get the most from a greenhouse, I think one needs a clear notion of its primary purpose. Is it to be a workshop or is it to be a special kind of living-room – a conservatory, in fact – where the plants and their appearance *in situ* are what count?

In the workshop greenhouse we can overwinter tender plants that will spend their summer months outside. We can bring on plants for house and conservatory; we can raise seedlings and root cuttings, grow tomatoes, melons, cucumbers, aubergines – a nectarine or two (peaches will do outside). Looks will count less than productivity.

The conservatory, which preferably is an extension of a living-room, can be devoted entirely to plants that are at their peak. Permanencies should be handsome evergreens that look smart at every season, as do, for instance, many of the tall-growing begonias. Much of its contents will be made up of plants having a temporary season, and these can be moved in and out accordingly. To this end it is a great advantage to have a service greenhouse nearby. What I'm really saying is that, ideally, you should work towards having two greenhouses, or divide one greenhouse into two sections, one for work and one for 'play'.

A certain amount of utilitarian ugliness is permissible in your workshop greenhouse, but in the conservatory a beady, vigilant eye will forestall your leaving around hideous equipment such as red plastic watering cans and hoses of virulent green. Appearance counts for everything here. Pots of a dull, neutral-coloured or black surface are far to be preferred to the all-too-prevalent, shiny red-brown kind. Manufacturers always tend to equate bright with beautiful. It is for the customer to set standards.

In whichever kind of greenhouse your plants are growing, their health must be your overriding concern. To have the right atmosphere in which they (cacti and other xerophytes apart) can flourish, the air must be humid, yet not close or stagnant if this can be avoided. This is not too easy to achieve the whole year round. In winter, humidity can be taken for granted; it will be too high – likely as not – and at low temperatures, destruction of soft-leaved plants by the grey mould fungus, *Botrytis cinerea*, which mantles them with a sort of grey fur coat, can be very serious.

Prevention is better than cure. Allow a through current of fresh air whenever the weather permits. Don't water too often. The best way is to let your plants get rather on the dry side before giving them a thorough soaking that will work right through their pots and last them for several days, perhaps a week in certain weathers. Water the pot soil rather than the plant itself, leaving as little water on the foliage as you can and, by the same token, water in the morning for preference, as foliage will then have its best chance of drying off before the night-time period of slowest evaporation. Life will be made easier if some heating is available, but it is surprising what can be achieved by keeping the temperature just above freezing point.

In summer, the problem is to keep the temperature down and the humidity up. It is at this season that I am most conscious of the unhappy atmosphere in many greenhouses – a lifeless, brittle feel. The fact that half their contents have been moved out does not help, because a luxuriance of vegetation means a great area of leafage to hold and give off moisture.

Slatted benches do not retain moisture. Solid benches are preferable by far. If you go in for capillary watering, they will be solid and covered in moist sand anyway, but if you have a varied collection of plants all with different watering requirements, the capillary method may give you insufficient control. In that event, benches covered with a 2.5cm (1in) layer of grit are more satisfactory.

An earth floor under the benches can be colonized by shade-loving plants which themselves act as a reservoir of moisture in summer. If the whole floor is concreted over it will be harder to keep up the humidity in summer, when you must also allow as much ventilation as possible. The door may be left open for weeks on end. Shading can be arranged with blinds or a sprayed-on wash. This will be obligatory if you are growing large numbers of ferns or orchids that would otherwise scorch ; smaller numbers can usually be grouped in the shade of taller plants. Given abundant reserves of moisture from water-holding surfaces, whether leafy or of earth or grit, it is possible to do without

shading altogether, but if you have trouble from red spider mites turning the foliage of peaches, primulas, daturas and other soft-leaved plants to parchment, it is a sure sign that the atmosphere is insufficiently humid.

And it is the humid atmosphere that imparts that pleasurable greenhouse smell and feel which we noted at the start. Please the plants and we shall please ourselves.

An amateur gardener's small but luxuriant greenhouse. The air must be correctly humid, yet not close or stagnant, to aid the well-being of your plants – and to create that distinctive greenhouse atmosphere.

MAKE READY FOR SUMMER

Spring is the most maddening and disappointing season of the year. That is not the fault of spring, of God, of the Fates or of anyone except ourselves. We expect too much.

We want sunshine, a rising thermometer, a hushed absence of wind that allows us to hear contented bees (our contentment, anyway, if not theirs) on pear blossom wafting its own sickly sweet but ever welcome scent. The first swallow is an event to chalk up, the first cuckoo likewise.

Not every year – but just once in a while – all these wishes do materialize simultaneously and then our country is as wonderful to be in as anywhere in the world. I say 'our country' rather than 'our gardens' because it is the countryside that is especially beguiling. Woods full of primroses, anemones and early purples do still exist in abundance, notwithstanding the depredations of 'flower-lovers' near populous roads. You need only take to your feet for a few minutes to find them or, for that matter, to look out of the train window at the railway cuttings as you are whisked through the countryside.

In our gardens we can only gild the lily at such a time. This we do with a will. Give a chap a mixed boundary hedge of hawthorn and other indigenous elements and, ten-to-one, he'll either grub it up and replace it with a low suburban wall to open up the prospect or he'll plant the hedge bottom between the garden and the road with a row of prize-size daffodils.

'Fair daffodils, we weep to see you fade away so soon,' will – with Herrick's – be his next lament, and the daffodil leaves will be tied into carefully made thumb knots. In this way we civilize our environment.

We must have our daffodils, of course, but they do need discretion in their choice and placing. A rough hedge looks best with a rough bottom from which dog violets, white stitchwort and blue granny's eyes can peer out. Wild daffodils will be in scale here, too, their diminutive leaves scarcely noticed when the flowers have faded.

The big daffodils, if you *must* grow them – though they really look much more in scale in a large town park or public garden – can be grouped in a shrubbery among hybrid rhododendrons. Even there, you'll have their leaves to worry about at least until May is finished.

Spring is still not too late for preparation. We should be planning ahead with special reference to late summer and autumn when the countryside has become heavy, tired and dusty and the garden itself an oasis. Too concentrated a burst of colour and blossom in the spring garden is almost inevitably followed by the glumness of out-of-season cherry trees and dark-leaved rhododendrons or the scruffiness of decayed aubretias, daffodils and bluebells.

Spring bedding, though, is fine. It is temporary and will make way when finished for summer's gauds. And the same applies to tubs and window boxes. Today's tulips and double daisies will be tomorrow's petunias and geraniums.

I would put in a plea for spring bedding. Do it wholeheartedly and make your splashes look as though you really meant them. Group your wallflowers closely, the leaves of each plant touching its neighbours, instead of dotting them weakly about with an infilling of no less weakly dotted bulbs. Group these closely too. A clump of ten or twenty-five tulips behind a thick cushion of blood-red or cloth-of-gold wallflowers will look far more effective than dots of the one scattered among spots of the other.

Likewise in tubs, troughs and boxes; no earth should be visible when their contents are in full bloom. If you can't afford to do this kind of bedding well (you can if you raise most of the plants yourself and look after the bulbs so that they can be used again and again), then be content

with some less vivid but more permanent substitute.

Heathers are all very well in their way and many will still be flowering in April but they hardly contribute to the freshness of the season. In borders of mixed shrubs and hardy perennials, on the other hand, you can already be revelling in the fresh young foliage of such plants as delphiniums, day lilies and peonies while interplanting the more permanent of them with tulips, hyacinths (especially good among the pink shoots of peonies) and Crown Imperial fritillaries. As the bulbs wither away, so their presence will be masked by a surge of new growth among their neighbours.

If you always think about what's coming next you will never be in the position of those who will soon be exclaiming: 'The spring garden is finished!' – by which they mean that their garden (apart from the statutory bed of roses) is finished for the year. April is the flow tide sweeping us forward to May, June and July. The water is still cold – but time is on our side.

Left: Spring flowers, like these daffodils, look their best in natural surroundings.

Right: Wallflowers, tulips and wistaria. Don't be cautious, make a bold splash of colour by close planting.

BEWARE THE FLORISTS' ZEAL

Florists, the men and women who have cultivated and improved flowers through the centuries, have tended to concentrate on certain genera for which they could create the greatest demand. These florists' flowers, as they are known, have been developed by the hybridization of a few species and the continual selection from further crosses of new forms.

The florists' standards of excellence have undoubtedly brought many benefits. Roses, for instance, could never have achieved their fantastic popularity if they still resembled their remote and modest ancestors. But the florists' zeal in the pursuit of flower power has often resulted in disastrous side effects. These are sometimes of a material kind, such as susceptibility to disease, or of an artistic nature, when the end product has become so bloated that new standards have at last started a trend in a different direction.

The flower-arranging movement of the past twenty years has played an important part in this counter-revolution. Gladioli on offer were all, in the quite recent past, of the brilliant yet top-heavy, large-flowered types that win prizes in local flower shows. But they make awkward plants to manage. In the garden they must be staked; picked for the house they sway and lurch ungovernably unless stuffed into a narrow chimneypot-shaped vase.

Yet the gladiolus should be an ideal cut flower and to satisfy this demand the far less clumsy 'Butterfly' strain and the still more elegant 'Primulinus' hybrids with hooded flowers have been bred. Even more to my taste are the 'Nanus' gladioli which can be treated as hardy perennials in some gardens, if planted in sheltered borders. Flowering early, in late June and July, they grow only 60cm (2ft) tall and need no support. As they leave a gap after flowering, the best way is to interplant them with low-growing perennials like catmint. The reason they need shelter is because their foliage appears in the autumn and suffers from frosts if severe. The carmine red 'Robinetta' is one of the most vigoroous and quickly spreading. It contrasts well with 'The Bride' and 'Albus' which are pure white.

Some of the wild gladiolus species, notably the green-flowered *G. tristis*, are deliciously night-scented and these have been hybridized a little giving us, for instance, 'Christabel', which has retained the scent: however, it is seldom offered and we need to take more interest in these lovely

Japanese flower arrangers place the emphasis on delicate blooms, varying their sizes for dramatic effect.

bird-like flowers. A satiety of florists' flowers often makes us wish to return to the charms of the original species although, alas, some of these have now vanished, and there is an urgent necessity for a gene bank of flower species as there is for cereals.

The florists' chrysanthemums are an example of man's desire for double flowers. Single, daisy-type chrysanthemums rarely win the highest awards in shows and the same can be said of dahlias. With both, increase in flower size has inevitably been accompanied by increase in leaf size so that the charmingly cut leaves of dahlia and chrysanthemum species have been replaced by coarse leathery foliage utterly devoid of charm. These vigorous chrysanthemums attain a most inconvenient height, but man's inventiveness has devised a dwarfing hormone spray that can keep them at the height of pygmies without reducing their flower size. Luckily for sanity there is an insatiable demand from the flower arrangers for spray chrysanthemums with long stems that have not been disbudded, and hence have small flowers.

We still have too few hardy chrysanthemums of a convenient height and reasonably early flowering that we can safely grow in our flower borders as permanencies. They tend to die out and so need lifting and overwintering under cover.

The florists' cyclamens were all developed, without hybridization, from the one species, *Cyclamen persicum*, which grows wild on the littoral of the eastern Mediterranean, usually in the dry-wall stone terracing between cultivated patches. The Arab name for it means gazelle's horns and you can see why, in the elegance of the unimproved plant with its slender, spirally twisted upward-pointing petals. The scent of this wilding is delicious and powerful but is apt to be lost almost as soon as improvement by selection starts. Colourful cyclamens for pot-work have been developed at London University's Wye College in Kent, retaining the elegance and scent of wild *C. persicum* (which is white with a magenta ring around the mouth); but they have not yet caught on with the public.

As for the rose as a florists' flower, there is a significant pointer in a recent publication by the Royal National Rose Society: *How to Grow Roses* by Jack Harkness. The longest chapter of twenty-six pages is on pests and diseases and their control, the next longest, on pruning, having fourteen pages. It is a sad fact that the more popular a flower becomes, the more difficulties attend its cultivation. The answer, surely, is not to specialize. Grow a wide range of plants and you'll sleep soundly at night.

UNLIKELY TALES

There seem to be an exceptional number of superstitions about vegetables. For instance, that sprouts must have had a frost on them before they are worth eating: in fact, if frost has any effect on them it is as a destroyer. Not long ago I found I'd grown a sprout variety, new to me, that was already in perfect condition in August. It was excellent in every way and so free of slug damage as to be scarcely recognizable as my own product. And really sprouts with roast lamb in high summer are every bit as welcome as they will be in the winter. And you can eat your own newly made rowan jelly with the same course, for the fruits of *Sorbus aucuparia*, the mountain ash, should not all be left to the birds.

Cucumbers, the outdoor ridge kind, grow best on my compost heap, sharing it with mushrooms which always turn up here, even though the heap (but not its site) is changed annually. Certainly, ridge cucumbers don't look as good as those grown under glass and they curl up into all kinds of awkward shapes, but they taste best of all and that is surely what counts above everything. Since they develop in super-abundance I make a lot of soup with them and deep-freeze some of it. The only hot cucumber soup recipe (it can also be eaten cold) in my books is one given by Katie Stewart. I have had to adapt it fairly heavily, for here again we are up against some curiously ingrained superstitions, notably that the pips and skins of cucumbers make them bitter. But well-selected strains, and especially the F1 hybrids, are not bitter and the whole cucumber can be eaten. So when Katie Stewart tells me first to skin and de-pip them, then at the end to add some green colouring matter, I think she's a little misguided.

By the same token, the fashion for seedless cucumbers – the all-female, unpollinated kind of which Joy Larkcom tells us – is misdirected. Cucumbers are less than half-grown when we eat them and their seeds are soft, sweet and altogether innocuous. That other practice of reducing raw cucumber to a pulp with salt so that all its crispness is lost, also strikes me as dubious. A gardener is supposed to eat his produce so I see no reason for holding my tongue on these culinary issues.

Anyway, the most exciting and also the most enjoyable salad I've ever eaten was mixed salad beautifully packaged by Joy Larkcom. She identified the ingredients for me over lunch – there were seventeen of them and although some were, individually, alarmingly hot, their heat was absorbed by the cool salad elements when it came to ingesting them. Incidentally, Joy Larkcom's recent paperback *Salads The Year Round* is a refreshingly original piece of work.

A long, tapering carrot may appeal to the judges when laid out for exhibition, but it has no practical value. The length means that you have to cultivate your ground exceptionally deep, and that's not funny on a clay soil. The taper ensures that the carrot will snap prematurely when you're scraping it in readiness for cooking. Stump-rooted carrots are far more practical in every way and the same remarks apply to parsnips. To create a parsnip for exhibition you have to make a deep hole with a crowbar, getting it into a parsnip shape by circular leverage and then filling this cavity with special soil. Fun's fun, but when the end product is a monster for which there isn't room in your kitchen let alone in your family's bellies, things have gone too far. And unless you're nuts on winning prizes don't grow any leek with a name like 'Prizetaker'. Huge and coarse, its size is won at the expense of flavour.

There seems to be an English tradition that parsley should be curled and mossy. I'm all in favour of that when I'm growing it as a bedding-out plant for display, but otherwise would plump for the plain-leaved parsley that's used on the Continent every time. Its delicious parsley flavour is far stronger. Last year I also grew turnip-rooted parsley for the first time, sown in June. This was a great success. After using its leaves all through the autumn and up till Christmas (Constance Spry has a recipe for parsley soup that I return to many times) we ate the roots – a lovely contrast to parsnips, artichokes, carrots and other roots, when cooked with oxtail. They say you can use every part of a pig except its squeal and I felt I'd had similar value from my turnip-rooted parsley.

Above left and left: Vegetables grown for exhibition have a different up-bringing to most – and amateur gardeners (unless you're a giant leek specialist) should steer clear of growing for size. Far better to have stumpy carrots like 'Early French Frame' than long, tapering and impractical ones.

Right: People wake up to the prospect of summer when the buds of the apple trees suddenly unfold in May.

ON THE BLOSSOM TRAIL

Hot strong sunshine and cold north-easterly winds with night frosts are standard ingredients in May's book of recipes. There are foretastes of summer in this spring month. You suddenly realize that the midday shadows are really short and that they are being cast by trees in leaf.

And such leaves. Horse chestnuts are surely the most dramatic in the way their foliage, limp and drooping at first like the undried wings of a newly emerged moth, quickly expands in a huge canopy of brilliant greenery – itself only the setting for a knockout display of blossom. What other flowering tree can compare with it ? Few private gardens can contain such monsters, alas.

But it is not necessary to own in order to enjoy. The season of garden-visiting is in full swing and there are blossom trails through Kent and the West Midlands for those who like to drive about the countryside in the warmth of a well-heated car,

insulated against biting winds and hail showers. The light between storms is never so brilliant nor the blossom more dazzling than when seen against a towering cloud castle.

In fact, however, a single fruiting apple tree in your own garden is likely to be a more beautiful object than all the carefully pruned, regularly sprayed but basically mechanical units that comprise the commercial plantations, impressive though these are in their way.

Pruning is necessary in order to contain the size and regulate the cropping of a tree, but an unpruned specimen develops its own personality. An unpruned 'Bramley's Seedling', for instance, will build into a large tree, as apples go, and for a few days its opening and newly opened blossom is as bright and fresh a shade of pink as you could wish to see on any ornamental *Malus*. Its fruits, albeit not highly coloured, will hang in gorgeous ropes in the autumn and those you pick and save will supply you with the best-flavoured, finest-textured cooked apples that there are to be had, from September till the following June, given cool but natural storage.

That's not a bad all-purpose record even if your *laissez-faire* non-pruning tactics do result in occasional years when there is no blossom or crop at all. On the other hand, in bumper years the ground will be decoratively strewn with a carpet of fruit that will regale blackbirds, redwings and

fieldfares right into the new year. There are few more entertaining home-made spectacles than a gang of greedy yet highly competitive blackbirds, as busy seeing each other off as feasting themselves. An earlier, non-keeping apple like the August-ripening 'Beauty of Bath' will attract hordes of wasps, and it has the further disadvantage of posing as a tasty fruit while actually being barely edible; but it makes a beautiful little tree, and its fruits are a treat to look at before and after falling.

Queen wasps are seen on the wing in May more than at any other season and they have a strange predilection for the blossom of *Cotoneaster horizontalis*. Some people have a mania for catching and killing them at this stage, but I doubt whether their efforts make a ha'p'orth of difference to the success or failure of the wasps' breeding season. Torrential rains in June, when new colonies are being established and may be flooded, seem to be far more effective wasp controllers. And anyway, if you do nothing about them until their nests are discovered objectionably close to your dwelling, you can comfort yourself with the thought that wasps do a great deal of good in controlling harmful insects and their larvae, which they feed to their own young.

Aphids always build to large and sometimes alarming populations in May-June. Their predators and, still more, their natural parasites will control them in time and I never, for my part, bother about them on my roses apart from giving these, together with bush fruits and tree fruits, a five per cent tar-oil wash during the winter.

But there are cases where immediate action with a suitable insecticide is essential. For instance, when your wall-trained morello cherries become infested with black fly and again when (not if, because they always do) they start on the developing blossom buds on your honeysuckles. The display on these can be completely ruined if you do nothing, the flower buds remaining green and becoming puffy and distorted without ever recovering. And if you notice black aphids on an ornamental spindle – species of *Euonymus* – spray this, not only to save its own foliage but because the insects will later migrate from spindle to broad beans, globe artichokes and many other crops.

There are many anxieties at this time of year, not least for the young foliage on such as hydrangeas and early-flushing rhododendrons, but it is a month full of excitement and activity. To catch the scent of wistaria blossom, as you take breath from your labours, is a reward for all those dour winter months of waiting.

BITES OF THE BEST

Some of the most luscious fruits that we grow outdoors can be grown more easily in southern European countries and then imported, but for this purpose they must be picked unripe whereas with your own fruit you can wait for the perfect moment, then let it fall into your mouth.

The kind of white-fleshed peaches that we grow in England – 'Peregrine', for instance – are anyway far juicier than the yellow kinds that are almost invariably offered in the shops, excellent though those are in their way. I'm sure the peach-fed pigs that are (said to be) raised in Canada and New England must likewise enjoy the idea of being made tastier by partaking of this ambrosial fare.

Whereas peaches can, in sheltered, warm conditions, be grown as free-standing bushes, an apricot in England really must have a wall. With its great vigour and the fact that it cannot be pruned on the renewal system like peaches and morello cherries (their fruited wood being entirely replaced by young shoots of the current season), the apricot is not so easily trained and needs plenty of space, but what a delectable fruit this is when eaten fresh and naturally ripened. As juicy as a peach too, and more easily eaten because the fruit divides into two so cleanly and the stone drops out.

Nectarines, alas, are tough-skinned outdoors and don't make much size. Given just the extra

Above: The white-fleshed peach 'Peregrine' – far juicier than the yellow varieties.

Left: The time to protect your figs from scavengers is when they turn from green to purplish-brown.

protection of cold glass, they will excel themselves but that makes them expensive. Still, at their best they're more transporting even than peaches or apricots.

Figs are best of all, for those of us who dote on them when they are green. This is an easy outdoor crop if you garden in the south or east. The less you prune them the more they fruit, so a fig needs and deserves space, whether trained to a wall or free-standing in a sunny corner or courtyard. It is also an ornamental plant. Even in winter its stems are a pleasingly pale grey. One reads *ad nauseam* (it's the one piece of misinformation that everyone remembers about figs) that their roots must be confined if they are to fruit freely. This is quite unnecessary and likely, on the contrary, to cause unproductive starvation, unless you remember to feed and water generously. Then they'll make good pot plants. Otherwise, the best policy is to plant where there is space enough for a bush to develop without needing to be butchered and then to let it get on with its job unassisted. Mind you, black-birds, starlings, earwigs, squirrels and even rats all adore figs, not usually waiting till they're ripe, so country gardeners have plenty of competition.

To protect figs, I use plastic lettuce bags, the kind in which you buy lettuces in shops. They are perforated and so the contents do not become over-humid and rot. If you find this is still happening, snip the lower corners of each bag away before adjusting it and this will drain any rainwater that has seeped in. The shape of a fig seems to be tailor-made for having a bag fixed to it. Nevertheless, having enclosed each individual fruit, avoid placing any weight or strain on it by twisting a wire stem-tie on to the supporting branch.

A routine that I find works well is to combine a bag-fixing with a fruit-picking session every third or fourth day (according to the weather). Put your bags on to fruits that have just started to change colour from green to browny purple. In three or four days' time they'll be dead ripe, nearly always splitting their skins longitudinally at this stage (my mouth waters as I write). So you can remove a bag and straightway fix it on to another fruit. I have never found that fruits picked prematurely continue ripening off the tree. They should be left till the last possible moment.

There are two schools of thought on how to eat them. I like to peel mine from the stalk end, banana-wise, and eat from the top down towards the bulbous base which is the juiciest part of the fruit. Or, using the stalk as a handle, you can eat from the bulb upwards and not bother too much about the skin, which is quite thin and palatable at the base of the fruit anyway.

Mulberries need picking straight off the tree and eating on the spot. They should be very nearly black before consigning them to your mouth. Although the birds will be at them from late July, the ideal stage is seldom reached before early September. Most people unfamiliar with them get the idea that the mulberry is a horribly sour fruit because they tackle them when merely red. They are always sharp but stimulatingly so at the right moment. The lower branches of a mulberry will hang almost vertically. These are the easiest for us to reach and the most awkward for the birds, so we both get our share.

The mulberry is a beautiful tree and that, on a more manageable scale, is also the medlar's particular asset. An old medlar is one of the most picturesque features you can have in a garden. The brown fruits, each with an enormous eye, are quaintly attractive too and the foliage turns to glorious shades of yellow and warm orange-brown in the autumn. Watch out for and remove hawthorn suckers that may mysteriously appear from the bottom of your medlar tree. Medlars are commonly grafted on to hawthorn stock and if this is allowed to take over you'll lose your medlar.

RUNNING RELAYS IN THE BORDER

Whereas the majority of the flowering shrubs appear at their best in late spring, our flower borders reach a later climax in July and we can, with a bit of organization, extend this season at both ends. June flowers must be chosen so as not to leave nasty scars of dereliction later on. Such in particular are flamboyant lupins, flag irises, delphiniums and peonies.

Lupins always look dreadful after flowering, whether you cut them back – subsequent foliage is invariably mildewed – or whether you merely remove their seeding spikes. You may care to try the technique I adopt of treating them as biennials. Sow seed each spring, line out the seedlings for the summer, plant them where they are to flower in the autumn and discard the plants after flowering, at the end of June. They can be replaced with late-struck dahlia cuttings or with annual seedlings sown in May and brought on in pots or boxes.

Delphiniums can be treated in the same way. From an April sowing they usually flower well in September-October and then again in June, after which bid them farewell. Peonies loathe disturbance but you can grow a late-flowering clematis or an everlasting pea (*Lathyrus*) behind them, and train its shoots to thread their way through the peony clumps and over their supports.

The rhizomes of the iris require a good baking in the sun, so irises should never be masked and it is better to set a bed aside for them alone; somewhere that can be enjoyed in its season yet ignored when the irises turn shabby.

However keen you may be on growing a wide range of plants, it is very important to do some massing for effect. Otherwise, your border will be spotty and, in the aggregate, confused. Oriental poppies provide a marvellous splash in late May and June and they need never become a liability. Without detriment to the plants you can cut them to the ground the moment they look tired and interplant them with dahlias or cannas.

Phloxes are a powerful border element from early July onwards, with the bulk of them peaking in early August. They are a mainstay among border perennials for those who garden in a cool, wet climate (terrific in Scotland) or on heavy soils. If the spent flower heads of the earlier flowering kinds are removed, the plants will often carry a second crop in September. This is more likely to happen in the south, where the warmer climate allows time for bonus flowerings. Dead-heading will similarly extend your border's season when applied to many other perennial flowers like *Campanula lactiflora*, *Helenium* 'Moorheim Beauty', *Salvia nemorosa* (*S. superba*).

Some of the best rent-payers are plants with a tremendously long flowering season that need little or no encouragement. Many of the cranesbills are outstanding in this way, especially the chalky pink *Geranium endressii*, excellent in sun or shade; the cheerful magenta 'Russell Prichard', which flowers from May till autumn, spreads into great pools over paving or climbs into its neighbours if taller than itself; and *G. wallichianum* 'Buxton's Blue', which has the same sort of habits but starts two months later.

In a small border, always beware of plants with a brilliant but short season that quickly become passengers. Such is the early, July-flowering *Lychnis chalcedonica*, and yet I rate its domed heads of brilliant scarlet flowers highly. Also, the beautiful azalea-like flowers of the Peruvian lily, *Alstroemeria ligtu* hybrids, in shades of pink, apricot and crimson, but just a mess from late July onwards. One solution is to plant a late developer in front of them that will grow up and conceal them when, but only when, they have gone over. One of the most obliging is the 2m (6ft) *Verbena bonariensis*, with heads packed with tiny purple flowers. Its season starts in late July and carries on till October. Although it grows so tall I always have some at the front of my border because it is so stemmy that you can see through it if you want to, and really a border that is carefully graded by height is a bit of a bore, like someone who is overtidy in the house.

I have written only of herbaceous plants, so far, but my own borders are mixed and include, for variety of habit and length of season, bulbs (starting with snowdrops), annuals, tender bedding plants and, most importantly, shrubs. These last contribute bulk and solidity with a greater air of permanence than is in the nature of herbaceous plants. It is also a good place for shrub roses, those having a double season being especially valued.

The organization of a mixed border requires thought and quite a lot of work; but this is interesting in itself, and nothing is more satisfying than to achieve a result that arouses admiration from friends and visitors whose appreciation you value. The best results always have an appearance of ease and relaxation. That is the art of being professional and is something the amateur can well develop, given enthusiasm, energy and an eye for what looks right.

Flowers massed together, like this splash of oriental poppies, provide a focus. Cut poppies down as soon as they fade.

SIZING UP THE FUTURE

The tree lupin (*Lupinus arboreus*) – a short-lived shrub – is a good species to plant in a seaside garden.

Trees and shrubs tend to occupy more space than other garden plants. They are also harder to remove. This point becomes especially significant to retired people who have settled in their last home. They do not, as their strength declines, want to become increasingly dominated by some monster which they are decreasingly capable of controlling or demolishing.

We need to be sure of enjoying value from what we acquire. Of course there'll be mistakes. Equally, our tastes will change and the plant that once satisfied us will cease to do so. There's no cause for resentment in that, but it is certainly worth pondering your choice of trees and shrubs.

How long, for example, in any year will they provide pleasure? If only for a week of blossom, as is the case with many ornamental cherries and crabs, that is a poor return. So, also, if they colour brilliantly – but briefly – in autumn, and scarcely attract our eye at other times. You need a very large garden to accommodate plants such as these. But if they flower well *and* colour up in the autumn and, perhaps, also have a pleasing shape or colourful, nicely textured bark, then we're getting somewhere.

Although I often do it myself, I think it is unwise to choose shrubs seen at a flower show, unless you have a fair idea of their background story and potential. Choose rather from gardens where you can see how a plant performs over a period. At a show, they are caught at their perfect moment and may not, indeed, be flowering at their natural time or in their natural colouring, for they will often be forced or held back to be right on the day. This sort of manipulation seldom presents us with a characteristic specimen.

If you know a bit, or can grab a friend or expert to advise you, it makes all the difference. At a recent late autumn show I admired a variety of *Aucuba japonica* that was covered in berries. Aucubas were among the most popular of evergreens in Victorian shrubberies, because they were so tolerant of soot and shade. The spotted laurels belong here, but not all aucubas are spotted. This one had an elegant lance leaf (they called it Lance Leaf), plain and glossy; a fitting setting for its wealth of red fruit. It was a female and would, I knew, need a male pollinator if it was ever to set crops of fruit again and I was already growing just such a male at home, a yellow-spotted and blotched aucuba called 'Crotonifolia', super if you like that kind of variegation and not in the least inhibited from growing in the shade. With this sort of information at my finger-tips, I had no hesitation in ordering one then and there. I have planted my new acquisition near to this and Lance Leaf is berrying for me like nobody's business.

Where trees are to be chosen I think a good outline counts for a very great deal, so that whenever your gaze strays towards it and you see it silhouetted against the sky, you'll think, 'I could never tire of that'. And you won't. Such trees may grow rapidly in youth but only acquire their character when growth slows down and they are mature. Our native Scots pine, *Pinus sylvestris*, looks nothing special when young but is, I would argue, as beautiful as any conifer on earth, in old age; and there are old specimens all around us, with their rose-glowing trunks that light up in evening sunshine and glisten after rain.

Of deciduous trees that develop character late but will also be rewarding from an early stage, I would put in a plea for the false acacia, *Robinia pseudoacacia*. Its pendent tresses of scented, white pea flowers are borne quite early, and its airy, pinnate foliage keeps its bright, fresh green right through until autumn. In old age, its trunk becomes nobly fissured and the branches take on that angularity that we associate with Chinese painting. But, as usual, there are drawbacks. It is a specially good town tree, seen everywhere in London but too brittle for planting in exposed places. And it suckers if its roots are damaged. That will not matter in a lawn specimen where the mowing-machine passes at regular intervals.

Shrubs like magnolias and flowering dogwoods develop character and a pleasing outline in time also, but most are fast-growing and valuable for other purposes. If being mixed with herbaceous plants, you'll be grateful to evergreens like *Mahonia undulata* that make solid features and backgrounds and are especially handsome in winter. Buddleias and other summer- or autumn-flowering shrubs grow like herbaceous plants and can be cut back each winter or early spring.

And there are also shrubs of rapid growth for which you will feel special gratitude in a garden's early years when you need bulk and an established air as quickly as possible. For you, the brooms (*Cytisus, Genista, Spartium*), the evergreen Cistus tribe from the Mediterranean with saucer flowers in shades of pink, carmine and white; tree lupins, *Lupinus arboreus*, with fresh bright evergreen foliage and spikes of scented white or soft yellow blossom; and the tree mallow, *Lavatera olbia*, with sombre, rounded leaves but a month-long display of mallow pink, hollyhock blossom on a shrub that makes 1.2m (4ft) of growth in a season. Easy come, easy go. These shrubs are not long-lived but by then you'll have others coming along.

SOMETHING'S IN THE AIR

Aromatic plants can give those of us who make use of our noses some of the pleasantest and most evocative moments in the garden. Most herbs are aromatic, but that is not to say that they necessarily impart their aroma to the air. I have always found lemon verbena, *Lippia citriodora*, a slight disappointment in that way. You have to grasp and bruise a leaf to enjoy it; the scent never comes to meet you. Rosemary, balm, sage – many familiar herbs are much the same, but surely, on a hot, steamy morning in its native Mediterranean, rosemary would be scented on the air. Lavender can be, though not so very often. If you have a hedge of it, you'll now and again catch its scent as you walk past, and it will stop you in your tracks. Gardens are made for moments such as this.

Of course, we don't necessarily grow the best of its kind from the aromatic aspect. Old English lavender (nothing English about it except by adoption) is immensely powerful, but the bush grows large and unwieldy, while the flowers are pasty mauve. More often we'll settle for the dwarf Hidcote with rich purple flowers, but its scent is not so strong nor its leaves so grey.

Mints don't smell of much in the ordinary way, but the sweet-sharp aroma of water mint, *Mentha aquatica*, is one of the smells associated with the margin of pond, dyke, river or marsh anywhere in this country. As these are nice places to be during the growing season, and are rich in fascinating flowers, insects and other fauna, the smell of water mint imbues me with a feeling of instant satisfaction. Whether this smell is present on the air before my arrival or whether I stimulate it by treading on the plant, I am not certain.

Creeping peppermint, *Mentha requienii*, is a delightful plant to have in the garden because you're sure to bruise it, whether you mean to or not, and it will then assail you with its delicious peppermint scent. It is a ground-hugging plant that makes a mat of tiny, green leaves and is especially lush in moist shady places, although in sunshine it will flower freely with tiny specks of mauve. It is usually planted in paving cracks, but if it invades a lawn where you do not get busy with weedkillers, you'll smell it every time you walk there and, still more so, when you mow. Use an

Above: Lavender arched over a path at Barnsley House creates the sort of aroma that stops visitors in their tracks.

Above right: Just can't resist it: roses run the gamut of summer scents, emanating not only from the flowers but also from the foliage.

electric or hand mower, otherwise the smell of petrol and oil fumes will drown all else.

There are some scents associated with one part of a plant that are equally to be located in another, though with a slight difference in quality. Everyone knows the smell of bay leaves, but they have to be crushed, boiled or baked before the oils release their aroma. The scent of bay blossom on the air in May, however, comes to greet you; it's the same scent, but less aggressive and softened by nectar. So too with myrtle, *Myrtus communis*, the scent of whose flowers in the late summer garden is one of the most beguiling I know. Its crushed leaves are just the same, without the honeyed element, and although I can find no reference in Mrs Grieve's *A Modern Herbal* to their use as a pot-herb, I should be surprised if they were not somewhere popular in cooking.

The flowers of primroses and violets have a more familiar scent than that of the plants, yet gardeners who split and replant their polyanthus and violets will confirm that the smell of the plants when handled is very like the flower's.

Roses have so many scents that it is hard to pin

BE BOLD IN THE BORDER

The keen plantsman will always garden on the borderlines of what it is possible and safe to grow. I'm sure this is the right attitude. If you get five or six years of pleasure, thanks to a mild run of winters, from a somewhat tender wall shrub – say the Californian *Dendromecon rigida*, a tree poppy with bright yellow flowers and waxy lance leaves, or even the intensely blue haze created by an evergreen ceanothus – there's no need to repine if a hard winter carries it off. Some people take their losses as a personal insult, instead of cheerfully starting again (most tender plants grow extremely fast anyway) with a resolution to do better next time.

There are precautions you can take. The great thing is to protect a somewhat tender plant from icy, desiccating winds. Plant it, initially, where these do not blow, or where they can be mitigated by some sort of shelter. You don't want to enclose a shrub too much throughout the winter, as it may suffer more from your attentions through lack of light and circulating air (promoting fungal diseases) than if you left it alone. A polythene enclosure, kept back from the plant by canes, can be a great help, especially if you pack dead bracken or fern fronds into the cavity when the weather turns really cold. But remember to set it aside during mild, wet spells.

Very often, if you can keep the lowest 90cm (3ft) or so of a shrub protected it will not matter too much if the top is killed. New shoots will break from live wood lower down.

Some plants that you expect to die back in winter anyway – less hardy bulbs, for instance, or large-flowered fuchsias or that beautiful, glaucous-leaved South African foliage plant *Melianthus major*, only need to have the ground they are growing in prevented from deep-freezing. You can pile their crowns over with a 15cm (6in) layer of grit or spread a thick fern carpet over them – or both.

The alternative precaution that most appeals to me in the majority of cases is to strike cuttings of your less hardy plants in the summer and

them down. I should say that the popular floribunda 'Rosemary Rose' was scented of apples and that would link it to the more pungent and infinitely satisfying aroma imparted on the air by a bush of sweet briar, *Rosa rubiginosa*. There are other roses with foliage of varying aromas. *R. serafinii* smells delicious in the white garden at Sissinghurst Castle, and Graham Thomas tells us in *Shrub Roses of Today* that *R. glutinosa*, a southeast European species, has aromatic foliage 'which smells like a pine forest on a hot day'. *Rosa primula* smells of incense, especially in muggy weather or after rain. As I rather enjoy the smell of censers in Roman Catholic churches and joss sticks in Indian shops, I also like *R. primula* in my garden.

Likewise, the powerful smell of stewed prunes that meets me from a cheerful evergreen Tasmanian shrub, *Ozothamnus ledifolius*. In certain weathers you can move through your garden from one orbit of scent to another. Thanks to our moist, mild climate, this can happen as freely in February as in July.

Gazanias (above) open with the warmth of the sun. It's worth a little extra care to grow half-hardy plants like this.

the centre of the bush or they may resurrect at or close to ground level. When you can see where the living wood is, cut away the rest so as to let in more light to the young shoots.

On the other hand, hopeful gardeners will sometimes cling to a shrub long after it has become clear to me that it is as dead as mutton. 'It's still green underneath,' they say, scratching a wafer of bark away with a fingernail. This really tells you very little. The tell-tale sign I look for – and it is especially significant in the hebes – is split bark. Any branches whose bark has split are probably dead, though there may be others that are still sound.

I am often surprised at the number of half-hardy and tender plants I grow, but they give so much pleasure over such a long stretch that the extra effort required on their behalf is repaid over and over again. For instance, gazanias, which love to bask in your hottest border. These are South African daisies that look dead and shrivelled until the sun comes out and the day warms up. Then they expand and relax, revealing the most extraordinary colours, varying from plant to plant. Orange and yellow are the commonest background shades, but towards the centre of each daisy is a pattern of dots and blotches that may be mole brown or speckled white or, most startling of all, vivid green.

Gazanias can be raised from seed and will flower like annuals in the first year, but there'll be a good proportion of rubbish among the seedlings and it is better to take cuttings from non-flowering shoots on your favourite plants and to overwinter them under glass from which frost need barely be excluded. Make your cuttings in late September or early October, trimming the base with a sharp blade (the kind used in a Stanley knife is excellent) and shortening the foliage, if lanky, to 8 or 10cm (3 or 4in). You can fit ten or twelve cuttings into a single 9cm ($3\frac{1}{3}$in) pot and root them in a frame kept closed only for the first fortnight or so. It is as well to spray with a fungicide once a week as rotting is the chief danger at this stage. When rooted, the pots can be overwintered on an open greenhouse bench where they'll occupy very little space. Then, when March and longer days arrive you can pot them off singly – a cold frame will be useful here, for gazanias will stand a bit of frost – plant them out in May and they'll flower from then until October.

This routine can be followed for many tender perennials and it greatly extends the range of plants that can enliven your garden in the summer months.

autumn and overwinter them under glass that is only just kept frost-free, if that. This will encourage you to keep on growing and replacing the glamorous hebes, for instance – shrubby veronicas carrying substantial spikes of pink, crimson, purple or lavender through a protracted season from late June until the frosts. Tip cuttings of their young shoots can even be rooted in a vase kept filled with water on a windowsill if no better facilities are to hand. Planted out in the spring they will already be flowering for you next summer and autumn.

When a hard winter has struck and a number of shrubs around your garden are as ornamental as scarecrows, you'll be sorely tempted to get rid of them. I shall not say you are wrong, especially if you are secretly rather pleased to be presented with a gap in which to grow something else. But the fact remains that many shrubs may look thoroughly dead for months on end, only to start breaking into new growth in June or July. Such might be a *Garrya elliptica*, an evergreen ceanothus or an Australian bottle brush (*Callistemon*), a mimosa (*Acacia dealbata*), a eucalyptus or even a bay laurel. They may break from thick old wood at

SEEDS OF HOPE

The gardener's year is never at an end. Before he has finished with one crop he is looking forward to the next. Cycles may be annual, biennial, or so long term, with trees for example, as to span generations.

Planning sets the imagination to work. When ordering seeds you will sometimes choose plants from a catalogue – trees, shrubs, hardy perennials, annuals or whatever – which are wholly strange to you but sound exciting from the description or look good in an illustration. You may have no idea of where you'll finally place them in your own garden. That, you think, can be worked out when the time arrives.

A certain amount of this kind of blind ordering of seed and raising of plants doesn't matter at all. True, you may find yourself landed with more material than you have room for, but too much is better than too little. Some plans will inevitably go awry and you'll then be thankful that there's spare stock to fall back on.

Another part of your order will be seeds of whose final use and destination you have a very definite idea. Bedding out should be planned, but it doesn't have to be. You can just plant out a hotch-potch of ingredients and be content with a riot of colour, but that isn't clever and it's messy. It is far more satisfactory to confine yourself to a combination of two or three species, and to grow enough of each for the scheme to look like a scheme and not like a rag bag.

So, at the same time as ordering seeds of annuals or biennials you think you would like to grow, you will be thinking about what will look well growing with what. Jot your thoughts down in a notebook, otherwise you may (if you're like

Pondering the display at the Chelsea Show. Glean new ideas from visits to gardens most relevant to your own back yard.

me) forget them again within seconds and a wonderful opportunity will have been lost.

A further use for your notebook throughout the year is for putting down the names, together with a thumb-nail description or sketch to jog your memory, of plants or combinations of plants which you have seen and admired in other gardens. Among the best quarries for these will be botanic gardens like Kew and Edinburgh, societies' gardens like Wisley and Harlow Car and nurseries where trial grounds are open to the public. The gardens of National Trust properties and private houses that are open to visitors from time to time may often seem to have the closest relevance to the kind of gardening you practise yourself.

Tracking down sources can be frustrating. You do not need to be adventurous when you first start gardening and one seed supplier or one local garden centre may serve your requirements well enough. But that won't satisfy any experimental gardener for long.

The trade would always like us to write about and recommend the plants of which they already have abundant supplies but I, for one, would find this limited diet boring. So we write about some of the more uncommon varieties that we enjoy growing or eating. Back comes the question: where can they be found and it's a question I cannot always answer, having only a limited range of catalogues to consult. But there are ways of finding out, if you persist.

If you're a member of the Royal Horticultural Society, of the Northern Horticultural Society, of the Alpine Garden Society or the Scottish Rock Garden Club, you can acquire some very unusual plants or – more particularly – seeds from them. Moreover, they may often be able to tell you of sources and so may the weekly horticultural journals like *Amateur Gardening* and *Popular Gardening*. Then there is the Hardy plant Directory, published by the Hardy Plant Society and obtainable from the Society's Hon. Directory Secretary, Mrs Joan Grout, Colt House, Thurgarton, Nottingham. There is a paperback called *Green Pages: A Guide to Nurseries and Garden Centres in Great Britain and Northern Ireland* (published by Hart-Davis, MacGibbon), which tells you who and where the specialist suppliers are.

Of course, even a specialist nursery when suddenly inundated with requests for the same rare plant is soon going to run out of supplies, but amateurs need never feel beleaguered. There'll always be help available if it is persistently sought. And we are, I think it is fair to say, a generous community and the dissemination of many rare plants and seeds is achieved by fair exchange between like-minded enthusiasts.

Christopher Lloyd

GENERAL HINTS

A mixed border of herbaceous plants.

THE ORIGIN OF SPECIES: PLANT BREEDING TERMS UNRAVELLED

You cannot garden for long without coming across the terms 'species', 'variety' and 'hybrid'. They can be puzzling.

Species are wild plants just as they grow in their native habitats. The daisies on your lawn are a species, known as *Bellis perennis*. For gardeners, the importance of species is that they are stable and vary very little.

Yet even species do vary a little and gardeners have always been quick to seize on any that looked more exciting and attempt to perpetuate them. The big double daisies produced in this way and used in flower beds in spring, often as a groundwork for tulips or hyacinths, are *varieties* of the common lawn daisy. If these are left to grow and reproduce themselves in the garden they will almost certainly interbreed with the common daisies and revert in a few generations to that original type. To keep them big and double they have to be grown in isolation and inspected frequently so any plants of inferior quality can be removed before they contaminate the rest. Varieties are usually described in print thus: *Bellis perennis* 'Monstrosa'.

Hybrids are produced by interbreeding one species with another. Some hybrids occur naturally but the majority of those grown in gardens are man-made. The symbol 'x' is widely used in books and catalogues to describe hybrids. Thus, *Aster* x *alpellus* is a cross between *A. alpinus* and *A. amellus*.

Nearly all the popular garden roses, the hybrid teas, floribundas, miniatures and large flowered climbers, are man-made hybrids, but their parentage is so complex that it is almost impossible to trace their genealogy completely. Because of their mixed parentage, seedlings raised from hybrids often vary a great deal, and to keep these plants true to type they have to be increased by other means such as divisions, cuttings, layers and grafts which are really extensions of the original hybrid and not new individuals as seedlings are.

Yet here again there are exceptions and they are important. Some hybrids are always raised from seed and they are re-created every time by repeating the same cross-breeding between parents skilfully selected and carefully maintained to produce precisely the required result. In your seed catalogues you will find them described as F1 hybrids, which stands for 'first filial', meaning 'first generation'. Good F1 hybrids are exceptionally uniform and sturdy and for some purposes extremely useful – even if they cost much more.

A H

THE ANSWER LIES IN THE SOIL

You can't grow worthwhile crops in a garden unless the soil is fertile. But what is fertile soil – indeed, what is soil?

In spite of its solid appearance, soil is generally slightly less than half solid matter, and slightly more than half water and air. The solid part consists of mineral particles and organic matter. The mineral elements are sand, silt and clay particles, which, apart from giving the plant anchorage, are the source of some essential nutrients, such as phosphorus and potash. The organic matter, which is rarely more than about 5 per cent of the solid matter in garden soils, is a mixture of decomposing vegetation and animal remains, which is being continually broken down into humus.

The water and air in the soil are essential for both plant and animal life. Ordinary plants, indeed, are 90 per cent water, so they need plenty of water. They also absorb their nutrients in dilute solutions through their roots: when the soil is dry no nutrients are absorbed. As for the air, plants take in oxygen through their roots as part of their respiration system, and oxygen is also essential for the worms and other living organisms in the soil, all of which play an important role in soil fertility.

A fertile soil is rich in nutrients and organic matter, well drained but retaining plenty of moisture, well aerated with plenty of worms and biological activity, slightly acid or neutral, and has a good crumbly soil structure. This last factor is a very large piece of the soil fertility jigsaw. The mineral and organic particles in the soil join together to form small lumps or 'crumbs', which vary in size but are very stable. Around and between them a network of spaces or pores is built up, the pores and crumbs together making up the soil structure.

The channels between the crumbs are the vital aeration and drainage system of the soil. Optimum conditions are created in a soil with crumb particles (and hence channels) of varying sizes – the 'good balanced loam' of textbooks. In such soils, surplus water drains off through the channels formed by the larger pores, leaving a moisture reservoir for roots and soil organisms in the smaller pores. When water cannot drain away freely the soil becomes waterlogged, animal life and plant roots are deprived of air and therefore oxygen, and the systems start to break down.

The ability to form crumbs distinguishes the different types of soil. At one extreme are light sandy soils with (contrary to what one might think) large particles which are reluctant to stick together and form crumbs. In sandy soils the spaces between crumbs are large, so sandy soils drain rapidly, warm up rapidly in spring, but may be short of nutrients which are often washed out of reach of the roots. At the other extreme are heavy clay soils, which consist of minute particles which stick together in often impenetrable lumps, making for poorly drained, poorly aerated and cold soils – though once brought under control clay soils, which are often rich in nutrients, can become very fertile.

In practice, the essence of improving soil fertility is creating a balanced loam, which boils down to making light soils heavier and heavy soils lighter. In both cases the main agent for improving soil structure is humus. Not only is humus a storehouse of nutrients, but because of its unique physical and chemical properties, it can coat particles of sand and silt (which falls between sand and clay), so that they can form crumbs; it also, somewhat conversely, facilitates the breakdown of large clay clods into smaller clods, which in turn break down into crumbs. So the time-honoured method of improving soil structure is to work in organic matter, which will be converted into humus by micro-organisms.

Another important aspect of soil fertility is its acidity, which, roughly speaking, reflects the amount of calcium in the soil. In this country there is a natural tendency for soil to become acid. This is particularly true in areas of high rainfall, in industrial areas where acids in the atmosphere accentuate the process, and on light sandy soils. Acidity can be tested with simple soil-testing kits. Soils with high acidity can be remedied by dressings of ground limestone. Over-alkaline soils are rare, but can be corrected gradually by working in acid peat, or by dressings of the fertilizer ammonium nitrate.

Soil fertility in gardens cannot be improved overnight, but will improve steadily by the regular addition of organic matter, and by the process of cultivating plants.

FERTILITY PROBLEMS

Occasionally, however, a radical problem has to be rectified before anything can be grown successfully. The most likely problems are poor drainage, very high acidity or simply extremely poor thin soil, such as builder's rubble.

If soil is badly drained, water lies on the surface or is encountered a few inches down when digging, there is poor vegetation, and there are no worms.

Working in bulky organic matter helps to 'mop up' the water, but where the problem persists after a year or two simple trench drains, again primarily to absorb water, should be made. These can be constructed either across the lower end of a slope, or down the sides of a more or less level piece of ground. Dig them 60–90cm (2–3ft) deep and about a foot wide, and fill the bottom third with clinker, stones, broken bricks, etc., before replacing the soil in the top layer. If these in turn fail, a proper system of piped drains, leading to an outlet such as a ditch or soakaway, would have to be laid.

Where the problem is extremely poor soil, a start can be made by blanketing the soil in the autumn with a layer at least 10–12cm (4–5in) deep of organic matter, such as mushroom compost, seaweed (marvellous if you can get it), farmyard manure, old leaves and home-made compost, and letting them rot down slowly. Alternatively, a green manure crop of mustard can be sown in spring or summer and dug in.

In the early stages of cultivating a poor garden,

it is worth creating 'pockets' of fertility, making small trenches, about 15cm (6in) deep, filling them with potting compost or any other compost available, covering them with soil and sowing there initially. Once *something* is growing, soil fertility starts to improve.   PD

HOME MADE COMPOSTS FOR SEEDS AND PLANTS

SEED MIXTURE WITH SOIL

1 part by bulk good garden soil
1 part by bulk sphagnum peat (medium grade)
1 part by bulk coarse sand

SEED MIXTURE WITHOUT SOIL

Equal parts by bulk sphagnum peat (medium grade) and coarse sand

There is little plant food in this mixture and so seedlings should be pricked out as soon as possible into a rather richer mixture.

POTTING MIXTURE WITH SOIL

2 parts by bulk good garden soil
1 part by bulk sphagnum peat (medium grade)
1 part by bulk coarse sand

To each 9 litre (2 gallon) bucketful of this mixture add 28g (1oz) of National Growmore fertilizer or a slow-release fertilizer such as En. Mag., Sustanum or Osmocote.

POTTING MIXTURE WITHOUT SOIL

2 parts by bulk sphagnum peat (medium grade)
1 part by bulk coarse sand

To each 9 litre (2 gallon) bucketful of this mixture add 14g ($\frac{1}{2}$oz) of Vitox Q4 or a slow-release fertilizer, as above.   AH

LOOK NO SEED

There are two basic systems of increasing plants: one, known as seminal, meaning from seed, the other vegetative, meaning from some portion of the plant that is not a seed. A seedling, whatever its source, is a new individual carrying virtually nothing from its parents except two sets of genes, one from the female, the other from the male, plus a minute quantity of cytoplasm from the female egg. In contrast, a vegetatively propagated plant is not a new 'individual', but an extension of another plant in another place deriving all its characteristics from those of its single parent.

This is not just a matter of academic interest but of great practical importance since seedlings, even of species, always show some variation from each other and their parents whereas plants vegetatively increased from a single original parent will usually be identical in every detail. Collectively such plants constitute a clone and if they are of special merit are often given a distinguishing clonal name, eg 'Peace' is the clonal name of all roses vegetatively propagated from a seedling rose of that name raised in 1945.

The advantage of growing plants from seed are that it gives this possibility for change, that it maintains vigour and generally produces a generation free, at the outset, from diseases acquired by the parent plants; it is also often the cheapest method of multiplying stock. (How to sow is described under 'Seed'.) The advantages of vegetative methods of propagation are that they enable even minute variations to be carried on, allow plants that are sterile or produce little good seed to be increased and in some instances provide very simple methods of increasing stocks of plants that anyone can use.

Gardeners use four principal methods of vegetative propagation: division, cuttings, layering and grafting.

DIVISION

Division is the simplest and is done by breaking the plant into several pieces. It is particularly suitable for herbaceous perennials. Those that are loosely structured can be pulled apart with the fingers or, if tougher, levered apart using a pair of forks back to back (*see* 'Herbaceous Plants'). Others, such as peonies, delphiniums and dahlias, make tough or woody crowns which may need to be cut through with a knife.

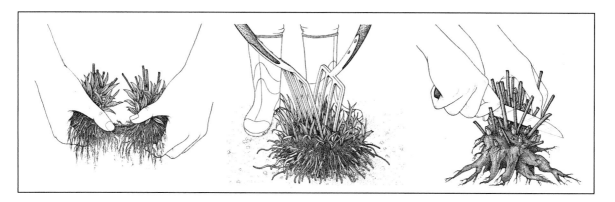

The essential feature of a division is that it must have roots and at least one growth bud. When big old plants are divided, it is the younger outside portions that usually provide the best specimens for replanting. Division of most hardy herbaceous plants is best done in March-April, but it can be carried out at any time of the year provided sufficient care is taken to re-establish the divided plant by suitable protection and watering. In spring neither may be required if the weather is mild and showery.

CUTTINGS

Cuttings differ from divisions in starting life with either top growth or roots, but not both. There are different forms of cuttings. Stem cuttings are made from a piece of stem, leaf cuttings from a single leaf usually with its leaf stalk attached, and root cuttings from a piece of root. The cutting, whatever its original character, must be induced to form the missing parts.

Stem cuttings may be prepared from young growth, semi-mature growth or end-of-season

Divide the plant by breaking it in pieces with your hands; if it's tougher, use two forks back to back to prise it apart or, if tougher still, cut with a sharp knife.

growth – these three types are known as soft, half-ripe and hardwood. Soft cuttings are taken mainly in spring for herbaceous or sub-shrubby plants, including dahlias and chrysanthemums. Half-ripe cuttings are usually taken in summer for a great many ornamental shrubs. Hardwood cuttings are taken mainly in autumn for increasing some shrubs and also for bush fruit, such as currants and gooseberries.

As a rule cuttings are severed just beneath a leaf or joint, because this is the point at which roots most readily develop. Sometimes half-ripe and hardwood cuttings are pulled off the parent plant with a sliver of older branch attached, and these are known as 'heel cuttings'. Soft cuttings must be solid flesh right through, not hollow at the

Treat your leaf cuttings with rooting compound and insert in cutting compost in the humid conditions of a propagator or in a pot covered with a polythene bag (note hoop); rooting should begin in about one month.

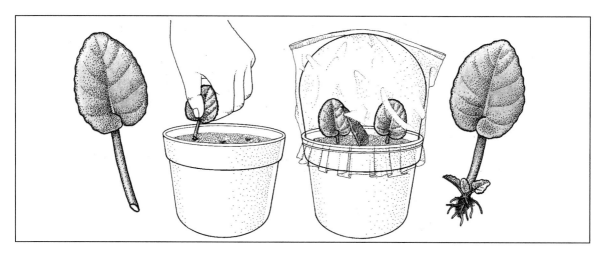

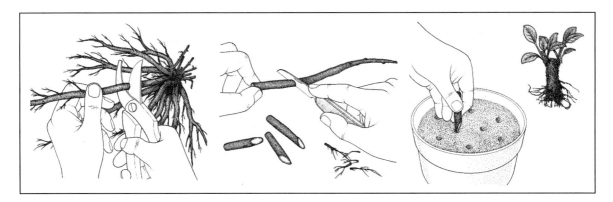

base; half-ripe cuttings need to be firm at the base, neither too immature nor too hard, which takes a little experience to gauge well, and ripe cuttings must really be firm and mature without being too woody.

Soft cuttings must be kept in a very humid, still atmosphere, or they will flag and quickly die. Firstly, insert them in cutting compost in a propagator, warming the soil to maintain a close atmosphere and stimulate the fastest possible root formation, ie in two or three weeks.

Half-ripe cuttings are just a little more resistant to collapse but also require damp, still air. Root them either in a propagator, a pot placed inside a polythene bag or in mist, a special device which sprays the cuttings with water automatically and keeps them constantly wet. Cuttings of this type usually take a month or so to root.

Hardwood cuttings have little or no tendency to flag and if they are of deciduous plants are likely to be bare of leaves when (or shortly after) they are taken. You can plant them outdoors if they are hardy, or in a frame or greenhouse if they are tender, but they take many months to root well.

Many different materials are used as cutting composts, the favourites being sand, Perlite, peat and leafmould. A mixture of equal parts peat and either Perlite or sand is a good basic formula.

Various chemicals, often referred to as root-forming hormones, can hasten or increase root formation. They are sold in the form of powders combined with a fungicide which prevents diseases from attacking the cutting while it is rooting. They are sometimes offered in three strengths, weak for soft cuttings, medium for half-ripe and strong for hardwood.

For soft and half-ripe cuttings it is usual to remove the lower leaves completely; large leaves may be cut in half to reduce the demand for moisture. When this has been done, place the base of the cutting in water, then dip it in the hormone

Sever your stem cuttings just below a joint, and after dipping in hormone rooting compound press them into a pot of cutting compost where rooting can begin.

rooting compound and finally press it gently into the rooting mixture in a pot, pan, tray or bed, whichever is most convenient. It may be necessary to use a dibber (a pencil-like piece of stick) to make holes for soft cuttings, and hardwood cuttings are usually lined out in little trenches chopped out with a spade, but half-ripe cuttings can usually simply be pushed in about half their length and made firm with the fingers. Water soft and half-ripe cuttings well, unless you are using mist which will take care of that automatically.

Once cuttings are rooted, they start to grow again but it may be worth lifting one or two carefully to see just how good the root formation is. When it seems satisfactory, pot the cuttings individually in a potting mixture and keep in a moist, unventilated atmosphere until they are established and air can be admitted. This can sometimes be the trickiest part of the whole operation. Hardwood cuttings can usually be replanted into nursery beds the autumn following insertion.

Layering

Layering might be described as taking cuttings without separating them from the parent plant until they are rooted. In some plants, strawberries for example, it is a natural means of increase, long runners being produced with plantlets along them. Where these touch the ground they root and form new plants and so the colony extends rapidly.

In many plants the rootings of young stems can be promoted by wounding, dusting with hormone rooting powder and covering with soil. This is the usual method of increasing border carnations, the non-flowering stems being partially slit through a

Layering is done by pressing a flexible stem into the ground, its underside slit at a joint to encourage rooting. Press the stem into a trench of cutting compost and (inset) hold it down with a hoop or a peg.

joint in summer and pegged to the soil around the parent. If this is done in July sufficient roots are likely to have been formed by September to allow the layers to be severed from the parent plants and then, a few days later, lifted and replanted elsewhere.

Many shrubs and climbers can be layered by bending a flexible stem and inserting it beside the parent plant in a shallow trench. Make a small slit on the underside of the stem to allow for rooting. Cover with cutting compost and hold securely in place with a hoop or peg. If this is done in spring it is possible that the layers will have made enough roots to be separated and transplanted by the autumn, but frequently shrub layers require at least a year, possibly two, before they are able to exist on their own. Brambles of most kinds will root from the tips of young canes if these are bent over and pegged to the soil.

It is also possible to layer shrubs and climbers without actually bringing stems to ground level. Instead, after suitable wounding and dusting with hormone rooting powder, they are wrapped in wet sphagnum moss, a sleeve of polythene film is pulled over this and tightly tied at each end to keep in the moisture. When sufficient roots have formed in the damp moss, the layer is severed and potted or planted. This is known as 'air-layering'.

GRAFTING

Grafting is the most complex method of propagation and consists of uniting two plants, one of which, known as the rootstock, will provide the roots and the other, the scion, all or most of the top growth. Each plant retains its separate identity and it is important to stop shoot growth from the rootstock because, if retained, it would have the characteristics of this and not of the plant grafted on to it. Nevertheless each can have some influence on the other and rootstocks are often chosen to control the vigour or precociousness of fruit trees.

Two of the many methods of grafting will illustrate the principles involved: splice-grafting and budding. Splice-grafting is suitable when there is not a great difference in thickness between rootstock and scion. Both are taken from year-old plants. The plant providing the rootstock is beheaded and a slice of bark and wood is removed

In grafting, select your scion and rootstock and cut matching grooves in each; then bind securely with raffia.

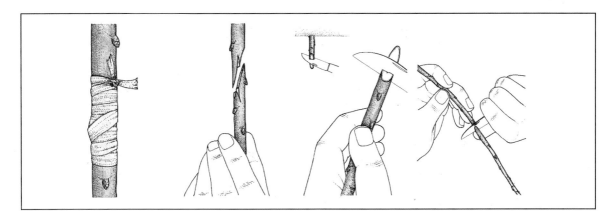

at the top of the stump. An exactly similar cut is made at the base of the scion, and the two cut surfaces are placed together and securely bound so that there can be no movement while they are uniting. As a rule the wound is further covered with grafting wax to prevent loss of moisture from the cut surfaces. This kind of grafting is usually done in early spring when growth is just starting and it is an advantage if scions can be a little retarded by being pre-cut in winter and partly buried in soil.

Budding, by contrast, is usually done in summer when plants are in full growth. It is the main method used for the commercial increase of roses. The scion is a single growth bud cut with a shield-shaped portion of bark and the rootstock is prepared to receive this by having a T-shaped incision made in its bark. The flaps of bark on each side of the T are gently raised and the bud bound in. No wax covering is required.

Buds are cut from well-developed young stems and it helps if you remove the sliver of wood which is cut with the bud as this will expose more of the active layer of cambium beneath the bark which has to unite with the cambium of the rootstock. It is usually possible to tell in a few weeks whether the union has occurred and the following spring the bud should start into growth. Before that date, cut off the stem just above the inserted bud so that rising sap is concentrated on it. The bud is now the source of all further top growth.

A H

YOUR GARDEN LABORATORY

The purpose of a greenhouse is to give the gardener much greater control of the environment for plants than is possible in the open. Plants too tender to be cultivated outdoors can be grown there and brought to flower or fruit at an earlier season. Greenhouses also make plant propagation easier: seeds can be sown earlier and will germinate with greater certainty, and many cuttings will root there that would have little or no chance of success out of doors. Frames can provide similar conditions and so fulfil some of these purposes but they contain only a small volume of air, making it more difficult to control temperature accurately, and cannot offer sufficient headroom for big plants. Nor do they provide any protection for the gardener. One of the great plusses about owning a greenhouse is that you can continue to work in it in comfort even when it is raining or freezing outside.

Greenhouses are of three main types: span-roof, lean-to and 'circular' (the last is usually hexagonal or octagonal rather than truly round). Each has its advantages and drawbacks. Span-roof houses are the most versatile in that they can be of any size and can be placed almost anywhere. Lean-to greenhouses need to be placed against a wall or building. They are often used as conservatories with direct access from a house and so virtually become an additional room. When used in this way they can draw quite a lot of warmth from the house, and with any lean-to built against a dwelling-house there is the possibility of combining both on the same central-heating system.

Circular houses are compact and often very pleasant to look at. They can sometimes be used as features in the garden design, whereas other types,

Greenhouse interior.

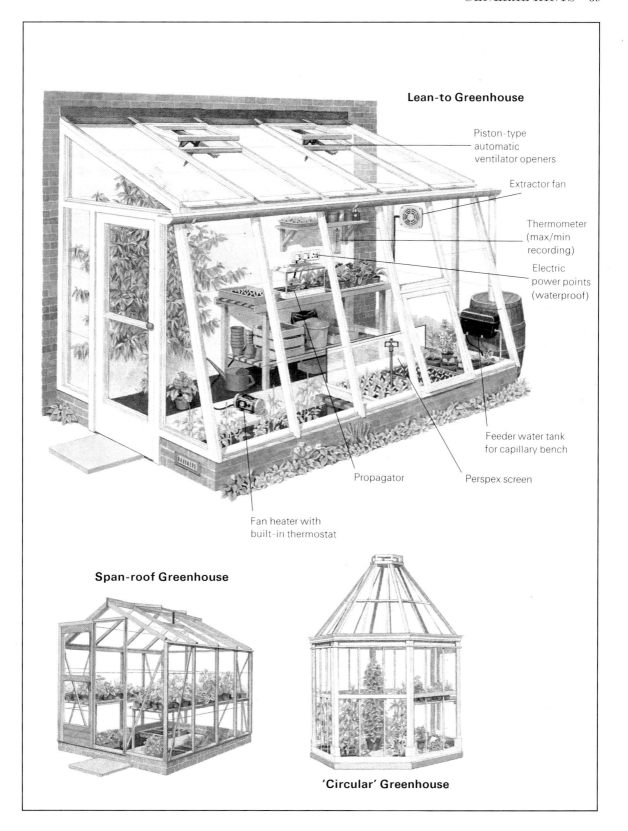

Lean-to Greenhouse

Piston-type automatic ventilator openers

Extractor fan

Thermometer (max/min recording)

Electric power points (waterproof)

Feeder water tank for capillary bench

Propagator

Perspex screen

Fan heater with built-in thermostat

Span-roof Greenhouse

'Circular' Greenhouse

unless elaborately made, tend to be less decorative and more obviously utilitarian. Most circular greenhouses are small, however, and this, as with frames, not only means restricted space for plants but also makes it harder to control temperature and humidity, both of which fluctuate more rapidly in a small volume of air.

Unless required for some special purpose such as the cultivation of ferns, greenhouses should always be sited in as sunny a place as possible.

HEATING SYSTEMS

Some means of heating a greenhouse artificially greatly increases its value since it increases the gardener's control over the climate. Except for tropical plants, few require any additional warmth from late May to early October, but in mid-winter it is usually impossible to keep the temperature above freezing point all the time and that can be critical for many tender plants. Most seeds only germinate freely at temperatures between 13–20°C (55–68°F) and without artificial heat it will probably be impossible to maintain any such level until April or even May. If early seedlings are required from sowings made in February and March, some heating is essential.

The most economical way to apply heat is in a propagator placed inside the greenhouse – really a little frame with its own heating system. Because of the double protection and the small area to be heated, the cost of running this can be negligible. However the seedlings or cuttings will soon outgrow the propagator and will have to be brought out into the greenhouse itself. Without some separate method of heating, the change of temperature may be too sudden and too great and the little plants will be killed or seriously checked.

The cost of heating a greenhouse roughly doubles for every 3°C (5°F) that the minimum winter temperature is raised. This is because, in addition to the extra heat needed to reach that temperature, there is the extra time during which it will be required. For this reason many privately owned greenhouses are now run at a winter temperature of 7°C (43°F) – enough to keep most plants alive if not always completely happy. A propagator can then be used in February and March to obtain the 16–18°C (61–65°F) which ensures rapid seed germination, and in April the minimum greenhouse temperature is raised to 13°C (55°F) to accommodate seedlings and young plants coming out of the propagator. This combines economy with a reasonable degree of safety for most popular greenhouse and bedding plants.

There are many ways of heating greenhouses. Electric fan heaters are convenient and most offer the additional advantage that they can be used without the heating element switched on to keep the air moving in warm, humid weather. Gas heaters burning natural gas, including bottled propane, can be used without flues inside greenhouses since the main by-products of combustion – water and carbon dioxide – are not harmful. However, damage can occur from very small quantities of other gases, mainly ethylene, and these heaters should never be used without a little ventilation despite the fact that this lowers their efficiency. Oil heaters suffer the same drawback and may become lethal if they are dirty, or do not get enough air, or if their combustion is disturbed by draughts. Hot-water pipes are safe but small boilers outside the house can require a lot of attention.

The ideal heating solution is to connect your pipes to the domestic central heating – provided this is not automatically cut off at night by a time switch. Wherever possible, heating should be controlled by a thermostat so that it is only used when necessary. Most electrical and gas heaters made for greenhouses have built-in thermostats and this can be very convenient though probably not quite as efficient as a thermostat placed well away from the source of heat.

AIR AND WATER SUPPLIES

Automation in the greenhouse is possible in other ways. Ventilators can be fitted with piston-type openers which are very sensitive to temperature changes. Another possibility is to fit an electrical extractor fan controlled by a thermostat, but this should be shielded from direct sunshine which can warm it unduly before the air temperature reaches the level set on the thermostat.

Watering can also be made automatic in a variety of ways, the simplest being the capillary bench. Any waterproof greenhouse staging can be employed as the base, covered with a thin layer of sand and small gravel or one of the special plastic mats made for the purpose. This is kept constantly wet by drip feed, float chamber or some other device, and the pots placed on it draw water through their drainage holes by capillary action. A variety of kits are available for this purpose. Capillary benches work best with plastic pots since these are sufficiently thin to allow the soil inside

them to come into direct contact with the wet mat or sand. If thicker clay pots are used, wicks of glass fibre should be passed through the holes to draw in the moisture.

Despite the labour- and time-saving attractions of automatic watering, there is really nothing to beat individual hand-watering provided it is done regularly and with understanding, and freshly potted plants should anyway be watered by hand for a week or so. Common faults are over- and under-watering, but the former is not likely to have serious effects if the potting compost used is adequately porous since it will allow surplus water to drain away quickly. Under-watering is much more serious and a common source of trouble. It can only be avoided by examining plants daily, watering any that appear dry and giving sufficient to soak right through the pot and trickle out the bottom. A H

THE COMPOST HEAP

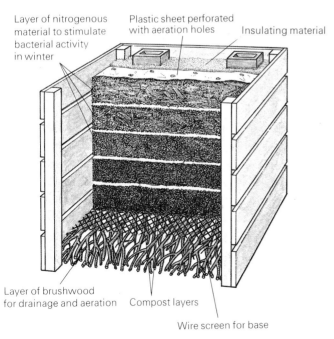

Layer of nitrogenous material to stimulate bacterial activity in winter

Plastic sheet perforated with aeration holes

Insulating material

Layer of brushwood for drainage and aeration

Compost layers

Wire screen for base

A home-made compost heap; make the front out of heavy wire mesh or loose planks for easy dismantling.

Soil fertility in gardens can not be improved overnight, but it will improve steadily by the regular addition of organic material. But getting hold of reasonable quantities is not always easy. What are some of the options? Any animal or poultry manure, always as well rotted as possible and mixed with plenty of litter and straw; *treated* sewage sludge and municipal waste, provided they are guaranteed free of toxic metals; seaweed, used fresh, dried or composted; spent mushroom compost; spent hops and slaughterhouse waste where obtainable; straw, which is best composted before use; peat, which is expensive and adds humus but no nutrients; leafmould; and last, but not least, home-made compost.

Compost can be made from any vegetable wastes – household, garden, or collected from the wild. Just avoid diseased material and weeds which have gone to seed, and chop up tough material such as cabbage stalks into pieces about 5cm (2in) long.

Of course, you can buy compost bins, but home-made ones are best, even for small amounts of waste.

Compost is best made in bins at least 90cm (3ft) square and 90cm (3ft) deep (otherwise heat is not built up), with three walls of good insulating material such as breeze blocks, bricks, timber or straw bales. Make the heap on a soil base so that worms can move in during the final stages.

Start with an 8cm (3in) deep layer of brushwood, broken bricks or pipe drains, to ensure drainage and aeration, if possible covered with a strong wire screen, about 2.5cm (1in) mesh, as a base for the compost. Ideally build the compost up in layers about 15-22cm (6–9in) thick, mixing together thoroughly different types of waste, which must be slightly moist. Never put in a mass of one substance, such as lawn mowings, which will simply form a nasty sludge. It is much better to accumulate a lot of waste in, say, a separate garden rubbish bin, to add to the heap in one go, than to add a little daily.

In winter, a source of nitrogen should be mixed into each layer to stimulate bacterial activity. This can be poultry or animal manure, a proprietary compost activator or concentrated seaweed extract, ammonium sulphate or other nitrogenous fertilizer. In summer there is so much nitrogen-rich fresh green material in the heap that this is unnecessary.

The complete heap can be held in place with a sheet of plastic, perforated with aeration holes about 2.5cm (1in) diameter, about 25cm (10in) apart. Cover this with an insulating layer of hessian sacks, matting, old carpets, old hay or straw, and the heap should be ready in about three to four months – rich-looking material with a soil-like texture.

Where this procedure is too much trouble, make a rough and ready pile of vegetable waste and cover it with plastic on completion. But it will need to be left for at least a year before it is sufficiently decomposed to use. If you are short of space, leave it uncovered and grow gourds and cucumbers on it while it rots.

HOW TO USE ORGANIC MATTER

Apply the material at 4.5kg (10lb), i.e. about 2–3 buckets per square metre. This should be done annually wherever possible, as soil reserves of organic matter are continually being depleted and much, of course, is removed from the soil when the vegetables are harvested. The most efficient way to use organic matter is to work it thoroughly and evenly into the soil when digging, not, as was traditionally advocated, putting it in a layer at the bottom of a trench. It can be spread on the surface in a layer several inches thick, allowing the worms to work it in. This method, which protects the surface, is especially useful on light soil where the soil structure is damaged by rain, although organic matter is not so evenly distributed through the soil.

In fertile garden soils very satisfactory crops can be grown without the use of artificial fertilizers. But many gardens lack essential nutrients: nitrogen in particular is washed out of soils during the winter and is often in short supply. In such cases yields can be boosted with artificial fertilizers.

There are so many variables – soils, crops, for example – that it is impossible to make specific recommendations on how much of which fertilizer to apply. But provided most of the plant waste in the garden is returned to the soil as compost, an annual dressing in spring, about a month before sowing, of a compound fertilizer containing equal quantities of nitrogen, phosphorus and potash (e.g. 10:10:10 as marked on the bag), applied at the rate of 60–90g (2–3oz) per square metre, would cater for most crops under average conditions.   J L

PESTS AND DISEASES

With pests, diseases and weeds the message must be: Anticipate. Be prepared, Take precautions. Check your plants in the very early stages, especially in spring when young plants are at risk.

Gardeners' attitudes to controlling these problems vary. There are those who want pristine produce from their garden and will spray for every possible pest and disease, and there are those who are 'anti chemical' and are prepared to put up with scabby apples and perforated peas. Most people,

however, will rely on cultural techniques to reduce the problems, only resorting to chemicals if and when things get out of hand.

There are several ways to lessen the problems caused by pests and diseases:

Rotate your crops.

Start with strong healthy plants and grow them well.

Remove the source of the problem as soon as it occurs.

Create an environment that discourages the development of pest or disease.

Potatoes grown in the same piece of ground year after year will suffer from a build up of eelworm in the soil. Similarly, brassicas will not do well if grown in the same spot each year as their roots become infected and grotesque with club-

Above: Ladybirds attacking a colony of blackfly.
Below: Greenfly.

Snail on hydrangea.

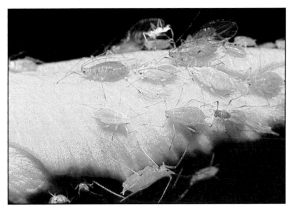

root. To avoid soil-borne pests and diseases, the vegetable gardener can divide up the plot and rotate crops.

Always buy healthy fruit plants, ornamental trees and shrubs. When buying herbaceous plants, look for obviously healthy and fresh material. Avoid wilting plants with dried up roots (unless you're short of material for your compost heap). When raising your own plants from seed, only use fresh seed from a reputable source or, if saving your own, only keep seed from healthy plants and store it carefully. Some bought seed will have been 'dressed' with a chemical to prevent problems later on (*see* 'Seeds'). When sowing seeds you should do everything you can to ensure rapid germination. In the glasshouse, seed should be shown thinly into sterile compost in clean trays. Warmth and moisture will encourage germination of many flower and vegetable seeds, but once through, lower the temperature and reduce the humidity to

Above left: Caterpillar on dahlia.

Above right: Peach leaf curl.

Left: Caterpillar damage on dahlia.

Right: Slugs attack a delphinium.

Below left: Grey mould (*Botrytis*) on cyclamen.

Below: 'Damping off' in tomato seedlings.

Far below: Codling moth damage.

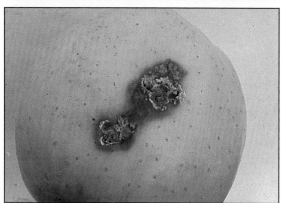

avoid soft growth. Avoid overwatering and too well-firmed compost as this combination leads to damping-off diseases. Prevention is far more effective than cure. Whether seedlings are of flowers or vegetables, do not overcrowd your plants as this sometimes results in poor growth and poorer air circulation which creates more problems.

Another way of stopping the spread of pests and diseases is to remove and destroy them as soon as they are spotted. For example, those white powdery tips of shoots on your apple tree should be cut off before the disease – powdery mildew – spreads. As the holes appear in your cabbage leaves, find the culprits – caterpillars, and pick them off.

Plants won't succumb to pests and disease if you create a healthy environment. For example, cabbages are less likely to get clubroot if the soil is not too acid and is well drained; and your strawberries or lettuces under cloches will not develop grey mould so easily if you provide good ventilation.

WAGING WAR BY OTHER MEANS

Using chemicals is the only way to control certain problems. But only use them if you really have to, and then only sparingly, as they often have undesirable side effects, particularly if used carelessly. You might be quite happy, for instance, to spray your apple trees regularly with an anti-mildew fungicide. But that fungicide may reduce the viability of the pollen and so perhaps reduce your crop. Similarly, the insecticide you put on to kill a few greenfly may also kill their natural predators and parasites.

The use of predators to keep pests in check has been developed in recent years. In a controlled environment, like a glasshouse, predators can reduce a number of pests that are otherwise difficult to control, even chemically. A good example is whitefly which affects many glasshouse

Top: Gooseberry mildew.
Centre above: Blackfly on broad bean.
Centre below: Cabbage root fly.
Left: Celery fly.

crops. A few small wasps, however, will reduce the whitefly population and prevent further serious damage.

This biological control is not so well developed outside the greenhouse, although gardeners can encourage natural predators to keep certain pests down. Birds like tits, for instance, should be encouraged for they will search out codling moth larvae which otherwise tunnel into your prize apples.

But birds are often pests in themselves – and one of the most difficult to control. How can we keep them off our valuable crops? Bird scarers, of course, but none of them work for long. The worst offenders in the garden are pigeons and bullfinches in winter, and starlings, thrushes, blackbirds and sparrows during the summer. When food is short in the depths of winter, pigeons will turn to the brassicas, especially early in the mornings. The only really effective way of keeping them off is to protect the crop with plastic pigeon netting either draped over the crop or supported on posts. Pigeon netting has large holes allowing snow to go through, so the risk of the whole lot collapsing under heavy snowfall is minimal. Bullfinches are the other winter pest, often creating havoc after Christmas when supplies of seeds become scarce. Their diet changes to swelling buds of forsythia, gooseberries, pears and plums as well as other fruits.

Young vegetable seedlings can be protected by a single strand of strong black cotton along the row about 5cm (2in) above ground level. Draping trees or bushes with black cotton can be effective, but only use cotton that breaks easily as the stronger synthetic threads will maim the birds. Far better to protect your fruit or shrubs with netting. You may prefer to grow all your fruit in a fruit cage, but draping netting over the plants is just as effective, and preferable for flowering shrubs that only need very temporary protection. The mesh size needs to be about 25mm (1in) and this will also do to protect your fruits from starlings, blackbirds and thrushes in the summer. I also use the same netting, supported on wire hoops from my low polythene tunnels, to keep sparrows off seedlings. Finally, in an attempt to blend in with the surroundings, most garden netting is made a lurid, bright green. if you have a choice, buy black.

WEEDING OUT THE WEEDS

The other major gardening problem to contend with is weeds. Perennial weeds such as couch, docks, ground elder and nettles should be eradicated either by digging out or using a weedkiller. You can easily dig out docks, particularly if you do so when the soil is moist. Just lever the soil gently with a fork and a steady tug should see them out in one piece. Couch and ground elder are much more difficult and invariably some pieces will be left behind to regenerate. The quickest way to deal with these is to spray with glyphosate (Tumbleweed). If the weeds are growing rapidly, this herbicide, which moves within the plant, will be more effective. In the case of tall nettles, for instance, it pays to cut them down and spray the next flush of growth.

Herbicides, such as glyphosate, are also very useful for keeping perennial weeds in check in an established garden. It's important to prevent the herbicides from contaminating your plants, so either spray or water them on when there is no wind; if you only have a few scattered weeds brush

Rotation of vegetable crops, To forestall build-up of crop disease, and profit from the nutrients left behind by previous crops, rotate your vegetables in the three-year cycle shown. Lettuce can be grown with the legumes (Plot 2), but provided some rotation is carried out this and other salad crops, celery and spinach can be placed anywhere convenient to the gardener.

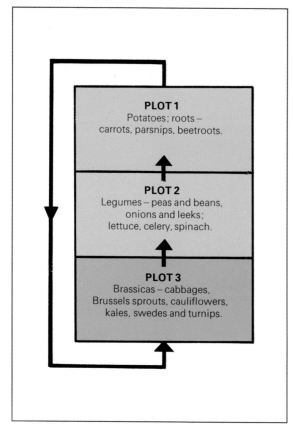

PLOT 1
Potatoes; roots –
carrots, parsnips, beetroots.

PLOT 2
Legumes – peas and beans,
onions and leeks;
lettuce, celery, spinach.

PLOT 3
Brassicas – cabbages,
Brussels sprouts, cauliflowers,
kales, swedes and turnips.

Common problems of ornamentals

Plant	Symptoms	Cause	Conditions	Cultural Control	Chemical Control
Many	Distorted growth. Stunted growth	Aphids	Warm conditions favour rapid reproduction	If no chemicals are used natural predators and parasites may control	Malathion
Many	Tattered, puckered and distorted leaves. Buds killed Misshapen flowers	Capsids	—	—	Malathion
Several	Stems severed at soil level	Cutworms	Weeds	Thorough and frequent cultivation. Control weeds	HCH
Several, inc. lawn grasses	Wilting, chewed roots and stems at soil level	Leatherjackets	Worst on uncultivated ground and that cultivated for first time	Frequent cultivation. On lawns cover patches with black polythene at night. Remove in morning. Birds will clear pests	Chlorpyrifos
Most having soft shoots at ground level	Chewed leaves, stems, roots, fruits	Slugs and snails	Mild, moist conditions. Soils with high organic content	Improve soil drainage	Metaldehyde, methiocarb
Many	Chewed leaves, roots, stems, fruit	Caterpillars	—	Hand-picking, crushing egg batches	HCH, trichlorphon, malathion, fenitrothion, derris, Bacterium-*Bacillus thuringiensis*
Many shrubs and trees, some herbaceous perennials	Plants die rapidly, honey-coloured toadstools	Honey fungus	Sites of old orchards or woodland	Remove infected plants with *all* their roots	Soak soil with creosote or 2% formalin before replanting
Several, esp. roses	White powdery fungus on leaves, stems and flowers	Powdery mildews	Sheltered conditions. Plants short of water	Remove infected leaves and shoots and burn	Dinocap, benomyl, thiophanate-methyl
Roses	Black spots on leaves	Black spot	Wet summers	Burn infected leaves. Mulch with thick layers of grass mowings	Captan

on glyphosate gel. Annual weeds such as chickweed, shepherds' purse and groundsel are best controlled with regular hoeing. The weeds should be cut down when young, and certainly before they can seed.

The saying 'one year's seeding gives seven years' weeding' is only too true. Whatever type of hoe you use, keep it sharp so that the tops of the weeds are cut off cleanly. Herbicides can also be used on annual weeds and one of the best for this purpose is paraquat (Weedol). Paraquat is not translocated in the plant like glyphosate, so it only kills those parts that it hits – in this case the tops of weed seedlings, acting like a chemical hoe. Paraquat is inactivated on contact with the soil, but residual herbicides such as simazine (Weedex) persist for several months in the soil and are therefore effective in preventing annual weed seedlings coming through. Simazine is best applied to compact moist soil in the spring and is particularly useful around roses and fruit trees. You can also use it on paths and drives to prevent weeds growing in those unsightly cracks which seem to increase after each winter.

Common problems of glasshouse crops

Crop	Symptoms	Cause	Conditions	Cultural Control	Chemical Control
Many	Poor growth, wilting	Aphids	Warm conditions favour multiplication	—	Malathion, nicotine, pirimicarb
Several, esp. chrysanthemums and cinerarias	Tunnels between upper and lower surfaces of leaves	Leaf miners	—	Remove affected leaves and burn them	Diazinon, HCH, nicotine
Several	Bronzing of the leaves, cobwebs and colonies of tiny mites	Red spider mites	Dry atmosphere and leaf surfaces	Keep plants moist. Use predator – *phytosieulus**	Derris, diazinon
Mainly house plants	Scales on stems and lower leaf surfaces. Leaves sticky and sooty	Scale insects	—	—	Diazinon, malathion
Many, esp. fuchsia	Adults fly when disturbed. Larvae suck sap and produce sticky honeydew	Whitefly	—	Use predator – *Encarsia* parasite**	Malathion or permethrin smokes
Seedlings	Collapse at base of stem	Damping-off disease	High humidity. Thickly-sown seedlings. Using unsterilized compost and dirty seed trays.	Ventilate. Sow thinly. Use sterile compost in clean trays	Cheshunt mixture
Several, esp. cuttings of soft plants	Rotting followed by grey fluffy down	Grey mould	High humidity. Still atmosphere. Low temperatures	Ventilate	Benomyl or thiophanate-methyl alternating with captan
Several, esp. tomatoes and cucumbers	Poor growth and wilting	Root diseases	Growing same crop in same soil year after year	Rotation. Replace soil with clean. Grow in containers	Best avoided
Many	Poor growth, distorted leaves, pale green or yellow blotches or streaks	Virus diseases	—	Remove and burn infected plants	Control aphids, etc. with insecticides to prevent spread

These predators can be bought from Natural Pest Control, Watermead, Yapton Road, Barnham, Bognor Regis, West Sussex PO22 0BQ. Use them in the glasshouse, where they attack the pests that are their natural victims.

Whatever chemicals you buy, please use them carefully. Only use them when it's really necessary and when you do, read the instructions. Never add a bit more for luck; measure out the exact amount and check the safe period between application and harvest to prevent harmful deposits being left on the crop. Never apply insecticides (or fungicides unless absolutely necessary) to flowering crops being visited by bees. Many of your crops depend on bees as pollinating agents.

Finally, wash out sprayers and watering cans thoroughly after use with at least two or three rinses. Sprayers are fairly cheap and there is a lot of sense in having one for pesticides and fungicides and another for weedkillers only. Keep these and any chemicals well out of reach of children and pets (including fish), preferably under lock and key.

In some areas of the country, the Ministry of Agriculture's Advisory Service provides a useful 'phone-in service where you can listen to a pre-recorded tape covering several aspects of horti-culture. These are usually changed weekly and include information on when to look out or spray for certain problems in your area.   P D

Common fruit problems

Crop	Symptoms	Cause	Conditions	Cultural Control	Chemical Control
Apples	Yellow or red curled leaves on young shoots. Small and distorted fruit	Aphids	—	—	Winter tar-oil wash. Dimethoate or formothion as leaves emerge
	Tunnels to the core	Codling moth	—	Trap overwintering caterpillars by tying cardboard around trunk in July. Remove in winter with cocoons and burr	Fenitrothion applied 4, 6 and 8 weeks after petal fall
	Ribbon-like scars on fruit surface	Sawfly	—	Pick damaged fruits in June	HCH, dimethoate or fenitrothion 1 week after petal fall
	Sunken patches on bark forming elliptical wounds	Canker	Poorly drained soil	Cut out diseased areas	Three sprays of copper fungicide after picking. Paint cleaned wounds with canker paint
	White powdery covering to young shoot tips	Mildew	Hot dry conditions	Cut out infected shoots in June and late summer. Water trees well in dry spells	Dinocap or thiophanate-methyl from leaf-emergence at 14-day intervals until mid-July
	Dark green blotches on leaves. Black scabs on fruit	Scab	Wet summers	Rake up leaves and burn. Cut off shoots with scab on	Captan from leaf emergence, every 2 weeks to July
Pears	Like apples, pears suffer from aphids, caterpillars, canker and scab. Treat as for apples	As for apples		As for apples	As for apples
Plums	Curled-up leaves on young shoots. Colonies of mealy aphids under leaves	Aphids	—	—	Early winter tar-oil wash. Dimethoate or formothion before and after flowering
	Silvery coloured leaves and die-back. Wood is stained	Silver leaf fungus	Rough pruning cuts	Cut back infected branches to 30cm (12in) beyond stained wood	—
Cherries	Leaves with brown spots. Cankers on branches	Bacterial canker	Wet summers. Rough pruning cuts	Cut out cankered branches in spring	Bordeaux mixture in August, September, October
Peaches	Distorted leaves	Peach leaf curl	—	Peaches under glass are not usually affected	Copper fungicide or Bordeaux mixture (Jan–Feb). again just before leaf fall.
Currants	Blistering of leaves. Distorted leaves	Aphids	—	—	Tar oil or DNOC/petroleum (Jan). Dimethoate or formothion (April)
(Black)	Swollen buds	Big bud mite	—	Cut out and burn affected shoots in January–March	Benomyl sprays for diseases also help control this mite
	Dark brown spots on leaves	Leaf spot disease	—	Collect diseased leaves and burn	Thiophanate-methyl from flowering
Gooseberries, redcurrants	Defoliation from middle of bush outwards	Gooseberry sawfly. Caterpillars	—	Pick off caterpillars in April and May	Derris or malathion
Gooseberries	White powdery coating on young leaves and fruits	American gooseberry mildew	Overcrowded bushes. Plants given too much nitrogen	Prune bushes to give good air circulation. Cut out and burn diseased shoots in September	Thiophanate-methyl or benomyl from flowering every 2 weeks until end of May
Raspberries, loganberries, blackberries	Grubs feeding as fruit turns pink and ripens	Raspberry beetle	—	—	Malathion or derris
	Dark purplish blotches around buds in August	Spur blight	Overcrowded canes	Cut out infected and surplus canes	Thiophanate-methyl or benomyl at 2-weekly intervals from bud-burst to just after flowering
	Small purple spots on canes in June, followed by canes splitting open	Cane spot	—	Cut out and burn badly spotted canes	As for spur blight
Strawberries	Brown patches on developing fruits, grey fluffy growth on ripe fruits	Grey mould (Botrytis)	Wet summers. Poorly ventilated cloches or tunnels	Remove infected fruits before they turn grey and fluffy	Benomyl or thiophanate-methyl at 2-weekly intervals from start to finish of flowering

Common vegetable problems

Crop	Symptoms	Cause	Conditions	Cultural Control	Chemical Control
Beans, esp. broad beans	Weak plants. Colonies of blackfly near shoot tips	Aphids	Later sowings of broad beans	Pinch out tops of broad bean plants when in full flower.	Dimethoate, formothion, malathion, pirimicarb
Brassicas (cabbages, cauliflowers, etc)	Yellow leaves on weak young plants	Mealy cabbage aphid	—	—	Dimethoate, formothion
	Holes in leaves, tunnels into the heart	Caterpillars	—	Pick off egg batches and young caterpillars	Trichlorphon, derris or carbaryl dust
	Weak plants, wilting, bluish leaves. Roots eaten	Cabbage root fly	—	Crop rotation. Put discs of flexible material around plants when planting	Treat soil when planting with bromophos, chlorpyrifos or diazinon granules
	Stunted plants, wilting, swollen distorted roots	Clubroot	Acid soils, poor drainage	Lime soil, improve drainage, crop rotation	At planting dip roots in calomel paste, benlate or thiophanate-methyl
Carrots	Tunnels under the root surface	Carrot root fly	Growing carrots near hedges which harbour adults. Thinning attracts adults	Delay sowing to end of May. Sow thinly. Thin only on dull wet evenings.	Treat soil before planting with bromophos, chlorpyrifos or diazinon granules
Celery and celeriac	Chewed areas on stems	Slugs	Poorly drained heavy soils	Improve drainage. Destroy slugs	Methiocarb pellets
	Leaves shrivel	Celery fly	—	Pick off affected leaves	Dimethoate, formothion
Lettuce	Greenfly on leaves	Leaf aphids	On crops under cloches	—	
	Plants weak and wilt	Root aphids	Aphids overwintering in poplars	'Avondefiance', 'Avoncrisp' are resistant	Diazinon
	Yellow blotches on upper surfaces of leaves and mealy underneath	Downy mildew	Overcrowded seedlings. Wet soil	Sow thinly. Thin early. Remove infected plants	Zineb or thiram
	Rot on plants just above soil surface	Grey mould (*Botrytis*)	Soil wet for long periods	Provide good tilth and avoid overwatering	Treat soil with quintozene, Thiram or thiophanate-methyl
Peas	Tunnels in pods, maggots in peas	Pea moth	Varieties flowering June to mid-August are prone	Early maturers, late sown varieties escape	Fenitrothion
Potatoes	Large tunnels in tubers	Slugs	Late varieties are attacked	Grow early varieties	Methiocarb or metaldehyde
	Narrow tunnels in tubers	Wireworms	Newly cultivated ground	Grow early varieties	Treat soil at planting with bromophos, chlorpyrifos or diazinon
Potatoes, tomatoes	Yellow brown patches on leaves. Potatoes develop red dry rots under skin. Tomatoes rot	Blight	Cold wet summers	Grow early varieties	Maneb, zineb or copper

FLOWERS

Richly coloured gloxinias, which thrive in a temperate atmosphere.

COLOURS OF SUMMER: GROWING ANNUALS AND BIENNIALS

Annuals are plants that complete their life cycle within one year and then die, leaving seed behind to germinate the following spring and continue the cycle. That is the strict definition but gardeners stretch it to include some plants that, though they do not automatically die after they have flowered and set seed, are nevertheless best renewed annually from seed.

Gardeners also, for convenience of handling, divide annuals into three groups: hardy, half-hardy and tender. The hardy kinds can be sown outdoors in spring where they are to flower in summer and little more will be needed except to

Verbena phlogiflora.

thin out the seedlings, if too many appear for comfort, and to keep them clear of weeds.

Half-hardy annuals can be sown outdoors in late spring as a rule, but then may start to flower so late in the summer that they make little effective contribution to the garden. If sown earlier out of doors they either fail to germinate because soil temperatures are too low, or they germinate but are then at risk from spring frosts which can continue well into May in many parts of Britain. To overcome these twin hazards they are sown in a controlled climate, in a greenhouse, frame or well-lighted room, in which a temperature of between 13–18°C (55–65°F) can be maintained. The seedlings are grown on in this same temperature range until it matches that outdoors, usually some time in late May or early June, when it is safe to plant them wherever they are required.

Tender annuals are those that are rarely happy in the open in the British Isles except perhaps for a few weeks in summer or in the mildest, mainly maritime districts. They are essentially greenhouse plants, to be grown throughout their short lives in a controlled climate in temperatures generally several degrees higher than those that suit the half-hardy kinds.

Biennials and monocarpic plants resemble annuals in dying after they have flowered and produced ripe seed but differ in the time they take to do this.

What Makes them Grow

Most annuals are sun-lovers though a few will succeed in shade. All like reasonably well drained, moderately fertile soil. In poor, dry soil they are unlikely to make sufficient growth to give a good display. Many hardy annuals have a fairly short flowering season but half-hardy annuals and the half-hardy perennials, grown from seed as if they were annuals, usually continue in bloom for much longer.

By contrast, hardy annuals are natives of temperate regions where the growing season is much shorter and they must hurry to ripen their

Convolvulus tricolor

Dimorphotheca

Limnanthes douglasii

Linum grandiflorum

Dianthus 'Queen of Hearts'

Oenothera

Verbascum

Try these less common annuals and biennials

Hardy annuals to sow outdoors in Spring

Acroclinium	pink, white	30–40cm (12–15in)
Amaranthus caudatus	crimson, lime green	60–80cm (2–2½ft)
Bartonia aurea	yellow	60cm (2ft)
Collinsia	lavender and white	30cm (1ft)
Convolvulus tricolor	blue, purple and white	trailing
Dimorphotheca	yellow, buff, orange, white	20–40cm (8–16in)
Echium (annual)	blue, purple, white	30cm (1ft)
Gypsophila (annual)	white, pink	40–50cm (16–20in)
Lavatera trimestris	rose, white	60–90cm (2–3ft)
Layia	yellow and white	30cm (1ft)
Leptosiphon	white, yellow, pink, carmine	10–15cm (4–6in)
Limnanthes	yellow and white	15–20cm (6–8in)
Linaria maroccana	blue, purple, pink, crimson, yellow	20–30cm (8–12in)
Linum grandiflorum	scarlet	30–40cm (12–16in)
Phacelia	blue	20cm (8in)
Salvia horminum	blue, pink, white	45–60cm (1½–2ft)
Saponaria vaccaria	pink, white	60cm (2ft)
Silene pendula	pink, red, white	15–30cm (6–12in)
Sweet Sultan (Centaurea moschatus)	pink, purple, yellow, white	40–50cm (16–20in)
Viscaria (Lychnis coeli-rosa)	pink, red, blue, white	30–40cm (12–16in)

Half-hardy annuals and related plants

Amaranthus tricolor	yellow, red and green leaves	60–90cm (2–3ft)
Arctotis	white, yellow, orange, red, purple	30–60cm (1–2ft)
Brachycome	blue, white	15–20cm (6–8in)
Celosia plumosa	red, yellow	30–60cm (1–2ft)
Cleome spinosa	pink, carmine, purple	60–90cm (2–3ft)
Cobaea	purple, white	climbing
Cosmos	pink, red, yellow, white	40–90cm (16–36in)
Dianthus sinensis	pink, red, mauve, white	15–30cm (6–12in)
Gaillardia picta	yellow, red	30–40cm (12–16in)
Ipomaea rubro-coerulea	blue	climbing
Kochia	finely divided green leaves becoming crimson	60cm (2ft)
Mesembryanthemum criniflorum	pink, red, apricot, orange	trailing
Petunia	pink, red, blue, purple, yellow, white	30–45cm (1–1½ft)
Phlox drummondii	pink, red, purple, white	15–30cm (6–12in)
Portulaca	pink, red, yellow, white	15cm (6in)
Ricinus	large, divided, bronze, purple or green leaves	60–150cm (1–5ft)
Rudbeckia hirta	yellow, crimson, bronze	40–90cm (16–36in)
Salpiglossis	pink, red, yellow, purple and blue	45–60cm (1½–2ft)
Scabious (annual)	pink, red, purple, lavender, white	45–90cm (1½–3ft)
Statice sinuata	blue, pink, red, yellow and white	45cm (1½ft)
Stock, Ten-week	pink, red, crimson, violet, lavender, cream and white	30–60cm (1–2ft)
Tagetes signata	yellow, orange, red	15–20cm (6–8in)
Ursinia	orange	30cm (1ft)
Venidium	yellow and black	60–90cm (2–3ft)
Zinnia	red, pink, orange, yellow	15–90cm (6–36in)

Biennials and related plants

Canterbury Bell	blue, pink, white	45–75cm (1½–2½ft)
Daisy, Double (Bellis)	white, pink, red	15cm (6in)
Forget-me-not (Myosotis)	blue, pink	15–30cm (6–12in)
Honesty (Lunaria)	purple, white	60–80cm (24–32in)
Oenothera biennis (Evening Primrose)	pale yellow	90cm (3ft)
Pansy	blue, purple, yellow, apricot, orange, bronze-red, white and black	15–20cm (6–8in)
Poppy, Iceland (Papaver nudicaule)	pink, yellow, orange, scarlet	60–80cm (24–32in)
Stock, Brompton	white, pink, red, lavender	40–50cm (16–20in)
Sweet William	pink, red and white	45–60cm (1½–2ft)
Verbascum bombyciferum	yellow flowers – grey woolly leaves	2m (6½ft)

Iceland poppy (*Papaver nudicaule*).

seeds before the autumn arrives to destroy them. This gives half-hardy annuals, such as petunias, French and African marigolds, scarlet salvias (*Salvia splendens*), *Begonia semperflorens*, antirrhinums and verbenas a special value in that they provide colour in the garden over a long period.

Annuals do not require much care once they are planted out. They suffer little from pests and diseases and rarely need to be sprayed. Plants look tidier and continue to flower longer if faded flowers are regularly removed. Weeds should be kept under control so the annuals have no competition.

Some hardy annuals spread freely by self-sown seed. Whether it is wise to let them do so depends a good deal on whether they are species or hybrids. Species, if not highly developed by selection, breed fairly true to type from seed and so self-sown seedlings can be accepted as a welcome bonus. Garden hybrids tend to break up and produce inferior plants; the deterioration continues with each succeeding generation.

Home-saved seed presents similar problems. The more highly developed the variety, the less likely it is to produce seedlings of its own character and quality. Worst of all in this respect are the F1 hybrids which have to be remade every year from parent plants which are never distributed by the raisers. So if you expect the seed from your pink petunias to give pink flowers next year, you could be sadly disappointed.

RULES FOR SOWING

The techniques of cultivation are much the same for all kinds. All seeds require warmth, moisture and air for germination which means that the soil in which they are sown must be crumbly so that water and air can penetrate freely, and moderately firm so that roots of seedlings make easy contact

Dianthus 'Cool Charm' and gypsophila.

with it. If seeds are sown under glass or in other protected places it will almost certainly be most convenient to have them in pots, pans or seed trays filled with growing mixtures specially prepared for the purpose (gardeners rather confusingly call them 'composts', a term they also use for decaying organic matter, a very different material). These mixtures may contain soil, the basic formulae usually being based on those devised at the John Innes Horticultural Institution in the 1930s and known as John Innes (JI) seed and potting compost. Or they may be 'soilless' or 'peat' types, and consist of peat, usually with sand or vermiculite added. All these composts can be prepared at home or purchased ready-mixed for use.

Outdoors, you must usually make do with the existing soil on the site, but this can often be improved out of recognition by digging, forking, raking and mixing in peat, coarse sand, old mushroom compost, decayed garden refuse or anything else that will open up the soil, making it more crumbly and therefore more like the special seed composts used under glass.

Lime is also an excellent improver of the texture of sticky clay soils but it has one drawback for gardens, namely that a good many ornamental plants thrive best in soils that are slightly acid or neutral and lime tends to make soil alkaline. This is less of a hazard for annuals than it is for shrubs and other perennials, for most annuals are fairly soil tolerant, at least as far as an acid/alkaline reaction is concerned. All the same it is best to be sparing with lime.

You can begin sowing some half-hardy annuals in heated greenhouses as early as January, but late February is a better time in home gardens because by then it is easier to maintain the necessary temperatures. The days are getting longer and the light more intense, factors which make it easier to keep seedlings growing sturdily. Sowing can be held back even later, but then flowering will be delayed. Outdoors it is rarely safe to sow annuals until mid-March and then only if the soil can be worked easily and is not sodden and lumpy. In many places mid-April sowings made in good soil and weather conditions can be more satisfactory than March sowings ; the plants, because they have never been checked, may be sturdier and start to flower just as early.

All seeds should be sown thinly since over-crowded seedlings quickly become weak and are much more likely to be attacked by disease. In pots, pans, seed trays or other containers, seeds are usually scattered evenly all over the surface, a method known as 'broadcasting'. Some of the larger seeds can be spaced out singly about $\frac{1}{2}$cm ($\frac{1}{4}$in) apart. The soil in the container should be perfectly level, moderately firm (a couple of sharp raps on a firm bench will settle it down nicely and

can be followed by a good watering from a can fitted with a fine rose) and reach to about 1cm ($\frac{1}{2}$in) below the rim of the container. The seeds are covered with a sprinkling of the same mixture, just sufficient to keep them out of sight but not to bury them to any depth. The compost can then be watered again, once more using a fine rose to prevent disturbance of the surface, then each container can be covered with a sheet of glass laid on top to keep in the moisture.

When all the containers have been sown and covered in this way, a single thickness of news-paper can be laid over them to shade the seeds until they have germinated. It must be removed directly seedlings start appearing, and a day or so later the sheets of glass can be tilted a little, then after another day or so removed altogether. From this time onwards, most seedlings will require all the light that is going. Only a few exceptional kinds will need any shade so early in the year.

Outdoors annuals may be sown broadcast, which is convenient if they are to be grown in patches of one kind, or in 'drills', the tiny furrows made with a pointed stick or the corner of a hoe or rake. The advantage of sowing in drills is that the seedlings of the garden plants will all appear in rows, whereas weed seedlings will be distributed at random and will be easier to spot and remove.

For most seeds the drills need be no more than 1cm ($\frac{1}{2}$cm) deep and they are refilled, after sowing, by drawing the displaced soil back into them. Seeds are sown just a little more deeply out of doors than under cover since they need protection from disturbance by wind and heavy rain.

PLANTING OUT THE SEEDLINGS

Seedlings grown in containers must be trans-planted after a few days before they become weakened by overcrowding. 'Pricking-out', as this is termed, is about the trickiest part of the whole operation as the tiny seedlings are fragile and

Prick out container-grown seedlings gently with a stick and replant in holes pressed out with a forefinger.

easily damaged. They can either be tipped out very carefully or lifted, a few at a time, with a sharpened stick (a wooden plant label will do). They are then separated and replanted 4–6cm ($1\frac{1}{2}$–$2\frac{1}{4}$in) apart in seed trays filled with the same type of compost as that used for germination. The same sharpened stick can be used to make little holes for them but the forefinger is quicker and even more efficient.

Seedlings raised under cover must be acclimatized to outdoor conditions before they are finally planted out. The most efficient way to do this is to move them into a frame for the last fortnight, for this can be left completely open by day if the weather is favourable and partly open at night if there is no threat of frost.

Outdoors, seedlings will need to be thinned out and many kinds can be transplanted elsewhere if they are dug up carefully with a little soil adhering to their roots. Transplanting is most successful on a damp day after rain but if there is none, the seedlings should be well watered a few hours in advance.

All that has been said about the cultivation of half-hardy annuals applies equally to tender annuals up to and including pricking-out, but slightly higher temperatures may be required for some. Pot on the seedlings singly, this time into a rather richer potting compost. They are then grown on under cover with no hardening-off or planting-out. Make sure that the final pot is large enough to cope with the fully grown plant. Biennials germinate one year but do not flower and produce seed until the next year. Monocarpic plants, which include many species of meconopsis and also *Saxifraga longifolia*, take an unspecified time to complete their cycle. Some actually live for a number of years before they flower but once they do their end is near.

Although biennials have a regular life extending over at least part of two years, it is necessary to raise them anew from seed every year if flowers are to be enjoyed every year. Just as with annuals, there are numerous plants that, though not truly biennial, are conveniently treated as such since they produce the best and most reliable results when grown in this way.

Seed of most biennials and monocarpic plants (also of most true herbaceous perennials) is best sown in May or June. Usually by then it will germinate quite well outdoors but it may be easier to care for some of the rarer, more expensive or more difficult seeds if they are sown in pots, pans or other containers and germinated in an unheated frame or greenhouse.   **A H**

THE ROSE GARDEN

Roses have been so intensively interbred and developed in gardens that a quite bewildering range of types and varieties has developed. Home gardeners, though, can safely think of them under three main headings: the climbers, the shrub and the bedding varieties.

Roses to be grown as climbers are trained against walls and screens, over pergolas and arches; the most vigorous kinds are allowed to scramble up into trees. Shrub roses can be planted on their own or in company with other shrubs. Bedding roses are most effective when planted together to make fine sheets of colour.

The bedding varieties come in various sizes of plant and flower. Some, traditionally known as hybrid tea roses, have large, notably well-shaped flowers and are the ones to choose if you value quality of bloom most highly. Others, traditionally called floribundas, carry their flowers in large clusters and do this so continuously from June to October that they are the best roses to grow when overall display is more important than individual perfection. A third sort, the miniature roses, are quite short, rarely above 30cm (1ft), with leaves and flowers to scale. They are the ideal roses to use as edgings or to make carpets of colour; some are attractive in rock gardens though they can be a little too sophisticated to look really in keeping with conventional rock-garden species.

There are many sub-divisions of the three main groups. These include roses with single, semi-double, fully double or pompon flowers; moss roses which have a curious development of moss-like glands on the calyx segments and flower stems, and roses which sprawl rather than climb and so can be used as ground cover. Also, by grafting garden roses on to tall briar stems, it is possible to create plants like miniature trees. These are knows as 'standards' or, if the rose grafted on the straight stem is a climbing variety, as 'weeping standards' since the long flexible stems will arch over and eventually touch the ground, making a specimen like a small weeping tree.

Climbers like 'Karlsruhe' make one major display each summer with intermittent flowerings later.

PLANTING

Roses will grow in all fertile soils, alkaline, neutral or moderately acid, light, medium or heavy. The two essentials are that the soil must be reasonably well drained and have a readily available supply of plant food. This last is particularly important for the bedding roses which must make continuous sturdy new growth if they are to perform well. Species, most of which flower only once a year, and that only for a week or so, make less urgent demands on the soil than hybrids.

Roses thrive best in open sunny places with a free circulation of air. A few will grow in shade but they are exceptional. In very enclosed places with little air movement they can suffer badly from mildew and some varieties, especially the ramblers which are vigorous climbers bearing clusters of relatively small flowers, are also specially vulnerable to mildew when trained against walls.

Soil for roses should be well dug and manured. Anything that makes it richer will help: animal manure, decayed garden refuse, prepared town waste or sewage sludge or old mushroom compost fortified with a little fertilizer. The best way to buy roses is lifted from the open ground but this can only be done safely from late October until late March. At other times roses must be obtained in containers from which they can be planted without disturbing the soil around their roots.

When you're planting roses, make the holes wide enough to accommodate all the roots – which should be spread in a natural manner – and deep enough to bring the junction between stems and rootstock to about 1cm ($\frac{1}{2}$in) below soil level. Plants dug up from nursery beds may have some long thin roots which can be shortened a little with secateurs. Broken roots can also be trimmed neatly at the same time. Plant securely, treading the soil in firmly around the roots, but only plant when conditions are favourable, ie not when the soil is so wet that it sticks to your spade and boots nor when it is frozen.

PRUNING

All newly planted roses should be pruned either before they are planted, which is often most convenient but in cold places can be a bit risky, or in March, which is safe since by the time new growth appears frosts are unlikely to be sufficiently severe to do the plant any harm. Even early

Hybrid Teas and Hybrid Perpetuals

Floribundas

Species and Shrub Roses

Climbers and Ramblers

FIRST YEAR PRUNING

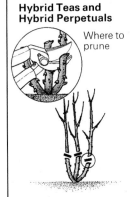
Where to prune

All strong stems should be cut back to 8–10cm (3–4in) and weak growth should then be removed altogether.

Cut back to 8–10cm (3–4in)

Cut back to 30cm (1ft)

Leave best stems to 60–90cm (2–3ft)

SECOND AND SUBSEQUENT YEAR PRUNING

Cutting out old wood.

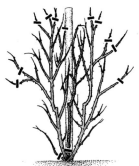

The thick, hard brown bark found in old bushes can be cut out completely. Cut back new growth to $\frac{1}{2}$ original length and thinner stems by $\frac{2}{3}$ or $\frac{3}{4}$. remove all broken branches.

Do not shorten new growth so radically; cut out some old wood. The best shoots should be shortened by $\frac{1}{3}$; and the weakest by $\frac{2}{3}$ – or else they could be removed altogether.

Important aspect is the thinning and removal of dead, damaged and decayed growth. Otherwise, only a little shortening is needed to maintain a good shape.

These roses can be left to grow almost naturally with just a sufficient amount of thinning and shortening to the branches to ensure they fit the area they are required to fill.

April is all right, provided the weather is not too warm. All strong stems of bedding roses should be cut back to 8–10cm (3–4in) and weak growths removed altogether. Vigorous shrub roses and species need not be pruned so severely and can be left with stems up to 30cm (1ft) long, and climbers can be given even more freedom, with the best stems left 60–90cm (2–3ft) long.

After the first year, pruning should be varied according to the type of rose, the way in which it is growing and the space it is required to fill. A fair general rule for all pruning is that the harder a plant is cut the stronger will be the new growth it makes. However, when a plant is in such poor condition that it has only a few hard old stems left, severe pruning will simply hasten its end. Even that may not be a bad thing, for there comes a stage when it is better to replace a weak plant than struggle to rejuvenate it.

The large-flowered bedding varieties, or hybrid teas, thrive on the hardest pruning. It can be done at any time from November until late March (but March pruning is safest in cold places, as already explained). With old bushes a few of the oldest stems, thick and with hard brown bark, may be cut out completely if they are carrying little young growth. Younger bushes will have no branches of this type but they may have some damaged or diseased stems which should be cut back to sound growth. Black or purple patches on the stems are tell-tale signs that fungi are at work and should be cut out if possible. When all this has been done the bush will probably look a good deal simpler and more open that it did at the start. It only remains to shorten the best of the remaining stems made the previous year (they are the ones with smooth green or reddish bark) by about half their length and thinner stems by two-thirds or even three-

Above: 'Priscilla Burton' (Floribunda).
Above left: 'Fruhlingsmorgen' (modern shrub).
Left: *Rosa canina* (species).

Below left: 'Fantin-Latour' (old rose).
Below: 'Madame Pierre Oger' (old rose).

Above: 'Handel' (climber).

Below: 'Coalite Flame' (hybrid tea).

quarters. Each cut should be made just above a growth bud facing as nearly as possible outwards from the centre of the bush. This helps to direct growth outwards and so prevent a tangle of branches at the centre.

The pruning of cluster-flowered bedding roses, or floribundas, is similar in principle but different in degree. It is just as necessary to cut out old or diseased wood but there is no need to shorten good young growth as much. The best can be tipped or shortened by a third, the weakest removed or shortened by two-thirds. Most of these varieties are naturally vigorous and capable of sustaining quite a lot of growth.

True shrub roses are even more vigorous and it is the thinning operation, the removal of dead, damaged or diseased growth, that is most important. This can be followed by a little shortening and thinning, enough to preserve a well-balanced shapely bush.

Right at the end of the pruning scale come the species and climbers, many of which can be allowed to grow almost naturally with enough thinning and shortening to fit them to the areas they have to fill.

The spectacular hip of *Rugosa* 'Frau Dagmar Hartopp' – a shrub rose that is good for hedging and wild places.

FEEDING

Pruning needs to be supplemented by feeding for the two have a similar purpose, to maintain a constant supply of sturdy new growth. If manure or garden compost is available, rose beds and the soil around specimen bushes and climbers can be given a good dressing or mulch every year, preferably in February or March though any time is better than not at all. On its own the mulch is unlikely to be enough, and should be supplemented by a scattering of fertilizer in April with a little more to follow in June just as the bushes are coming into flower. A compound fertilizer containing about equal percentages of nitrogen, phosphoric acid and potash is best, and if the 7:7:7 National Growmore formula is chosen it should be applied at 100g (3½oz) per square metre in April and about half that quantity in June.

Faded flowers should be removed, and with bedding varieties this can be the opportunity for a mild summer pruning, the stems with dead flowers being cut back to a young growth or, if none can be seen, to a fat growth bud where a leaf stalk is attached to the stem. A H

WINTER AND SPRING GREENHOUSE FLOWERS

A greenhouse with good light and sufficient warmth to prevent the temperature ever falling below 7°C (45°F) can be a flowery place throughout the year but many home gardeners may prefer to use it for crops such as tomatoes, cucumbers and aubergines in the summer and concentrate more on flowers from about October, when chrysanthemums begin to require protection, until the spring, when it may be required mainly for raising seedlings before it would be safe to do so outdoors. Among the best plants for this purpose are various kinds of winter-flowering primulas, cinerarias, cyclamen, greenhouse azaleas and early bulbs, particularly hyacinths, daffodils and specially prepared hippeastrums, some of which have already been described,. There are also winter-flowering begonias and poinsettias as well as various winter-flowering heaths (ericas) but these are not generally as easy to manage.

AZALEAS

One section of the evergreen azaleas, usually described as Indian azaleas, is derived from the distinctly tender Chinese and Formosan species *Rhododendron simsii*. The garden hybrids from this have fairly large double flowers, white, pink, salmon, orange-red, scarlet and crimson, often with one colour splashed on another, and as they can be gently forced into flower from October until March, they have become very popular as winter-flowering pot plants. Vast numbers of them are sold in the florist and plant shops, especially at Christmas, and this is the way most amateurs acquire them in the first place. Though they make excellent room plants for a few weeks, they usually deteriorate in time partly for lack of light, even more because they like a moderately moist, fresh atmosphere and find it too dry indoors.

During the summer they are quite happy standing outdoors in a light but not too hot place but they must be watered well and they also like to

be sprayed overhead so that the leaves are damp.

In October they should be brought into a cool greenhouse, conservatory or light room and should continue to be watered fairly freely. They are usually grown in a compost containing a lot of peat which, if it gets dry, is difficult to wet again. Should this happen the pot should be stood for ten minutes or so in a bucket of water and then allowed to drain. Peat contains little plant food, so azaleas should be fed every ten to fourteen days in spring and summer, preferably with a liquid fertilizer (a seaweed extract is ideal) diluted in water according to label instructions. Failure to flower after the first year is usually due to inadequate watering and/or feeding. Repotting is not, as a rule, necessary annually but when it is required a mixture of three parts peat, one part lime-free loam and one part lime-free sand is suitable.

There are early, mid-season and late-flowering varieties. The first are used for Christmas flowering and are grown in a temperature of 13–18°C (55–60°F) from the moment they are housed in October. Mid-season varieties are grown at a few degrees less until December, when the temperature is raised to bring them into flower in late January or February. Late varieties can be left to flower naturally in April-May or given a little extra warmth from January to start flowering in April.

BROWALLIA

Browallia speciosa is another attractive annual which will make a good pot plant for winter flowering. An early sowing in March in a temperature of 15°C (60°F) will give plants to flower from July to October, a second, made in May or June, will provide a succession until December. Treatment is exactly as for exacum and 10cm (4in) pots are suitable for the fully grown plants. Bushiness will be improved if the tips of shoots are pinched out occasionally during the summer. Plants are about 30cm (12in) high and have bright blue flowers.

CALCEOLARIA

These are the gayest of the spring-flowering greenhouse biennials, at their peak in May but continuing into June to link up with the summer flowers. There are a number of different species,

Spring greenhouses (*left*) can be very colourful places with displays such as these calceolaria (*above right*) and cineraria (*below right*).

many perennial and even sub-shrubby, but the popular greenhouse varieties are all biennials sown one year to flower the next. They are bushy, rather leafy plants with big clusters of distinctively pouched flowers, yellow, orange, red and crimson often with one colour splashed or spotted on another so that the display is very striking. There are several types including Large Flowered and Multiflora Nana, the latter rather shorter, 20cm (8in) instead of 30–40cm (12–16in), compact and with smaller flowers.

Seed should be sown in May or June as described for primulas and pricking out and first potting are also the same. These are also plants that like cool conditions in summer and so are easier to manage in a frame, which can be left wide open when the weather is warm, than in a greenhouse, which can become uncomfortably hot. Even in winter there is no need for much artificial heat provided the temperature never drops below 7°C (45°F) but plants do want all the light possible and careful watering, with the leafy crowns of the plants kept as dry as possible. Big plants will need to be potted on into 15cm (6in) pots in September or October and will need some staking in spring because of the weight of the flowers they will carry.

CINERARIAS

These plants belong to the daisy family and are really perennials but in gardens are invariably renewed each year from seed, which is sown in April, May or June. Often two sowings are made, one early to give flowers from November until about January and another late to carry on until April or May. There are several different types, all bushy plants but differing in size and flower character. The Grandiflora varieties, with flowers up to 10cm (4in) across, are the most popular but the Stellata varieties, with much smaller, more numerous flowers, are very attractive and the Multiflora varieties, with flowers of intermediate size, have the additional merit of being compact in habit, a characteristic even more marked in the Nana Multiflora varieties which are very suitable for small greenhouses. Colours in all these types are rich and varied, blue, violet, purple, crimson and red, often with a white zone around a dark central disk.

Cinerarias are almost hardy and require little artificial heat. Seed should be sown from April to June in a peat or soil-based seed compost in a temperature of 15–16°C (60°F). Seedlings are pricked out into trays of similar compost and later potted singly, as advised for primulas except that the largest plants may require 15cm (6in) pots and the final potting will be in September or October. Like primulas, cinerarias will be happier in a frame in summer and, even when returned to the greenhouse in late September, they should be given maximum light and as much ventilation as is compatible with a minimum temperature of 8°C (46°F). They need a fair amount of water in summer while growing fast, but in autumn and winter should be kept no more than moist and great care should be taken to keep water off the leaves and crowns which rot readily if constantly wet.

Cyclamens will flower for most of the winter if the conditions are right.

Cyclamen persicum is available in a variety of colours, including white.

CYCLAMEN

It is the garden varieties of *Cyclamen persicum* that are grown as winter-flowering greenhouse plants. There are a great many of them, some with very heavily silvered leaves which are as decorative as the flowers themselves, some with extra large flowers, or flowers that have a slight but very pleasant perfume, in a variety of colours from white and palest pink to crimson. They are perennials which make bun-shaped tubers sitting more or less on the surface of the soil, getting larger each year until they eventually become unwieldly. Propagation is by seed which is traditionally sown in an unheated greenhouse in August though some of the modern, fast-maturing varieties can be sown in January or February in a temperature of 15°C (60°F) with good prospect of having plants in flower by the autumn.

Germination can be erratic and it is wise to prick out seedlings as they appear but not to discard the seed pan for several months in case later seedlings appear. Plants will grow well in peat or soil-based potting composts in a temperature around 13–15°C (55–60°F) with a minimum of 7°C (45°F) in good light but with shade from hot sunshine. From early June to late September they will be just as happy in a frame, or even standing outdoors provided they are not neglected. They should be potted on as necessary, the largest plants reaching 12–13cm (5in) pots by September.

The first year they must be watered throughout and fed occasionally with liquid fertilizer. Flowering can continue most of the winter but when it is over the water supply should be gradually reduced and from June to August the soil need be no more than just damp. Plants can be repotted in August, all the old soil being shaken off and the tubers kept almost completely on top of the new soil. Though cyclamen will live for many years it is usually best to limit their life to two or three years and then replace with seedlings.

EXACUM

Exacum affine is an easily grown annual which deserves to be better known. It makes a neat bushy plant about 30cm (12in) high with lilac-blue sweetly scented flowers. If seed is sown in a cool greenhouse in March plants will flower from August to about October. A second sowing in June will give a succession of flowers from about October until Christmas or later. Seed germinates readily in a temperature of 15°C (60°F), seedlings thrive in a peat or soil-based potting compost, will need no artificial heat in summer, should have normal watering and will reach full size in 10cm (4in) pots.

KALANCHOE

Kalanchoe blossfeldiana is a small, bushy succulent cultivated for its abundant sprays of small scarlet or yellow flowers in winter. It is an easy plant to grow, readily raised from seed sown in March or April in a temperature of around 18°C (65°F) or from cuttings rooted in sand and peat any time in summer. It will grow in a mixture of equal parts soil, peat and coarse grit or sand with just a peppering of fertilizer such as John Innes base or En Mag. Watering is normal and artificial heat is unnecessary in summer and is only necessary at other times to maintain a temperature between 7 and 13°C (45–55°F). Plants require all the light possible. Good flowering plants can be produced in 8–10cm (3 to 4in) pots.

POINSETTIAS

The botanical name of the poinsettia is *Euphorbia pulcherrima* and it is a deciduous shrub from Mexico, cultivated for the large scarlet or pink bracts which surround the insignificant flowers in winter. It is forced in large numbers for the Christmas trade and this is how most gardeners acquire it. It is not difficult to retain plants for several years but it is almost impossible to keep them as short and compact as they were when bought as they were sprayed in the nursery with growth-retarding chemicals which are not readily available for home use. If taller plants are acceptable there remains the problem of making certain that they produce flowers and bracts, which are only initiated when the night length is sixteen hours or more. Difficulty arises mainly when plants are grown in rooms, for even an electric light, switched on in the evening, can inhibit the formation of the flower buds and their accompanying bracts. The way to prevent this is to cover plants from mid-September onwards with a black out each evening sufficiently early to ensure at least sixteen hours of complete darkness.

After flowering, poinsettias are best kept in a greenhouse with a temperature range of 15 to 20°C (59–68°F) with plenty of moisture in the air and light shading in summer. For two or three weeks in April the soil is kept almost dry so that leaves fall. The stems are then shortened by two-thirds, watering is resumed and the temperature raised a little to re-start the plants into growth. If desired the prunings can be prepared as cuttings and rooted in a warm propagator. Old plants and rooted cuttings can be potted in a fairly rich, soil-based compost and, after about a month, should be given supplementary liquid feeding every seven to ten days throughout the summer.

PRIMULAS

The four most useful primulas for winter flowering are *P. obconica*, *P. malacoides*, *P. sinensis* and *P. kewensis*. With the exception of the last, which is only available in one yellow-flowered variety, all have been highly developed by plant breeders and many varieties differing in flower colour and form are offered. All can be raised from seed and are generally treated as annuals and discarded after flowering but *P. obconica* and *P. kewensis* are, in fact, perennials which, under favourable conditions, will live for years.

Primula obconica carries its flowers in loose

Primula.

clusters on stems up to 30cm (1ft) high and though there are starry flowered (stellata) varieties it is those with quite big, round flowers that are most popular. They are available in shades of blue, pink and red as well as white, in mixture and also in some separate colours. Though winter and spring are their main flowering season, they will continue to flower less freely for many months, sometimes virtually the year round. Seed should be sown in March or April for winter flowering and in June or July to give vigorous young plants to carry on flowering freely in spring. Seed will germinate in a peat or soil-based seed compost in a temperature of 15°C (60°F) but seed pans should be covered with glass only, no paper, as these are seeds that germinate better in the light.

Seedlings should be pricked out into seed trays filled with a low fertilizer content potting compost

Above: polyanthus.

Polyanthus are hybrids of the Primula species. They are available in a variety of colours.

as soon as they can be handled conveniently. When they have made a few more leaves, they should be potted singly in a similar compost in 7.5cm (3in) pots and be moved on to 12–13cm (5–5½in) pots and a rather richer compost when the small pots are comfortably filled with roots. Much of this time, certainly from June to September, the plants will be as happy in a well-ventilated frame as in a greenhouse, and if kept in the latter should be lightly shaded and not allowed to get hot or dry at any time, certainly not above 24°C (75°F) with the average around 18°C (65°F). In autumn and winter the plants will do better in a light greenhouse or sunny window and it will not matter if the temperature occasionally drops to 7°C (45°F) though the 13–15°C (55–60°F) range suits them best.

The leaves of *Primula obconica* are covered beneath with short glandular hairs which can cause a severe skin rash in some people. As a precaution it is wise to wear rubber gloves when handling these plants.

Primula sinensis is a rather shorter plant, often with attractively fringed petals, and a colour range that includes orange and scarlet as well as blue and white. Though very beautiful, it has never been quite as popular as *P. obconica*, perhaps because of its less extended flowering season and greater tendency to decay in winter if kept too wet and cool. Nevertheless it is not a difficult plant to grow and the details of cultivation are the same as for *P. obconica*, with an even greater emphasis on equable temperatures and careful watering, especially in winter when water should be applied direct to the soil and not splashed over the leaves.

Primula malacoides is one of the easiest winter-flowering plants, almost hardy and actually capable of growing out of doors in some mild places. The flowers are small but numerous, in large sprays, mauve-pink and single in the wild species but in various shades of pink and carmine, occasionally double, in the garden varieties. The chief difference of cultivation is that, since this primula grows fast, it is unnecessary to sow seed until June for winter flowering and it can be grown with even less artificial heat.

Primula kewensis is also nearly hardy. The leaves and stems are usually covered with white meal but this is lacking in some forms. The flowers are invariably bright yellow and are pleasantly, though not strongly, scented. Cultivation is identical to that of *P. malacoides* with the one exception that this is quite a good perennial, so it may be worth while retaining some plants to flower another year. It is mainly spring flowering.

WINTER-FLOWERING BEGONIAS

Several races of begonia, particularly 'Gloire de Lorraine', 'Optima' and varieties related to them, are exclusively winter flowering. They can be grown from cuttings rooted in a warm propagator in spring and need to be grown on in a greenhouse with a minimum temperature of 15°C (60°F), in a moderately moist atmosphere and with shade from direct sunshine. Even in winter a temperature of 13–18°C (55–65°F) must be maintained.

'Gloire de Lorraine' and other varieties of its type produce large sprays of small pink flowers not unlike those of *Begonia semperflorens*, so popular for summer bedding. Their roots are wholly fibrous. 'Optima' is taller and has larger, single pink flowers and the roots are partly fibrous, partly tuberous owing to their hybrid origin. This makes them more sensitive to overwatering in winter, when the soil needs to be kept moist but never sodden. This is made easier if the potting compost is really porous, with plenty of peat and/or leafmould and sand.

WINTER-FLOWERING HEATHS

The three heaths mainly grown for winter flowering are *Erica hyemalis*, with pink and white flowers; *E. gracilis*, rosy-purple and *E. nivalis*, white. All are native to South Africa, require acid, humus-rich soil and are often grown in almost pure peat with a little lime-free sand or grit to make it more porous. These heathers are grown in large numbers for sale as pot plants, particularly at Christmas, and this is how they usually find their way into home greenhouses. Unfortunately for easy market handling the plants are frequently removed from the fairly large pots in which they have been grown, the root balls are reduced in size and squeezed into much smaller pots. Such plants are very difficult to keep alive for more than a few weeks.

Winter-flowering heathers are nearly hardy and can be grown in a minimum temperature of 7°C (45°F). They need all the light available and very careful watering since the peat compost must not be allowed to become dry but should never be saturated for long. In practice, with a well blended mixture, surplus water should drain away quite rapidly. From June to September plants can be placed in a frame or even stood outside provided they are not neglected and allowed to become dry.

A H

AN EXOTIC ATMOSPHERE

BEGONIAS AND GLOXINIAS

Tuberous-rooted begonias and gloxinias are two of the most gorgeous, exotic plants that can be grown easily in greenhouses, conservatories or sunny windows. February is a good time to start, either with seed or with tubers; you can begin later, but flowering will then be delayed.

Tubers should be raised in a greenhouse maintained at an initial temperature of 15–18°C (59–65°F). Bed them side by side in moist peat in shallow seed trays and keep them moist until they have two or three leaves each. Then lift them carefully out of the peat and transfer them singly to 12-15cm (5–6in) pots containing any good soil- or peat-based potting compost. Keep the tubers almost on the surface.

Once potted-on, both begonias and gloxinias like to grow in a temperate atmosphere. They do not like great heat or intense light. The temperature range should be 15–21°C (59–70°F) with the sunny side of the greenhouse kept shaded in summer. The begonias can also be planted outdoors from June to September, though it is best to limit yourself to plants producing medium-sized

Below right: Gloxinias are almost stemless with dark velvety leaves.

Below: Full-bodied blooms of tuberous-rooted begonias on display at a show held by the Royal Horticultural Society.

flowers since the larger flowers tend to get battered by wind and rain.

Water the greenhouse plants fairly freely in spring and summer but less and less from early autumn and not at all in winter. By November they can be tapped out of their pots, the remaining stems and leaves cut off and the soil shaken from the roots, after which the tubers can be stored dry in any cool frost-proof place. Alternatively, leave the tubers in their pots and lay these on their sides in a frost-proof place so that no water gets into the soil. There the tubers can stay until it is time to start them again the following year.

If you decide to grow begonias and gloxinias from seed you must be very careful when sowing because the seed is very fine, almost dust-like. It is best sown in pans filled with a peat-based seed compost made very smooth and level so that the tiny seeds do not drop down into crevices and get smothered. After sowing, the seed may either be covered with the lightest peppering of fine silver sand or left uncovered with a sheet of glass laid over the pan and a single sheet of newspaper laid on top. Pans are best watered by holding them for a few moments almost to their rims in a basin of water; the moisture then rises from below and the surface is not disturbed. A temperature of 18–21°(65–70°F) will ensure good germination but it may be up to four weeks before all the seedlings appear.

Prick out the seedlings while they are still tiny into a peat compost no less fine than the one you used for sowing. A few weeks later the seedlings can be potted singly in small 6cm (2½in) pots using a slightly richer mixture which may contain a little soil if preferred. As these pots become filled with roots, move the plants on to larger pots. When the tubers start to form, they should be kept quite close to the surface when repotting, only just covered with soil. Continue to cultivate exactly as for plants grown from tubers.

There are many other types of begonia which do not make tubers and therefore cannot be stored dry during the winter. Some actually choose winter as their flowering season and are among the most beautiful plants then in bloom. This group includes 'Gloire de Lorraine', with dense sprays of small pink flowers, the larger-flowered 'Optima' and other associated varieties. Grown from cuttings of young shoots rooted in a warm

Begonia 'Bali Hi' on display.

Below right: Tuberous begonia 'Picotee Edge'.

Below: Tuberous begonia 'Alan Melville'.

propagator in spring, they require similar conditions to the summer-flowering begonias except that they are never deprived of water and are kept growing throughout the winter in a temperature of 15–18°C (59–65°F).

The 'Rex' begonias, and also a species named *B. masoniana*, often called 'Iron Cross' because of the black cross-shaped marking on each leaf, are grown for their foliage. In the 'Rex' varieties the leaves are large, heart-shaped and richly coloured – green, silver and metallic purple. These begonias are not difficult to grow, they will put up with a lot of shade and will survive even when the temperature falls to 10°C (50°F), but they are happier with a few degrees more. They should be watered moderately, even in winter, and can be increased by division when repotting in spring.

There are also numerous species, such as *B. manicata* with large loose sprays of pink flowers, *B. haageana* with leaves green above and light purple beneath, *B. lucerna* with sprays of large pink flowers and *B. fuchsioides* with long stems that can be trained to wires or canes, all of which are beautiful in both flower and leaf. They need very much the same conditions as the tuberous-rooted kinds except that they must be watered moderately throughout the winter and kept in a temperature which should never fall below 10°C (50°F).

A H

ORCHIDS

This is a vast race of plants embracing a great many genera, a far larger number of species and innumerable man-made hybrids. It is the last that are now most popular as greenhouse plants, particularly those derived from a relatively few species such as cattleya, cymbidium, dendrobium, lycaste, miltonia, odontoglossum, oncidium, paphiopedilum, and phalaenopsis.

Many orchids are quite hardy and grow in ordinary soil. Some are British wild plants, to be found growing freely in meadows, hedgerows, woodlands, etc. Such orchids are known as 'terrestrial' because they grow on the ground like the majority of plants and a few of the exotic kinds cultivated in greenhouses are also terrestrial. Others, and they are the majority, are epiphytic, ie they have adapted themselves to grow in trees or on rocks and to obtain much of their food from the air or from the plant debris which accumulates in such places. Such plants are not necessarily difficult to grow but they do require a totally different cultural technique from that used for terrestrial plants.

They are grown in very spongy composts, traditionally in a mixture of osmunda fibre (the fibrous roots of the osmunda fern) and living sphagnum moss, but now that osmunda fibre has become scarce and expensive, in all manner of substitutes including the chopped up roots of other ferns, pulverized or shredded bark or even fragments of polystyrene which provide the necessary firm yet very porous medium to which the orchids can anchor themselves. Different mixtures are used for different genera and experts vary greatly in their recommendations. A typical mixture, suitable for many orchids, is three parts of chopped sphagnum moss, two parts bark chippings and one part of perlite or polystyrene granules. For cymoidiums, lycastes and paphiopedilums, which need a firmer more terrestrial type of compost, a mixture could be used of two parts sphagnum moss, one part well rotted beech or oak leafmould, one part of fibrous loam, broken up by hand but not sieved, and one part of perlite or polystyrene granules.

Orchids are grown in well drained pots or in special baskets which can be suspended from the roof rafters. It is not, as a rule, necessary to repot annually and when repotting is done, usually just as new root growth is starting, no attempt is made to firm the compost around the roots but it is carefully inserted all round and between the roots so that there are no open places.

Nearly all orchids like a very humid atmosphere and it is natural for the epiphytic kinds to hang their roots down to collect moisture and food from the atmosphere. Trays of water may be required in the house to maintain this moisture; paths and stages may need to be wetted several times a day and plants sprayed with water. Automatic humidifiers may also be used to keep the air at predetermined levels of humidity.

An alternative, almost essential if orchids are to be grown indoors, is a terrarium or plant cabinet, a kind of tiny, portable greenhouse which can be kept tightly closed and in which any degree of humidity can be maintained.

Some orchids want a good deal of warmth but most of the popular kinds will grow in what is known as an intermediate temperature range, 13–16°C (55–61°F) in winter rising to 16–21°C (61–70°F) in summer. Some of the hardier kinds will take temperatures at least 3°C below these and the little pleiones are virtually hardy and can be grown in any greenhouse from which frost can be excluded.

Nearly all orchids need shade from direct sunshine but few like dense shade. Orchid houses are often fitted with lath shades on the sunny side, a few inches above the glass with the spaces between the laths about equal to their own width. Such houses also often have two stagings inside, the upper one of slats to carry the orchid pots, the lower one, a few inches below, solid to take gravel, coarse sand or leca (expanded clay granules) which can be kept constantly moist.

Many orchids form bulb-like stems, known as 'pseudo-bulbs', which serve as storage organs and are formed, one in front of another, as the plant grows. Old pseudo-bulbs gradually wither away and are discarded, but when orchids are repotted, the younger back pseudo-bulbs can be detached and potted separately to grow into new plants.

Many orchids, particularly those with well developed pseudo-bulbs, have a marked resting season each year when temperatures can be allowed to drop a little and watering can be considerably reduced. Part of the skill in growing orchids well is in knowing when to rest them, for how long and how much.

A magnificent display of orchids in the orchid house of the Botanic Gardens in Durban.

Cattleya 'Nature's Masterpiece'.

Above: Cymbidium
'Monterey Hills'.

RECOMMENDED ORCHIDS

Cattleya Showy epiphytic orchids with large flowers, often in shades of purple, crimson, mauve and white. They flower at different times, should not be kept dry at any time but need far less water in winter than in summer. There are a great many varieties.

Coclogyne cristata A small epiphytic species with white flowers in February and March. It is one of the easiest to grow and it rests in winter.

Cymbidium Probably the most popular genus today, with arching sprays of bird-like flowers in a wide range of colours many of which are seldom seen in other plants. There are a great many varieties, some relatively small, some large and most semi-terrestrial in habit, best grown in peat plus perlite or polystyrene granules. The main flowering season is March to June and they rest in winter.

Dendrobium Epiphytes with cane-like pseudo-bulbs and sprays of white, yellow, purple or pink flowers in winter and spring. They rest in autumn or early winter.

Lycaste Superficially rather like cymbidiums except that the flowers are carried singly, not in sprays. They require similar treatment.

Miltonia Often strikingly coloured epiphytic orchids with flat flowers rather like enormous

Right: Pigeon orchid.

pansies. They flower mainly in spring and summer and have no very marked resting period.

Odontoglossum A large and varied genus, mainly cultivated as hybrids. Those derived from *O. crispum* carry their white or purple blotched flowers in arching sprays at various seasons, whereas *O. grande* has much larger yellow and chestnut-red flowers carried in twos and threes in autumn or winter. It needs little water in winter but the *O. crispum* hybrids should be kept moist at all seasons.

Oncidium A large and varied genus of epiphytes in which some of the most beautiful kinds make large, branched sprays of relatively small yellow- or brown-spotted flowers. They flower at various times but most rest in winter.

Paphiopedilum These are the orchids which most gardeners still call by their old name cymbidium.

Popularly they are known as slipper orchids because of the large pouched lower petal. Some are epiphytes, some terrestrial, but most will grow in a sphagnum moss and fibre mixture to which a little loam has been added. They have no pseudo-bulbs and so no resting season.

Phalaenopsis Often called moth orchids because of a supposed resemblance to moths in their white or pink flowers carried in arching sprays. They are epiphytic, flower at various times and have no pseudo-bulbs and therefore no resting season.

Pleione Small, almost hardy, easily grown, semi-epiphytic orchids with funnel-shaped white, pink, rose or pale yellow flowers in spring. They rest in winter.

Vanda caerulea A beautiful epiphyte with large sprays of pale blue flowers in autumn. It has no resting season. A H

Above: Slipper orchid.

Above left: Tiger orchid.

Vanda 'Marguerite'.

BORDER COUNTRY

'Herbaceous' plants are soft-stemmed and not woody like shrubs. Although the term by itself includes both annuals and biennials, gardeners nearly always use it instead with two other adjectives – 'hardy' and 'perennial'. These in effect limit herbaceous plants to those that live for some years and are sufficiently resistant to cold to be grown outdoors in most parts of the country. They include such favourites as peonies, lupins, delphiniums, phloxes and Michaelmas daisies and they play an important role in the stocking of most gardens.

They are more permanent than annuals and biennials, and less so than shrubs, but they reach maturity quickly and so can give gardens a well-furnished appearance long before trees and shrubs are of comparable size. Many of them associate well with shrubs and vigorous bush roses, and one currently popular planting scheme is to make a permanent framework of shrubs and roses filled in with a semi-permanent planting of hardy herbaceous perennials, with bulbs, annuals and biennials added as fillers and to keep the display going for longer.

A few hardy herbaceous perennials, such as hellebores and peonies, are best left undisturbed for a good many years. A few others, such as lupins and delphiniums, age rather quickly and are best renewed quite frequently. Most benefit from lifting and replanting every three or four years and this can provide a welcome opportunity to re-model the planting, correct mistakes, and introduce new varieties and generally indulge in second thoughts.

Not many hardy herbaceous perennials, and certainly none of the popular kinds, are fussy about soil, most thriving in anything that is reasonably fertile and well drained. A few like abundant moisture, and though most prefer light places, enough either prefer or tolerate shade to make it easy to find candidates for every growing position.

Most herbaceous perennials are easy to manage. Some of the taller kinds, or those with slender stems, may require support and there are numerous ways to do this. One is to push twiggy branches into the soil in spring so that stems grow up through them; another is to use metal hoops or half-circles in much the same way. Canes or stakes with encircling ties of soft string are another possibility, and you can also buy miniature hurdles which look picturesque and can be used to prevent plants flopping over paths and lawns.

Right: Stretch of border at Clare College, Cambridge: herbaceous plants look good in irregular colonies.
Below: Eryngium alpinum.

Above: Hemerocallis 'Pink Damask'.

Below: Crocosmia masonorum.

Below: Euphorbia griffithii.

Above: Acanthus mollis.

Below: Campanula glomerata 'Superba'.

Twenty not-so-common herbaceous plants

Acanthus mollis	June–August	90cm (3ft)	Handsome foliage, stiff purple and white flower spikes
Agapanthus 'Headbourne Hybrid'	July–August	75–90cm (2½–3ft)	Heads of blue or white flowers
Anaphalis triplinervis	July–September	30–45cm (12–18in)	Wide-spreading with grey-green leaves, clusters of small creamy flowers
Anthemis cupaniana	May–August	20–30cm (8–12in)	Ferny grey leaves and white daisies
Artemisia lactiflora	August–October	120cm (4ft)	Plumes of small cream flowers
Astrantia carniolica	May–July	30–40cm (12–16in)	Small heads of lilac-pink or reddish-purple flowers
Bergenia cordifolia	April–May	30cm (12in)	Pink flowers and large, rounded shiny green leaves
Campanula glomerata	June–July	40cm (16in)	Heads of violet-purple flowers
Campanula lactiflora	July–August	30–150cm (1–5ft)	Sprays of blue, lilac or white bells. Several varieties
Crocosmia masonorum	July–August	60cm (2ft)	Orange flower and sword-shaped leaves. The variety 'Lucifer' is a bright red hybrid. Both resemble montbretias but are less invasive
Dierama pendulum	July–August	75cm (2½ft)	Arching wands bearing pendant pink flowers
Eryngium alpinum	July–August	75cm (2½ft)	Cone-shaped blue flower heads surrounded by lacy metallic blue ruffs
Euphorbia griffithii	May–June	75cm (2½ft)	Flat heads of small orange-red flowers
Helleborus corsicus	February–April	60cm (2ft)	Apple-green flowers, handsome deeply divided leaves
Hemerocallis hybrids	June–July	60–90cm (2–3ft)	The 'day lily' with trumpet-shaped flowers, yellow, orange, pink or crimson
Hosta fortunei	July–August	70cm (28in)	Large blue-grey leaves and lilac-blue flowers
Hosta undulata	July–August	30cm (1ft)	Shiny green and white leaves and pale violet flowers. Many hybrids, some with variegated leaves
Liatris callilepis	July–August	60cm (2ft)	Spikes of fluffy magenta flowers
Rodgersia pinnata	July–August	90cm (3ft)	Large fingered leaves and compact plumes of pink or white flowers
Thalictrum dipterocarpum	July–August	150–180cm (5–6ft)	Ferny leaves and loose sprays of small lilac or white flowers

Keeping them Healthy

Herbaceous plants suffer very little from pests and diseases and only occasionally require spraying with insecticides or fungicides. They may require watering in dry weather and will grow more vigorously if fed in spring – and possibly again in early summer – with a well-balanced compound fertilizer containing nitrogen, phosphate and potash in more or less equal proportions. They should be kept clear of weeds and in autumn the stems of deciduous kinds should be cut off a little above ground-level. Faded flowers or seed heads can be removed much earlier, but this depends on whether or not you regard them as unsightly, or need to take them for home-produced seed.

Weeds should be removed regularly by hand-weeding or hoeing, and in autumn the soil can be lightly forked to remove any remaining weeds and loosen the surface. It is unwise to disturb the soil to a greater depth than 5–6cm (2–2½in) as there may be many feeding roots quite close to the surface.

Where they Flourish

Herbaceous plants are usually grown in borders, most of which are usually rectangular or curving, or in island beds which are almost always irregular in shape and size and are usually separated by grass paths or wider expanses of lawn. Both borders and beds need to be fairly large for an effective display (180cm/6ft minimum width for borders), especially if roses and shrubs are to be mixed with the herbaceous plants – a useful device for prolonging the flowering season. If you add some evergreen shrubs and varieties with coloured stems, these will provide a permanent framework which will remain interesting in winter when nearly all the herbaceous plants have died down to ground level.

Shrubs and shrub roses may be planted singly but herbaceous plants, except for a few very large kinds, are usually best planted in groups, forming irregular colonies of various shapes and sizes. Obviously, most of the short plants should be at the front and the tall ones at the back, but there should be some flexibility so that the final effect is of sweeping bays of foliage and flowers not a regularly graded slope.

If you are aiming for a long flowering season, you can avoid being stuck intermittently with uninteresting patches by making each group rather long and narrow, with something else in front or behind that will flower at a different time and conceal the plants that have finished or are yet to flower. The use of plenty of good foliage plants can also make amends for seasonal shortages of bloom. Spring-flowering bulbs will add early colour, dying down by the time most of the herbaceous perennials are coming into full growth. In summer other temporary plants with an extended flowering season can be used to maintain continuous interest and colour.

A H

Shrubs and flowers mingle in an overflowing border.

SPACE CONTROL

Many gardeners, faced with a tiny space to fill, will be quite content with a few carefully selected plants where arrangement is all-important. Others, perhaps more interested in plants than in design, will fret at the restrictions placed on them by lack of space. They need not despair, for there are ways to overcome these problems.

There are four principal avenues of approach:

To seek out plants that are naturally small.

To look for plants that grow upwards without a corresponding lateral spread.

To plan for successional planting or better still two-tier planting which may double the capacity of the garden to produce beautiful flowers, foliage and fruit.

To grow plants in pots, tubs and so on.

SMALL BUT PERFECTLY FORMED

Plants may be small by nature or they may be small varieties of normally much bigger plants. Many alpines and rock plants are of the former type, natural miniatures which could only survive in the native habitat they have chosen by remaining tiny, at any rate above ground. Below, the roots of these tiny mountain plants travel far in search of food and water.

Rock plants of all kinds are very suitable for growing on raised beds (see 'Rock Plants'), and in walls built with soil in place of mortar. Even in a tiny back yard you can pack in several hundred alpines this way, many of them growing in the crevices between the bricks or stones of the walls where they will find just the sharp drainage they most enjoy. There are many small plants, not actually alpines, that will thrive under these conditions, glad of the quick drainage in winter and the freedom from aggressive competition.

Plants a-top a wall provide a colourful welcome for visitors to this house.

Right: Old chimney-pots act as plant stands for this group of plants.

Below: Going up for air and light are roses trained on a trellis, their colours accented by the white-painted background.

The snaky branches of the wistaria contrast with the vertical bars of the railings.

Small varieties of normally much larger plants occur in the wild and gardeners are constantly searching them out and introducing them to gardens. There are small forms of naturally large herbaceous plants. For example, *Campanula* 'Pouffe' is a dwarf variety of the normally tall *C. lactiflora*, and there are dwarf Michaelmas daisies such as 'Audrey', 'Lady in Blue', 'Little Pink Beauty' and 'Snowsprite'. There are also numerous dwarf varieties of normally large shrubs: *Berberis* 'Bagatelle' is a 30cm (12in) high form of *B. thunbergii*, which can reach 2m (6ft), or *Spiraea* 'Alpina' and 'Bullata', both much-reduced versions of their parent *S. japonica*.

In some ways, the most remarkable of all are the dwarf conifers. A whole new industry has sprung up to satisfy the enthusiasts. Dwarf conifers look particularly good with heathers which form ideal carpets of green, grey, yellow or copper beneath. However, not all the conifers sold as 'dwarf' are permanently so. Some are very slow growing: they may appear dwarf for many years but will eventually become quite large. This may not matter if you are prepared to renew plants occasionally, but it is as well to know at the outset exactly what the plant is likely to do.

Dwarf conifers for small gardens

Chamaecyparis lawsoniana 'Minima Aurea'	Golden pincushion cypress
Chamaecyparis obtusa 'Nana'	Dense dark green 'bun'
Juniperus communis 'Compressa'	Tight, blue grey columna. Takes years to reach 30cm (12in)
Juniperus horizontalis	Spreads flat along the ground. Several good varieties
Juniperus sabina 'Tamariscifolia'	A low, but wide, blue-green dome
Picea pungens globosa	Dwarf Blue Spruce with silvery blue young needles
Pinus mugo 'Humpy'	Dwarf form of a compact mountain pine

Planting for shape and effect: low-growing clumps arranged around a dwarf conifer, masking its base.

UPWARDS NOT OUTWARDS

Climbing plants have suffered from a considerable amount of misapprehension and misuse. Many people believe that they ruin buildings, bring insects into the house and are difficult to control. Under certain conditions all these things can happen, but it is equally true that, given proper selection and care, none of them need, or indeed should occur, so shattering your faith.

Damage to buildings nearly always results from choosing too vigorous climbers. Wistaria, vines and ampelopsis, planted against house walls and not kept under proper control, are likely to finish up under the tiles or blocking the gutters; yet climbing up an old and otherwise valueless tree they can be delightful. Ivy does not ruin modern mortar made with cement, but it can get into all sorts of unwanted places and its dense foliage does provide safe harbourage for many insects. It is better kept off house walls though it may be admirable on old tree stumps or ruined buildings.

But there is no need to court any disasters with climbing plants, for there are plenty that are of moderate vigour and easily controlled. Their merits are that they provide the garden with delightful drapes and that they are space saving since they ascend more or less vertically, making use of areas which would otherwise remain empty.

True climbers ascend by different means. Ivy and ampelopsis (*Parthenocissus tricuspidata*) cling, the former holding on to any firm surface by means of aerial roots, the latter with little adhesive pads. Honeysuckles and wistarias twine, lashing themselves around branches, poles, pillars and pergolas. The tendrils of clematis and vines (as well as the annual sweet peas) twist around twigs, trellis, netting or stretched wires. Climbing roses and brambles are thrusters, pushing their strong stems through bushes or even into trees, finding necessary support among their branches.

In addition to these true climbers, there are numerous shrubs which are not really climbers at all but are readily trained against walls and can be almost self supporting if wisely pruned and given an occasional tie to a wire or vine eye to keep them from toppling forward. Some of the best are house-wall plants like pyracanthus, cotoneasters and ceanothus, for they are the least likely to get out of hand.

But don't restrict climbers solely to use on buildings; they can grow on fences and screens, as live coverings for terraces, patios and barbecues, covering arches, pergolas and arbours, scrambling into shrubs and trees (the most natural location for many of them), and sometimes flat on the ground as dense, weed-smothering cover.

Like other plants, climbers may be evergreen

or deciduous, grown primarily for their foliage, for their flowers or for their fruits, and with preferences for sun or shade, warm places or cool. Most will grow in any reasonably fertile soil and only a very few have any marked dislikes – lime-haters, for example.

When climbers are used to clothe walls they can easily become excessively dry because the wall will shelter the soil from a great deal of rain. Part of the remedy is to plant at least 50cm (20in) away from the base of the wall where the protection is a little less intense, and also to pay particular attention to the preparation of the site, digging in plenty of peat, leafmould, garden compost, rotted manure, spent mushroom compost or other humus-forming material. This will make the soil more spongy and therefore more able to draw water to it and to retain it without becoming waterlogged.

Apart from this, planting is the same as for other plants. Nearly all climbers are supplied in pots or other containers from which they should be removed carefully. Since the soil in the container is likely to be even more porous and humus-rich than that of the site, it is wise to prepare a planting mixture of equal parts garden soil, peat, leafmould or pulverized bark and coarse sand, and to work half a bucketful of this around each plant when it has been placed in its planting hole, which should be just sufficiently deep to allow the top of the pot-ball to be 1–2cm ($\frac{1}{2}$–$\frac{3}{4}$in) below soil level. If roots are wound round fairly tightly in the pot-ball, particularly at the bottom, they should be very carefully loosened with the fingers into this planting mixture.

Here are some useful and attractive garden climbers.

Actinidia *A. chinensis* is a fast grower with stems covered in red hairs and large, round leaves. Flowers are buff white and the hairy fruits edible, but its chief value is for its foliage. This applies also to *A. kolomikta*, a far less rampant plant with medium size leaves attractively coloured green, pink and cream, suitable for training on a sunny house wall. *A. chinensis* is for an old tree or a ruin. Either can have stems shortened occasionally in summer and cut back more severely in winter.

Ceanothus Shrubs, not climbers, but all, and particularly the small-leaved evergreen kinds, make excellent covering for sunny walls. Small blue flowers carried in spring or early summer in thimble-like clusters. Should be pruned immediately they fade. Important to shorten the

stems growing away from the wall or fence which cannot easily be tied back.

Chaenomeles Botanical name for Japanese quinces or 'Japonicas'. Deciduous shrubs flowering in late winter and spring, ideal for training against walls and almost self supporting. Clusters of scarlet, crimson or orange-red 'apple blossom' flowers; pruning best done from May to August as for ceanothus.

Clematis Great variety. Most familiar are the very vigorous May flowering *Clematis montana*, with small but numerous white or pink flowers, and the many summer flowering hybrids, with much larger flowers, and of various colours. All deciduous, as are spring flowering *C. macropetala*, with lavender or pink nodding flowers, and August-September flowering *C. tangutica*, with bell-shaped yellow flowers, followed by silken seed heads. Spring flowering *C. armandii* is evergreen, with clusters of small white flowers. Needs a warm sheltered place.

Pruning is determined by vigour and flowering time. Spring and early summer flowering kinds, eg *armandii*, *macropetala*, *alpina*, *montana*, 'Henri' and 'Nellie Moser', are pruned immediately after flowering when stems can be shortened to fit available space. Later summer or early autumn flowering kinds, eg *tangutica*, *orientalis*, *viticella*, *flammula*, 'Jackmanii', 'Comtesse de Bouchaud', 'Ernest Markham', 'Hagley Hybrid', 'Marie Boisselot', 'The President', and 'Ville de Lyon', are best pruned in February-March, when they can be cut back quite severely. All varieties enjoy lime and like to grow with their roots shaded but their leaves in the sun.

Cobaea scandens Very fast-growing perennial. Too tender to live outdoors in winter except in the mildest parts of Britain but grown successfully as a half-hardy annual. Unusual, attractive flowers, rather like Canterbury Bells and either green and violet or greenish white, ideal for use as a quick cover. It climbs by tendrils.

Eccremocarpus scaber Fast-growing tendril climber often treated as a half-hardy annual, but will survive outdoors in many warm, sunny places. It has small divided leaves and dangling clusters of tubular yellow, orange or carmine flowers all summer. Dead growth should be cut out each April.

Hedera Botanical name for ivy. Three species are especially useful. Common ivy is *H. helix* with numerous varieties of leaf colour and shape. All completely hardy, and will grow in sun or shade, but the yellow-leaved varieties develop their best colour in good light. All can be clipped or cut back in spring or summer if they extend too far. *H. colchica* has the largest leaves of all, unlobed and sometimes 20cm (8in) long and almost as much across. It has a very handsome cream variegated variety, 'Dentata variegata'.

Hydrangea petiolaris and *Schizophragma integrifolia* Two very vigorous climbing hydrangeas clinging, like ivy, with aerial roots. Look splendid growing up big tree trunks. *Schizophragma* is the more spectacular of the two but less common. Both can be cut back as necessary in winter.

Jasminum The yellow winter flowering *J. nudiflorum* is quite hardy, will grow in sun or shade and is a sprawler or thruster requiring a few ties. An ideal wall plant and can be pruned as necessary after flowering. *J. officinalis*, the sweet-scented, white-flowered summer jasmine, is a vigorous twiner for a warm sunny place. It can be thinned and shortened in March-April.

Lonicera Honeysuckles, the climbing kinds, are all vigorous twiners. The varieties sold as 'Early Dutch' and 'Late Dutch' flower respectively in June and July-August, are yellow and red and are spicily fragrant. *L. japonica* has pale yellow, sweetly scented flowers. *L. sempervirens* has tubular scarlet flowers and *L. tellmanniana* is red in bud and deep yellow when open, but both these lack scent. All honeysuckles dislike very hot dry places. Most can be thinned and cut back after flowering, but *L. japonica* is best pruned in spring.

Parthenocissus Correct current name for the Virginia Creepers and Boston Ivies. All vigorous vine-like creepers with brilliant coloured leaves in autumn. Most like sun but *P. henryana* will thrive in light shade. All can be cut back as much as necessary in winter.

Passiflora coerulea The Passion Flower and the only species sufficiently hardy to be grown outdoors in Britain; even so requires a particularly warm, sunny, sheltered place. It is a very vigorous tendril climber with unusual, saucer-shaped, white flowers with a ring of violet purple filaments around the prominent central anthers and stigma. Plants can be pruned as necessary each April.

Pyracantha The Firethorns are evergreen shrubs readily trained against walls and fences and virtually self supporting. Good foliage, clusters of small white flowers in summer followed by fine crops of red, orange or yellow berries in autumn. Numerous species and hybrids, all excellent and all particularly fond of limy soils.

Polygonum baldschuanicum The Russian Vine, possibly the most rampant of all hardy climbers and ideal for covering a ruin or scrambling high into a worthless tree from which it will cascade in billowy cream and pink flowers in late summer. Can be a bit of a handful.

Trachelospermum Deliciously scented evergreen twiners for warm, sunny sheltered places. There are two species, *T. asiaticum* and *T. jasminoides*, both much alike in their clusters of small white flowers but *T. asiaticum* is slightly more hardy and therefore the better one to buy. Ideal for walls, and rarely needing much pruning but they can be thinned or shortened in April-May.

Vitis The vines are excellent tendril climbers which thrive on chalk and limestone and do not mind a relatively small amount of soil. Ideal for patios and terraces.

Wistaria Popular twiners more suitable for pergolas and for growing into trees than for training on houses, where they require a lot of pruning to keep them within bounds. *W. floribunda* is a good deal less rampant than *W. sinensis* and there are some very beautiful varieties of it. All can be thinned and cut back in winter and pruned in summer by shortening all side growths to about five leaves.

BLOOM AND BLOOM AGAIN

If you only have a small space to cultivate, you can make the ground work extra hard. It can be made to produce more than one crop of flowers each year either by successional planting, which can be extremely effective but fairly costly in plants and time, or by two-, or even three-tier planting. Successional planting relies largely on temporary plants, mainly annuals and bedding plants, most of which are discarded after flowering. Two-tier planting can be much more permanent and depends on matching plants that flower at different times and at least some of which die down naturally at a convenient time to make way for others. Bulbs, corms and tubers figure prominently in any such scheme: for example, in spring come daffodils, tulips, crocuses, scillas, chionodoxas and so on, which have finished their growth by the end of May, and make way for summer-flowering herbaceous perennials which do not start to grow freely until April. Roses and hardy fuchsias fit nicely into this scheme of things since neither makes any serious claim on space until well into the spring, and both flower for a long time in summer.

Summer-flowering lilies can be planted among short herbaceous plants and shrubs to grow up through them; indeed, lilies actually derive benefit from the shade cast on their roots. Dahlia tubers can be planted in early May to fill gaps or replace early flowering perennials cut down before the dahlias take over in late summer.

There are even a few herbaceous perennials that reverse the normal course of summer growth and winter rest. The most notable example is *Arum italicum*, a handsome foliage plant with dark green, white-veined leaves which appear in autumn and conveniently die down in late spring in time to let other plants take over.

GROWING ON CONCRETE

There is no end to the ingenuity for growing plants in containers. I have seen plants in pots suspended on the walls of an otherwise barren yard and watered by an ingenious tipping bucket on a pole. I know of many tiny city courtyards in which there is no soil at all but which have been transformed into charming little gardens with small evergreen shrubs, ivies and a few long-flowering bedding plants in an immense variety of old and new pots, troughs or plant holders.

There is not a balcony in the land that could not be made beautiful with plants grown in these ways. Growing bags, introduced to combat soil-borne diseases in nurseries but now universally available, have made this easier because the peat these bags contain is so much lighter and easier to carry than soil. Lay them down on any firm surface, partially slit open on the upper side so that plants can be put into them and after that it's a matter of water and feed.

The plastic bag contains the water so that there is a minimum mess and there is sufficient food mixed with the peat to keep the plants growing vigorously for about a month or six weeks. After that they will need to be fed by mixing plant food, such as a seaweed extract, with the water. There is scarcely anything that cannot be grown in this way, from tulips and daffodils in spring to scarlet salvias and dahlias which will still be flowering in autumn until stopped by frost.

A H

Hanging baskets containing lobelia and geraniums.

SHOW PIECES

There's nothing quite like the flower show block-busters for size and colour – and, of course, they can look even better in the border.

CHRYSANTHEMUMS

We have become so accustomed to seeing chrysanthemums offered for sale every week of the year that it may come as a surprise to some people that all the year round flowering is not a characteristic of the plant. Autumn is its natural flowering season, and though by skilful breeding and selection this season has been extended, chrysanthemums are basically what scientists call 'short-day plants', meaning that they flower when days are short and nights are long.

Commercial growers produce these conditions artificially with black-outs by day and lighting at night but though these techniques are not impossible for the home gardener they are difficult, and it is far better to grow chrysanthemums naturally in the traditional way.

For August and September flowering outdoors, obtain early-flowering varieties, and for flowering in greenhouses, conservatories and so on, choose mid-season and late varieties which flower from October to January.

Chrysanthemums can be grown from seed sown in a temperature of 15–18°C (60–65°F) in February or March but this method is used mainly for varieties producing an abundance of single flowers such as the 'Charm', 'Cascade' and 'Korean' chrysanthemums. Most other types are grown between January and April, and rooted in a propagator inside a greenhouse. The cuttings (or seedlings) are potted singly as soon as they are well rooted and are moved on to larger pots as they fill the smaller ones with roots. Soil-based or soilless (peat) composts can be used, but if the latter are chosen feeding must being after a few weeks as chrysanthemums are hungry plants requiring fairly rich soil.

Outdoor varieties are hardened off for planting out from mid-April to late-May in well cultivated soil in an open, sunny position. Late flowering varieties are usually grown in pots throughout, but are stood outdoors from about mid May until early September when they are brought into a light, airy greenhouse. Extra heat is only required to exclude

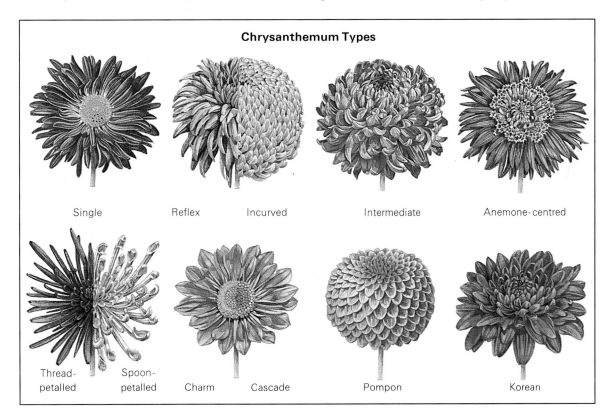

Chrysanthemum Types

Single   Reflex   Incurved   Intermediate   Anemone-centred

Thread-petalled   Spoon-petalled   Charm   Cascade   Pompon   Korean frost or to dry the atmosphere when it is very humid, as chrysanthemums are nearly hardy and it is the flowers which are most in need of protection from frost and rain.

Big plants may need pots up to 20cm (8in) in diameter. They must be kept well watered and regularly fed. Stems are usually reduced to about six to seven per plant, less for really big flowers, and are securely tied to canes. Usually it is wise to pinch out the tips of plants (known as 'stopping') some time in May to ensure early branching, and occasionally a second pinching is given in June. If large flowers are required, the side buds are removed and only the terminal bud on each stem is retained. If sprays of smaller flowers are required the terminal bud is removed and the side buds are retained.

When flowering is over, the stems are cut off a few centimetres above soil level, surplus plants are discarded and only just enough are kept to provide cuttings for the following year. Outdoor plants are dug up in autumn and replanted in boxes to provide cuttings. They require the protection of a frame or greenhouse but need little artificial warmth until a few weeks before cuttings are to be taken, when the minimum temperature should be raised to about 10°C (50°F).

Dahlias

The spectacularly showy dahlias are among the most highly developed garden flowers. Until autumn frosts cut them down they bloom from about mid-July in a dazzling range of colours, including almost everything except pure blue, in many different shapes and sizes.

Dahlias are tender but can be grown outdoors from May until October. They make clusters of large tubers, and in mild places these will survive underground all winter, but the usual practice is to dig them up in the autumn, when their top growth has been destroyed by frost, cut off all stems 5cm (2in) above the tubers, lift the tubers from the soil and store them in a cool but frost-proof place in shallow boxes barely covered in peat.

In spring, the tubers are either replanted outdoors in early May or are started into growth earlier in a frost-proof greenhouse either to provide cuttings to be rooted in a propagator and planted out in early June after hardening off, or to be split up into several pieces and planted out when danger of frost is over.

Dahlias can be purchased as rooted cuttings in spring or as pot tubers, that is, small tubers produced the previous year and packaged dry, like

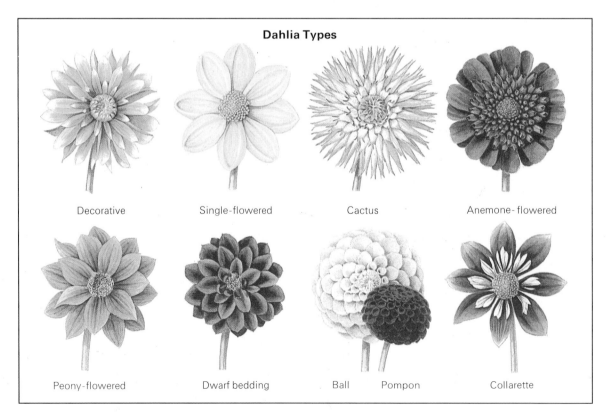

Dahlia Types

Decorative   Single-flowered   Cactus   Anemone-flowered

Peony-flowered   Dwarf bedding   Ball   Pompon   Collarette

A dazzling border of mixed varieties of dahlia.

Gladiolus 'Classic'.

of moisture while they are growing. They also like fairly rich soil. Make sure you stake large plants carefully as the stems are heavy and brittle.

GLADIOLI

There are gladioli that flower in spring and early summer and others that delay their flowering until late summer and early autumn. It is the latter type that are the most useful since they can be grown all the year round in the open whereas, except in the very mildest places, the early-flowering or 'Nanus' varieties must be cared for in greenhouses. This is because the corms start to grow in autumn and because their leaves are quite tender they are at constant risk all winter from frost. The late summer-flowering gladioli remain dormant in winter (store them dry in any frost-proof place such as a cool cupboard), and are then planted in spring, from mid-March to mid-May, about 15cm (6in) apart, their corms covered with 5–8cm (2–3in) of soil sufficient to protect them from frosts. By the time their leaves appear the weather should do them no harm.

The late-flowering gladioli are also by far the most spectacular, with medium to large sized flowers, in long tapering spikes which look well in the border and are excellent as cut flowers. Their colours include practically everything, except pure blue.

All gladioli are grown from corms which, besides producing leaves and flowers, also form new corms above the old ones. These gradually wither away and are discarded when the plants are dug up for storage about six weeks after the last flowers fade. It is the new corms that are retained; the top growth cut off half an inch above them. There may also be a lot of tiny corms or cormels clustered around the main corms and these can also be kept and planted, but as they are unlikely to flower until the second or third year they are best put aside in a reserve bed where their lack of colour will not matter.

All gladioli like sunny places, reasonably fertile soil and plenty of moisture while in growth. Only in the mildest places should you leave them in the soil summer and winter. The only exception to this rule is with *Gladiolus byzantinus*, a European species (all the rest are hybrids derived from South African species), which has long slender spikes of rich magenta flowers, magnificent in the right setting with plenty of green to tone the strong colours down but disastrous in the wrong company. This gladiolus is sufficiently hardy to be planted permanently in warm sunny places. A H

bulbs. These are best started into growth individually in pots in a greenhouse or on a sunny window ledge, and planted out in early June. But they can be planted 5cm (2in) deep outdoors during May with reasonable success.

Dahlias can also be raised from seed sown in spring in a temperature of around 18°C (65°F). The seedlings are potted singly and hardened off for planting out in early June. They will flower that same summer but the flowers may differ in colour and character from their parents.

All dahlias enjoy sunshine, warmth and plenty

STATELY BLOOMS

Most people immediately think of irises as the large flamboyant flowers, in all manner of wonderful colours, which grace the garden in May and June. These are the flag, German or bearded irises which have been so intensively bred and selected that the number of varieties now available is quite bewildering. Yet they are only one section of an immense family of herbaceous perennials and bulbs – some are quite tiny plants suitable for rock gardens, while others are tall and suitable for wet places or the shallow water at the edge of lakes. Collectively, they have a flowering season extending from January to July.

The 'bearded' flag or German irises all make substantial rhizomes, that is, thick stems which lie flat on the ground and make roots from their undersides. 'Bearded' means that on the centre of each of the three broad outer segments of the flower, the 'falls', there is a line of short coloured filaments like a beard. 'Flag' refers to the size of the three upstanding central segments of the flower and 'German' to the fact that *Iris germanica* was one of the important early parents of these hybrids, although other species have also been involved.

For many years the bearded iris has been a cult: societies have been formed to promote it, shows organized to display it and books devoted to it. Thousands of varieties have been raised and named, the size of the flowers has been greatly increased, their placement on the stems improved and their colour range extended to include many shades that are found in few other plants except orchids.

As usual, advance has not been gained without some loss. Some of the varieties are so tall that they require staking, some are more prone to disease than the wild species and most require more care. As a rule they benefit from being dug up and divided every second or third year which provides an opportunity to cut off a lot of the old half-dead rhizome that has formed in the centre of the clump and to replant the vigorous outer portions in fresh soil. The best time to do this is in late June or early July as soon as the flowers fade, for it is shortly after this that the rhizomes start to make new roots.

Bearded irises like sunny places and fertile, well-drained soils containing some lime. Plant the rhizome, which need be no more than 10–15cm (4–6in) long, covered just enough with soil to keep the plant firm and erect while it is establishing itself. After a while, the rhizomes will work themselves out on top, but do not attempt to cover them again. They benefit from annual feeding in spring with a good general fertilizer, and an extra dressing of superphosphate of lime at 50g (1¾oz) per square metre can be given in July.

Enthusiasts usually grow bearded irises in beds by themselves, and even make iris gardens, but they can perfectly well be mixed with other plants so long as the irises are not overrun or deprived of light and can be lifted and replanted in fresh soil every few years.

A great many iris varieties flower in June and are from 75–100cm (30–40in) high but there is also a race of smaller, intermediate bearded irises

Iris 'Blue Petticoats' have the characteristic 'beard' of short coloured filaments on the outer 'falls'.

Flowers emerge on the elegant spikes of these delphiniums which can reach up to 2.4m (8ft) high.

under its old name *I. stylosa*), which likes a warm, sunny, well-drained place, and the summer-flowering Siberian iris, *I. sibirica*, which enjoys moist soil and is never happier than when planted at the water's edge.

DELPHINIUMS

Some plants resolutely refuse to be 'improved' and others seem purpose-built for domestication, ready to develop in ways that could not have been dreamt of from an examination of the original wild 'material'. *Delphinium elatum* is emphatically adaptable, and with help from a few other species has produced, in a hundred years or so, all the wonderful garden varieties which are the back-bone of the flower border in late June and July.

Modern garden delphiniums – with their longer and larger flowers and greater colour – are not so tough and long-lived as their ancestors. To keep them in peak condition they must be renewed fairly frequently and be grown in rather rich soil, well drained in winter yet well supplied with water in summer. The real giants have such heavy spikes of bloom that they need to be staked individually to prevent them being blown over by the wind.

The best delphiniums used to be clones, that is, each variety was increased by cutting or division from an original seedling sufficiently distinct and good to be selected for this purpose and given a distinguishing name. Then it was discovered that it was possible to produce seed that would give plants of uniformly high quality and even, in some cases, of all one colour. So the age of the Pacific hybrids, of 'Astolat', 'Black Knight', 'Galahad', 'Guinevere' and 'King Arthur' had arrived and from them seed selections began to take over from clones, not because they were better in themselves but because they were cheaper to rear and easier to keep free of pests and diseases.

Delphinium seed, though fairly large, loses vitality rather rapidly and, where good germination is the only consideration, it should be sown in late summer or early autumn. The snag is that the seedlings are still so small when winter comes that they need protection, more from wet and slugs than from cold. So most gardeners delay sowing until March and either store seed in the bottom of a refrigerator or in hermetically sealed packets. The seed is sown in a cool greenhouse or frame, the seedlings are planted outdoors in a nursery bed in June and many of them will produce a small spike of flowers by late summer or early autumn. The next year they will flower at the normal time, about midsummer.

which flower in May. They do not require staking and are often easier to accommodate with other herbaceous plants. They usefully extend the iris flowering season but they are neither so numerous nor quite so magnificent as the June-flowering varieties.

Bulbous irises include small winter-flowering species, such as the blue *Iris histrioides*, violet-purple *I. reticulata* and yellow *I. danfordiae*, as well as much taller May- and June-flowering kinds such as the Spanish irises derived from *I. xiphium* and the English irises derived from *I. xiphioides*. These tall kinds make excellent cut flowers, while small early-flowering bulbous irises look good in rock gardens and raised rock beds where they benefit from the good drainage provided by a porous, rather gritty soil. They are best planted in September 58cm (2–3in) deep, but as much as 12cm (5in) for *I. danfordiae*.

Fibrous-rooted irises include such very different species as the winter-flowering Algerian iris, *I. unguicularis* (still more familiar to many gardeners

The single-flowered
P. mlokosewitschii.

Delphinium clones are usually increased by cuttings rooted in a frame or cool greenhouse in spring. Cuttings are prepared from the young growth when this is 8–10cm (3–4in) long. Each shoot is severed close to the crown of the plant so that it is firm and solid, not hollow, at the base. The cut surface is moistened and dipped in hormone rooting powder and the cutting is then inserted 4–5cm (1½–2in) deep in a mixture of equal parts peat and either sand or Perlite. Keep cuttings moist and shaded until they are rooted; then they can be potted individually in a good soil or peat potting mixture and gradually hardened off in readiness for planting out. Clones can also be increased by division in spring but are seldom as vigorous and healthy as plants raised from cuttings.

PEONIES

Peonies make a resounding splash in the summer border, their large, strikingly coloured flowers and rich veined leaves a head-turning focus of attention. In autumn the herbaceous sorts die down to fleshy crowns with buds which produce new growth the following spring. Other peonies are shrubby, and often go under the grander but visually quite unmerited name of 'tree peonies'. These have woody stems which remain all winter and form a permanent framework of growth.

Some herbaceous peonies cultivated in gardens are species appearing just as they would in the wild, but most are either hybrids or special selections, often with very large double or semi-double flowers. Among the best species, all with

single flowers, are *Paeonia peregrina*, often called *P. lobata*, with scarlet, goblet-shaped flowers; *P. mlokosewitschii*, with very large primrose yellow flowers; *P. obovata*, with white or magenta flowers, and *P. tenuifolia*, with very finely divided leaves and light crimson flowers.

The garden varieties fall into two main groups, one derived largely from *Paeonia lactiflora* and known as the Chinese peonies, the other from *P. officinalis* and often referred to as the Cottage Garden peonies. The Chinese peonies have the greatest range of colour and flower forms, white, pink, lilac, rose, carmine and crimson, single, semi-double, fully-double and anemone-centred. Most are also scented and their peak flowering season is in June. The Cottage Garden peonies are all very fully double, white, pink or crimson and not scented. They flower in May.

All herbaceous peonies like rather rich soil and a sunny or partly shaded position. They dislike being disturbed, and if grown in mixed borders they should be so placed that they can be left alone when other plants are lifted and divided. Increase is by division in spring or autumn but this usually stops plants flowering for a year or so until they have re-established themselves. The species can all be increased by seed sown outdoors or under glass in April-May or as soon as ripe, but it may be a few years before seedlings are large enough to flower.

Tree peonies are also divided into species and hybrids, the former with single flowers, the latter usually double. The best species are *Paeonia*

Cottage Garden peonies like this *P. officinalis* flower in May.

delavayi, a big bush with rather small deep crimson flowers; *P. lutea*, even bigger in growth with yellow flowers which are a little larger in the variety 'Ludlowii', and *P. suffruticosa*, usually smaller in growth but with much larger white, pink or magenta flowers often with blotches of darker colour at the centre of the bloom. The hybrid tree peonies are derived mainly from *P. suffruticosa* with some interbreeding with *P. lutea* to introduce yellow. This gives a very wide colour range including white, pink, carmine, crimson, orange and yellow often with two colours combined. The flowers are sometimes so immense that they hang downwards under their own weight and require some support.

These hybrid tree peonies are a little more difficult to grow than the species. Less hardy, more susceptible to spring frosts which can damage the young growths, they particularly need good rich soil with plenty of moisture in spring and summer but reasonably good drainage in winter.

The species are easily raised from seed and often produce numbers of self-sown seedlings. The big double tree peonies produce little or no seed which would not, in any case, produce flowers of identical character and so they are either layered in spring or, less satisfactorily, grafted on to herbaceous rootstocks. AH

BUILDING ON ROCKY FOUNDATIONS

Plants that have learnt to exist naturally among rocks are often small, at least above ground, though their roots may extend a long way in search of food and water. Some of these plants live in the mountains and are sometimes referred to as 'alpines', but the broader term 'rock plants' embraces these and also those that dwell in rocky places at much lower levels, even beside the sea.

For gardeners they all have a special value because their smallness gives them a particular charm and makes it possible to grow a considerable variety of plants in a small space.

A rock garden makes it possible to grow a number of different species in a small space.

ROCK GARDENS

You can make an attractive setting for your rock plants by grouping them together in a rock garden – a miniature rocky landscape that you can build yourself, with stones inserted into a basic earthmound. Although a rock garden will look more 'natural' sited away from buildings in a wilder part of the garden, not everyone has the space for this and it is by no means essential. Many people like to combine a pool (*see* 'Water Plants') with their rock garden, and it is as well to plan for this from the outset.

When deciding which kind of stone to use, consider how it will look beside the plants you wish to grow. Provided it is likely to give a pleasing effect, there is much to be said for using a local stone. Not only will it look more natural in its new setting, you will also save on transport costs, which can be considerable.

Most rock plants are accustomed to growing naturally in well-drained conditions, though often with access to considerable reserves of water retained beneath the rocks. In a garden you can simulate these conditions by adding plenty of peat or leafmould plus sharp grit or sand to the natural

soil of the garden. A surfacing of stone chippings can increase the natural appearance of the rock garden and provide extra drainage around the collars of the plants, where it is most needed. Limestone chippings can be used for lime-loving plants and granite or sandstone chippings for those that dislike lime. Make sure the soil is at least 40cm (16in) deep in all parts of the rock garden.

In general, a few large rocks give a better appearance than a greater number of small ones. Almost invariably the rocks need to be well bedded in the soil so that they appear to be part of a much more extensive rock formation, the rest of which is hidden from sight. Often the easiest and most satisfactory method of producing this effect is to lay rocks almost side by side to form a series of low, irregularly shaped shelves in the way that naturally stratified rock so often appears when exposed by weather and erosion on a hillside. Rock dug out of the surface, rather than excavated from quarries, will probably have natural markings caused by frost and water on exposed surfaces, and if you keep these areas visible when re-laying in the garden, they will enhance the illusion of a natural outcrop.

Soil should be packed in behind and between rocks so that there are no loose or open places. Roots should be able to grow unchecked wherever there is soil to sustain them; left to their own devices they will find their way deep into crevices and flatten themselves against the cool, moist undersurface of the rocks.

Dry Walls and Raised Beds

These are both devices which can make it possible to grow rock plants very successfully in surroundings which may seem incongruously formal for 'natural' rock gardens. A dry wall in the garden is one built with soil in place of mortar and it may be used as a retaining wall for a terrace or as a free-standing wall to divide one part of the garden from another. If plants are to be grown in a free-standing wall it should be built double, with a core of soil between the two courses of stone, so that plants can root into this and down through it into the bedrock soil beneath.

A raised bed is a development of both these ideas. A wall, or walls, are built without mortar to enclose any convenient area and shape, which is then filled with soil, peat, sand and grit in whatever proportions are most suitable for the plants to be grown in it. Convenient dimensions for such beds are between 60–100cm (2–3½ft) high and not more than 2m (6½ft) wide at any point so that they can be tended conveniently without actually having to climb up on to them. Plants can be grown in the faces of the walls as well as on top of the beds, giving you a variety of sun and shade to suit a rather broader range of plants. All dry walls, for whatever purpose they are made, should be built of good-sized blocks of stone with plenty of soil rammed behind and between them so that they sit firmly one on another. Bed the first course firmly into the natural soil to provide a firm foundation, and stagger the stones in the upper courses so that the vertical crevices are broken and a bond is formed just as in a wall built with mortar. Since the dry wall will lack the adhesive qualities of mortar, it may be necessary to give each stone a slight downward slope and build the walls themselves sloping a little backwards or inwards so that their own weight helps to hold them in place. As soil settles and plant roots fill most of the crevices, these walls become increasingly stable and, if well built, can stand for years.

Troughs and Tufa Blocks

There are yet other ways in which rock plants can be grown, making it possible to use them as ornamental features even in the most sophisticated surroundings of terrace, courtyard and patio gardens. Genuine old stone troughs and sinks are becoming a rarity but excellent reproductions are available. Tufa, which is a very porous type of limestone, can be obtained in blocks of any convenient size and many small rock plants can live on it, actually penetrating it with their roots. For new plants, gouge out a small hole and fill it with a core of soil.

All sinks and troughs must be provided with at least one good-sized hole in the base to allow surplus water to drain away. Place some pieces of broken pot or stones around and over the hole to prevent soil blocking it. Also for drainage, raise the trough or sink a little off the ground. Soil used for filling should be adequately porous as well as suited to the plants to be grown: a good average mixture is equal parts of good soil (loam, if available), sphagnum peat and coarse sand. The surface can be covered with stone chippings (as for rock gardens). A few small pieces of rock may be bedded into the surface both for appearance and to provide the roots with additional cool, moist surfaces to cling to.

Raised stone troughs containing an abundance of alpine plants.

Planting and Cultivation

Saxifraga paniculata flourishes in crevices in a wall.

Rock plants are almost invariably sold in pots or other small containers from which they can be planted at any time of the year when soil and weather conditions are favourable. The methods of planting are the same as for other small plants except that it is sometimes difficult to plant in narrow crevices between rocks or blocks of stone in a wall. The easiest is to build the plants into place while the rock garden or wall is being constructed, but you will have to find other methods if planting in established constructions.

See if you can dislodge a rock, introduce the plant, and then replace it. Alternatively, shake a lot of the soil from the roots, scrape soil out of the crevices, and then carefully press the roots into place with a little soil around them. This kind of planting, involving considerable disturbance of the plants, is best done in spring or early autumn when conditions are usually most favourable for re-establishment. Even so, it will probably be necessary to water the new plants well for a few weeks.

Rock plants, being mostly small, are even more in need than most of protection from weeds, which can quickly destroy them (*see* 'Pests and Disease'). Most weeding must be done by hand but when difficult weeds, such as couch grass, sheep's sorrel, bindweed and ground elder, become established, you will need herbicides. Glyphosate is an almost universal killer which will, in time, eliminate most weeds. Paraquat is rapid in action and particularly effective against grasses of all kinds. 2,4-D kills bindweed efficiently. Make sure you keep these herbicides off the rock plants. The best methods of application are either to use a very small hand-sprayer with the nozzle held close to the weed and a card placed behind it to prevent drift, or to wear a rubber glove with a woollen glove pulled over it; you then dip your hand in a bucket of herbicide and coat the weeds.

Some rock plants, particularly high-altitude alpines, accustomed to being protected in winter by deep snow, suffer badly from wet in winter in our climate and may need to be covered with cloches or sheets of glass. Leave these open at the

Autumn-flowering *Gentiana sino-ornata*.

sides to permit free circulation of air and no undue rise of temperature that might cause premature growth. Apart from this, the main requirement is for protection from slugs and snails. You can either go out at night with a torch and pick them off, or put down metaldehyde or methiocarb slug baits from time to time. Alternatively, place beer in partly covered containers; the slugs are attracted to the beer, find their way in and drown themselves.

Here is a short list of rock plants:

Achillea Some are large plants for borders; there are also small carpeters such as *A. argentea* with white flowers and silvery leaves and *A. tomentosa* with yellow flowers and green leaves.

Arabis caucasica A trailing plant with abundant white flowers in spring. There is an even more effective double-flowered variety, named 'Plena', and another, named 'Rosabella', with pink flowers. All like lime and are excellent for dry walls and sunny banks.

Cyclamen Small hardy kinds suitable for shady rock gardens include *C. coum*, pink to crimson flowers in winter and spring; *C. europaeum*, rose pink or carmine, summer flowering and *C. hederaefolium*, often called *C. neapolitanum*, with ivy-like leaves and pink or white flowers in autumn.

Dianthus Some kinds are too large, too short-lived or too sophisticated. Recommended are *D. alpinus*, with carmine flowers displayed on a mat of green leaves; *D. deltoides*, a slender-stemmed sprawler with pink to deep carmine flowers; *D. gratianopolitanus*, with grey tufted leaves and pink flowers and *D. neglectus* with rose-coloured flowers on hummocks of narrow leaves. All like lime.

Gentiana Easiest to grow of these rich blue-flowering plants are the summer species *G. freyniana*, *G. lagodechiana* and *G. septemfida*. Spring-flowering *G. acaulis*, with large blue trumpets, does not always flower freely. *G. verna*, with small intensely blue flowers in spring, likes to grow in moist peat among limestone rocks. The autumn-flowering kinds *G. farreri*, *G. sino-ornata* and the hybrids require an acid, peaty soil.

Above: *Iberis sempervirens* (candytuft).   *Below*: *Polygonum affine*.

Gypsophila repens   A small gypsophila with white or pink flowers. All forms like lime.

Hypericum   The big shrubby kinds are quite unsuitable for rock gardens but there are prostrate or tufted species, such as *H. coris*, *H. olympicum*, and *H. repens*, which are excellent. *H. reptans* is another fine prostrate species but a little more difficult to grow well.

Iberis   The perennial candytufts are all easily grown plants suitable for rock gardens and walls. *I. saxatilis* is one of the neatest, *I. sempervirens* one of the most showy. Both have white flowers.

Lithosperum diffusum   Carpets of narrow green leaves covered in the bluest of flowers for many weeks in summer. There are several selected forms such as 'Heavenly Blue' and 'Grace Ward'.

Phlox   The prostrate, mat-forming kinds are most suitable, such as *P. douglasii*, with white, lavender, pink or crimson flowers, and *P. subulata*, with a similar colour range but a more spreading habit.

Polygonum   The two best rock garden kinds are *P. affine*, which has short spikes of carmine flowers, and *P. vaccinifolium*, a more sprawling plant with slender spikes of pale pink flowers. Both flower in late summer and autumn and their leaves turn red in autumn.

Potentilla   Good mat- or mound-forming kinds including *P. alba*, with white flowers; *P. aurea*, with yellow or orange flowers; *P. nitida*, with silvery leaves and pink flowers (but this needs perfect drainage), and *P. tonguei*, with apricot and crimson flowers.

Primula   Some kinds require moist soil and are best grown beside water, but good primulas for rock gardens are *P. auricula*, with leathery leaves and yellow, purple or bronzy flowers; *P. edgeworthii* and *P. marginata*, both with grey leaves and lavender flowers; *P. juliae*, with deep magenta flowers, and *P. pubescens*, an omnibus name given to hybrids of *P. auricula* with flowers in a wide range of colours.

Saxifraga   The saxifrages, a large and very variable genus including the mossy sorts which make wide mats of soft green leaves studded in spring with white, pink or crimson flowers on slender stems. All like slightly moist soils and shade from hot sunshine. Cushion or Kabschia saxifrages make firm mounds of grey-green, often rather spiky leaves and have sprays of white, pink or yellow flowers on short slender stems in early spring. They like to grow in sun, with plenty of limestone chippings. *S. griesbachii* has stouter stems covered in crimson bracts. Silver or encrusted saxifrages have flat rosettes of grey or silvery leaves with loose sprays of white or pale yellow flowers, sometimes speckled with crimson. They like to grow in crevices between limestone rocks. The 'London Prides' have rosettes of soft green leaves and loose sprays of pink flowers. They like cool, partially shady places. So does *S. fortunei*, with quite large, shining, bronzy leaves and sprays of white flowers in early autumn. *S. oppositifolia* is prostrate and creeping, has heather pink or carmine flowers and it prefers peaty lime-free soil.

Sedum spectabile 'Carmen'.

Sedum   The stonecrops, many of which are prostrate plants. All have fleshy leaves and starry flowers. Specially recommended are *S. cauticolum*, with blue-grey leaves and crimson flowers; *S. dasyphyllum*, with tiny grey leaves and pale pink flowers; *S. kamtschaticum* 'Variegatum', with green and yellow leaves and yellow flowers; *S. lydium*, with small green leaves turning red in summer; *S. pulchellum*, with green leaves and clusters of pink flowers; *S. spathulifolium*, with rosettes of spoon-shaped, grey or reddish-purple leaves, and *S. spurium* 'Erdblut', with green leaves and carmine flowers.

Sempervivum   The houseleeks, succulent plants making tight rosettes of green or bronzy red leaves. They need very good drainage and not much soil. Some have rosettes covered in white filament, like cobwebs, but these are more difficult to grow unless protected from wet in winter.

Thymus   The thymes, of which the best rock-garden kinds are the completely prostrate, mat-forming *T. serpyllum*, with heather-pink, carmine or white flowers, and *T. lanuginosus*, with little leaves covered in grey down. Both can be walked on and make delightful aromatic 'lawns'.

Veronica prostata   A carpet-forming species with blue flowers.

Viola   Several species are suitable, including *V. cornuta*, with light blue or white flowers; *V. gracilis*, with deep violet blue flowers; *V. cucullata*, with white flowers, and *V. labradorica purpurea*, with dark violet flowers and purple leaves. All like cool, partly shady places.

Plants to Walk on

Grass is not the only plant that can be walked on,

Pavement planting between the crevices with ground-hugging sagina, cotula and mentha. Avoid overall concreting between and under the slabs to allow the plants to root.

though it is probably the best to withstand hard wear. Lawns of chamomile or thyme have been popular for centuries and both have the added merit of being aromatic.

Chamomile is *Anthemis nobilis*, a native herb with feathery leaves, sprawling stems and small white daisy-type flowers. It can be raised from seed or divided and either seedlings or divisions can be planted 15–20cm (6–8in) apart to form a lawn. It will take some time before they cover the ground completely and they will need to be cut from time to time to make them branch freely, though cutting need not be so frequent as for a lawn of grass, nor should it be closer than 3cm (1¼in) or the plants may be destroyed.

Chamomile is more drought-resistant than grass and can be used for lawns in places that might be too hot and dry for grass lawns. The same

is true of thyme, which also thrives particularly well on alkaline soils over chalk or limestone, conditions that do not suit the finer grasses. *Thymus serpyllum* and *T. lanuginosus* are the two best species to use since both are naturally mat-forming and require no cutting at all. Space the plants 15–20cm (6–8in) apart. The only subsequent care needed is to remove weeds.

Another idea is to make a flowery pavement by growing prostrate plants in the crevices between paving slabs. This reduces the amount of wear the plants get, since most people, using the paving, will step over the plants rather than on them. The choice of plants therefore becomes very much greater and includes many of the small dianthus species and hybrids, all the helianthemums, prostrate veronicas, the mat-forming phloxes, acaenas, cotulas, *Mentha requienii*, all the small arenarias, all the prostrate sedums, the small creeping or mat-forming erodiums, ajugas, prunellas, *Lysimachia nummularia*, and small campanulas such as *C. cochlearifolia* and *C. posharskyana*.

The plants must be able to root down into soil beneath the paving. This does not mean that no cement can be used to hold the paving slabs firmly in place, but it should be restricted to one or two blobs beneath each slab, with the rest filled in with soil, including the crevices between the slabs.

Plants for Dry Places

Plants have found many methods for coping with heat and drought. Some, like the cacti and other succulents, have developed fleshy leaves, stems or 'bodies' which can store considerable quantities of water to last them until rain arrives to replenish these reserves. Others cover their leaves with scales or hairs which insulate them from the heat and cut down the rate at which water evaporates from them. Yet others reduce the size of their leaves to tiny needles, which also reduces evaporation. Some thrust strong roots deeply and almost vertically downwards in search of sub-soil moisture, and there are also bulbous- and tuberous-rooted plants which make all their growth in a limited season, when water is available, and then die down, relying on the moisture stored in their bulbs or tubers to keep them alive for many months.

These are the plants to look for when you want to fill a dry space in the garden. Most cacti are too tender to be grown out of doors in Britain, except temporarily in summer, but there are quite a lot of hardy succulents or semi-succulents including all the stonecrops (sedums) and houseleeks (sempervivums). In tribute to its hardiness, the common houseleek, *Sempervivum tectorum*, acquired its name because it will thrive on roofs with no more 'soil' than the dead leaves and other debris which may have collected in the corrugations of the tiles. Others are echeverias, which somewhat resemble sempervivums in their succulent grey rosettes, but are less hardy and usually in need of protection in winter. The same is true of the agaves, large rosette-forming plants from Central America with fleshy, often spine-tipped leaves which in some varieties are conspicuously variegated with white or yellow. All the plants loosely known as mesembryanthemums are drought-resistant and so are gazanias and the succulent-leafed annual, portulacca.

The scaly, downy or hairy-leaved plants are usually silver or grey and this can be very useful

This little garden of succulent plants includes aeoniums, crassulas, echeverias and sedums. The plant flowering in the foreground is a South African osteospermum and is not succulent though it likes similar warmth and sun.

from a decorative as well as from a utilitarian point of view. Grey borders, or borders in which greys and silvers predominate, perhaps with white, blue and pink flowers to complete a restful colour scheme, are much in fashion and almost all such plants prefer situations that are rather dry, certainly well drained in winter and summer. The list includes a great many species and varieties of achillea, anaphalis, anthemis, artemisia, chrysanthemum, cistus, convolvulus, dianthus, eucalyptus, helianthemum, helichrysum, hieraceum, hippophae, lavandula, lychnis, olearia, onopordon, perovskia, phlomis, santolina, senecio, stachys, teucrium, verbascum and zauschneria.

Brooms, genistas and gorse are familiar examples of shrubs with very small leaves, the green stems performing some of the functions normally associated with leaves. Incidentally, all belong to the great pea family, Leguminoseae, which is notably rich in plants that have adapted themselves to grow in dry places. Every lawn owner will be aware of the annoying way in which clovers and medicks, both members of the pea family, will survive long after grass is half dead through drought.

Many conifers use the device of small leaves to survive both dryness and intense cold and none is more adept at existing in extremely dry places than the juniper family with their tiny, awl-like leaves. Heathers, though also small-leaved, vary considerably in their tolerance of drought, some being accustomed to growing on very moist, acid moorland, but the taller kinds, such as *Erica arborea*, *E. mediterranea* and *E. terminalis*, will all survive a considerable degree of dryness. Tamarisks of all kinds survive dryness and are particularly good near the sea as they are also salt-tolerant.

Deep-rooted plants which grow well in dry soil include acanthus, anchusa, echinops, eryngium, hollyhocks, *Papaver orientale* and verbascums.

The best bulbous- or tuberous-rooted plants for such places are those that make most of their growth in winter or spring, when the soil in Britain is rarely very dry, and then become partly or fully dormant in summer when it may well be dry. This group includes daffodils, tulips and hyacinths and also a lot of smaller bulbs such as winter aconites (eranthis), crocuses, muscaris, scillas and chionodoxas. *Nerine bowdenii* and, where winters are mild, *Amaryllis belladonna* are other possibilities.

It is not so easy to find plants for places that are both dry and shady but there are a few that will survive even this awkward combination. They include ivies of all kinds, *Hypericum calycinum*, *Iris foetidissima* and *Ruscus aculaetus*.   A H

CACTI AND OTHER SUCCULENTS

Succulents are plants that have evolved to grow in dry places by storing water and food in fleshy leaves or stems. Cacti are just one class of succulents in which the stem is the storage organ, often so swollen that it forms the major part of the plant and is sometimes referred to as the 'body'. Cactus stems are spiny and the spines are borne in clusters on aureoles or small protuberances. This is the botanical feature which immediately distinguishes them from other succulents.

All succulents, including cacti, like porous, well-drained soil but it is a popular fallacy that

A rock and cactus garden.

they thrive best in poor, sandy soil. A good mixture for most kinds is equal parts loam, peat and very coarse sand plus 50g John Innes Base Fertilizer to each 10 litres (bucketful) of the mixture.

For the Christmas and Easter Cacti, which are epiphytic, ie normally live in trees or on rocks out of direct contact with the soil, a more humusy mixture is better and they will enjoy shade from direct sunshine in summer, whereas most other succulents can take all the sunshine that is going.

Another common fallacy is that cacti and succulents require little water. In fact, from April to September, they need to be watered about as frequently and freely as most other greenhouse plants and it is only in winter that they need to be kept rather dry, though not completely so. Again an exception must be made for the epiphytes which need to be kept just nicely moist even in winter.

The third popular fallacy is that cacti and other succulents want a lot of heat. In fact in winter most of them like to be cool so long as they do not actually freeze, and a minimum temperature of 6°C (43°F) will suit most of them well. This enables them to rest properly and will ensure better growth and flowering when temperatures rise naturally with sun heat in spring and summer.

A peculiarity of the Christmas Cactus, *Schlumbergera buckleyi*, is that its flower buds are only formed when nights are long. When grown in rooms, artificial lighting may interfere with this, making the plants behave as if they were still growing in long days and short nights and so making new leaves but no flowers. The remedy is to remove plants to an unlighted room late each afternoon or cover them with an efficient blackout.

Cacti and other succulents can be raised from seed sown as soon as possible after it is ripe on the surface of sandy soil and germinated in a temperature of 16–18°C (61–65°F). Some kinds can be divided and some can be grown from cuttings or leaves, in fact there are some succulents that use leaves as a normal means of increase since they root when they fall to the ground and soon grow into new plants.

Most cacti and succulents are easy to grow and will withstand a good deal of mismanagement. Many are fascinating, strange and beautiful and a number have very showy flowers.

A cactus house.

Recommended Succulents (including Cacti)

Aporocactus flagelliformis   The Rat-tailed Cactus with long, narrow trailing stems and cerise flowers.

Cephalocereus senilis   The Old Man Cactus with cylindrical bodies covered in long silky white hairs.

Cereus   The Column Cacti with tall columnar bodies, sometimes branches, and flowers that, in some kinds, open at night.

Crassula   Numerous species with fleshy leaves and often showy orange or red flowers. Some are much branched like shrubs.

Echeveria   Rosettes of grey leaves and narrow sprays of flowers, usually orange or red.

Echinopsis   Barrel-like bodies often deeply ribbed and covered in spines.

Epiphyllum   Epiphytic cacti with flattened, jointed stems and large, showy flowers, pink, red, yellow or white.

Euphorbia   A number of succulent species including *E. obesa*, with a dome-shaped body, and *E. caputmedusae* (Medusa's Head) with a ball-like body and snaky stems.

Kalanchoe blossfeldiana   A leafy succulent with sprays of scarlet or yellow flowers in winter.

Lampranthus   Commonly known as mesembryanthemums. They are like small, branched shrubs with fleshy leaves and showy daisy-like flowers.

Mammillaria   The Pincushion Cacti with globular or cylindrical bodies and flower clusters in circles around the top.

Opuntia   The Prickly Pears, with pad-shaped bodies joined together to form large branched plants.

Rhipsalidopsis gaertneri   The Easter Cactus with flattened, jointed stems and sprays of carmine flowers in spring.

Schlumbergeria buckleyi   The Christmas Cactus, much like rhipsalidopsis but flowering in winter. There are pink and white as well as carmine-flowered varieties.

Selenicereus   The Night Flowering Cacti with snaky stems and large, white-scented flowers which open at night.

A H

The pincushion cactus (*Mammillaria*).

The prickly pear (*Opuntia*).

WOODLAND WONDERS

Of all flowering shrubs, with the solitary exception of roses, rhododendrons make the greatest contribution to the flower colour of gardens. At their peak in May and June they are terrific and people flock to enjoy the display made by such famous collections as those at the Saville Gardens and Valley Gardens, Windsor Great Park, the Isabella Plantation, Richmond Park, the two fine woodland gardens in Bushey Park, Hampton Court, and such gardens as Bodnant in Gwynedd, Exbury, Hampshire, and Wisley, Surrey.

The family is immense, including all those plants commonly known as azaleas; varieties vary enormously in size, habit, colour and appearance, many being so different from the popular conception of a rhododendron that most people without specialist knowledge would not recognize them as such. There are something like six hundred known species growing in the wild besides many thousands of garden varieties either selected from these species or made by hybridization between them. Many are easy to grow but all dislike lime, though the degree of dislike varies and the common purple *Rhododendron ponticum*, which has naturalized itself in many parts of Britain, will actually survive in soils that are neutral or even very slightly alkaline.

Most prefer to grow in semi-shade, preferably the dappled or intermittent shade cast by trees fairly widely spaced. They are the most popular shrubs for planting in woodland gardens; indeed you could even say that in Britain the woodland garden owes its existence to the great increase of interest in rhododendrons during the past hundred years. Yet some kinds will grow very well in full sun and these include some of the small-leaved mountain rhododendrons that are popular rock-garden shrubs as well as the very different hardy hybrids and the deciduous azaleas.

The hardy hybrids are what most people think of as typical rhododendrons, but in fact they are not natural species but man-made hybrids – the result of a long continued effort on the part of rhododendron enthusiasts to perfect and extend a race of evergreen rhododendrons capable of

Free-flowering clusters of azaleas – now officially classified as rhododendrons – at Bickling Hall.

flowering regularly and reliably outdoors in all parts of Britain. Since it is the open flowers that are most at risk, this has meant producing rhododendrons which will flower between mid-May and late June when the risk of severe and sustained frost is not great. The hardy hybrids mostly have fairly large leaves and dome-shaped clusters of large flowers. The colour range is wide, including pink, rose, red, carmine, crimson, purple, blue, light yellow and white, and most of them grow fairly slowly into large bushes. They are among the easiest to grow, surpassed only in this respect by *R. ponticum* which lacks their colour range and quality of bloom.

The hardy hybrids are of very mixed parentage whereas there are many other hybrids which are the result of crossing two species. These are often given distinguishing names, eg all hybrids between *R. fortunei* and *R. griffithianum* are known as *R. loderi*. Since they will not all be of similar merit, particularly good forms are increased vegetatively, by cuttings, layering or grafting, each selected form being given an additional distinguishing name; for example 'King George' is a particularly fine pink and white form (a clone) of *R. loderi*.

Rhododendrons differ enormously in size, habit and leaf as well as in their flowers. At one extreme are prostrate species, such as the scarlet-flowered *R. forrestii*, at the other tree-like shrubs, such as the red, pink or white *R. arboreum*. There are kinds with tiny leaves and small flowers, such as the purplish-blue *R. impeditum*, and others with enormous leaves and flower trusses to match, such as *R. sinogrande*. Some are completely hardy, some are only satisfactory in the milder maritime localities and some require greenhouse protection. In addition to the familiar type of bell-shaped flower packed into quite dense clusters there are rhododendrons with tubular flowers, almost flat flowers, funnel-shaped flowers and many other variations.

The azaleas can be split between evergreen and deciduous kinds. The hybrid evergreens are all fairly low-growing but rather wide-spreading shrubs with small evergreen leaves and small to medium sized flowers produced very freely, mainly in May and early June. Many are sufficiently hardy to be grown in all but the coldest parts of Britain. All prefer some shade and protection from searing winds.

The hardy deciduous azaleas are medium-sized shrubs, usually rather open-branched, with mainly medium-sized flowers in May and June. They will tolerate more sunshine and exposure

Sparkling blooms of the hybrid rhododendron 'Britannia'.

than the evergreen azaleas and can be grown outdoors virtually throughout the British Isles provided the soil is acid. The leaves of many colour well before they fall in autumn. These azaleas can also be purchased in excellent mixtures of colours such as the Knap Hill and Exbury strains.

To bring some kind of order into all this, botanists have divided the genus into groups, which they call 'series', the members of which have obvious characteristics in common. The Royal Horticultural Society's Rhododendron Group has published several useful handbooks on the species and hybrids. These use a system for assessing hardiness based on four grades: H-4 for a rhododendron that is hardy anywhere in Britain; H-3 for those hardy in the South and West in maritime areas and sheltered gardens inland; H-2 for those requiring protection even in the most sheltered gardens, and H-1 for rhododendrons normally requiring greenhouse protection. Some nurserymen use this classification in their catalogues but, in general, only varieties in classes H-4 and H-3 are readily available.

All are easy to grow provided the soil is not alkaline or liable to dry out badly at any time. Rhododendrons enjoy humus and benefit from generous annual mulches of leafmould or peat, but peat is not essential and excellent plants can be seen on acid clay soils. They benefit from spring feeding with a high-nitrogen compound fertilizer preferably including iron, magnesium and manganese as well as the usual phosphorus and potash. If they become overgrown they can be thinned or cut back in May or June, preferably immediately after flowering, but will not then flower the following year.

Although the peak flowering season for rhododendrons is May-June, some kinds flower as early as January in very sheltered places and a few do not start flowering until July.

CAMELLIAS

When these beautiful and early-flowering, ever-green shrubs first arrived in Britain in the mid eighteenth century they had already been highly developed by the Chinese and were available in numerous single, semi-double and double-flowered varieties. At that time they were considered far too tender to be planted outdoors and shared the orangeries and conservatories in which other exotic 'greens' were cultivated. Gradually, how-ever, it dawned on gardeners that most camellias were almost fully hardy and it was only their flowers that were at risk. Planted in suitably sheltered places, and in particular in woodland gardens which, by the late nineteenth century, were being made all over the place primarily for rhododendrons, they were quite happy in the open. Today camellias are in great demand both for this purpose and for cultivation in pots, tubs and other containers as terrace and patio plants.

The number of varieties is legion and has been swelled by the introduction of other species in addition to the original *Camellia japonica*, and the hybridization of these with existing varieties. The *Williamsii* hybrids, for example, are the result of crossing *C. japonica* with the smaller-leaved, thinner-stemmed *C. saluenensis*. 'Donation', a double pink-flowered variety of this parentage, has become one of the most popular of all camellias because it produces flowers with astonishing freedom; successive batches of flowers will open even after earlier ones have been spoiled by frost.

A very large-flowered species with a rather lax habit, named *C. reticulata*, has given rise to another race of camellias notable for the size and beauty of their flowers but these are, in general, a little more tender than *C. japonica* and *C. williamsii* varieties and, except in mild districts, may need to be trained against walls or given specially sheltered places. The same is true of the lovely forms and hybrids of *C. sasanqua*, not least because they can begin flowering in autumn and continue most of the winter if the weather is kind.

The colour range of camellias is not great, from white and palest pink to crimson, but flower size and form are varied, from singles with a single circle of petals and a central tuft of golden anthers to fully double flowers which may be completely formal, almost as if carved out of wood, or completely informal or anything between these two extremes. There are anemone-centred camel-lias, peony-flowered varieties, semi-doubles, large-flowered, medium-flowered and small-flowered kinds. The only serious lack is of camellias that flower really late, in May and June – rather than March or April – when their flowers would be much less at risk from frost.

Like rhododendrons, camellias dislike lime but they have a greater tolerance of soils that are near-neutral or only very slightly acid. They are also far more tolerant of dry soil and seem to be almost immune to attacks by the honey fungus (*Armill-aria mellea*) which does a lot of damage to rhododendrons. They enjoy dappled or intermit-tent shade but will also grow in full sun, though less vigorously and often with yellowed leaves. The two genera combine well and are frequently planted in association, the camellias preceding the rhododendrons in their main flower display.

Leaves of all camellias are evergreen and most are dark green, shining and handsome, and make first-rate foliage shrubs. They transplant well and are tolerant of very hard pruning in May, which can be useful if they become overgrown but should not be taken advantage of unnecessarily since it reduces or even eliminates the flower display the following year. If a few stems are cut with flowers for indoor decoration this is usually all the pruning that camellias require.

They benefit from annual top dressings of peat or leafmould supplemented by moderate appli-cations of a compound fertilizer, preferably one containing minor elements such as iron, man-ganese and magnesium as well as nitrogen, phosphorus and potash. They suffer very little from either pests or diseases but scale insects, looking rather like minute limpets, can attach themselves to stems and leaves and should be removed by sponging with soapy water or spray-ing with diazinon, malathion or petroleum-oil insecticide. A H

A BLOOMING LONG LIFE

I have always enjoyed the story of the visitor who, on being taken to admire the finest beds of scarlet geraniums, begged to be led away to cool his eyes on the parsley. For generations, these bedding geraniums, which are really 'zonal' pelargoniums, have been among the brightest of summer flowers and the most continuous in display (rivalled only by the scarlet salvias), but they are not the only important garden race of pelargoniums. Others are the ivy-leaved varieties which are sprawling in habit, the 'regal' pelargoniums, mainly valued as pot plants for greenhouse and conservatory, and the scented-leaved pelargoniums, grown more for

Zonal pelargoniums are those bedding plants much favoured by municipal parks – a sensible decision since they bloom and bloom, as long as they are dead-headed.

the many shapes and scents of their leaves than for their flowers which are often rather dowdy.

Zonal pelargoniums flower non-stop from the moment they can be safely planted outdoors in late May or early June until they have to be returned to the safety of a frost-proof greenhouse or other well-lighted shelter some time in October. Given a minimum temperature of about 13°C (55°F), many will continue to flower much of the winter and spring as well, and all zonal pelargoniums make excellent pot plants in sunny spots.

They are bushy plants with stems that become increasingly woody with age. The name 'zonal' refers to a zone or ring of dark colour on the leaves, but not all varieties have this, some being green all over and some variegated, with several colours including cream, yellow and red. Flower colours range from white and pale pink to cherry red, scarlet and crimson and there are double-flowered as well as single-flowered varieties. With the exception of the variegated-leaved varieties, which must be increased from stem cuttings, all can be grown from seed or cuttings: the seed should be sown in a warm greenhouse between

January and March, the cuttings rooted in a propagator or frame in spring or late summer. Seedlings are sometimes a little slow coming into flower the first summer, although the F1 hybrids such as 'Sprinter' and 'Carefree' are much better than the old non-hybrid varieties in this respect. All like warm, sunny places, do not require very rich soil and must be given complete protection from frost.

Ivy-leaved pelargoniums, though natural sprawlers, can be readily trained as climbers to wires or a trellis. Alternatively, they can be grown in hanging baskets, window boxes and other containers. The leaves are smooth and angular in contrast to the more rounded, softly downy leaves of the zonals. The colour range is also more restricted, mainly white, pink, lilac and scarlet, but flowers are produced almost continuously and the plants are equally sun-loving. Increase is by cuttings.

Regal pelargoniums are bushy, like the zonals, and most have larger flowers often handsomely blotched with a dark colour. The flowering season is shorter – at its peak in May and June.

Scented-leaved pelargoniums have small, not very showy flowers and are grown as foliage plants. They are bushy, like the zonals and regals, but the leaves are of many different shapes. The scents, too, vary as much as the leaf shapes and include lemon, rose and peppermint. They are grown as pot plants in much the same way as the regals.

All pelargoniums flower most freely and continuously if the faded flowers are removed regularly. The regal varieties can be pruned in August to prevent them getting too large or straggly, and the scented-leaved varieties can be similarly pruned at any time in summer. Zonal and ivy-leaved pelargoniums are usually cut back quite a lot when they are lifted in autumn and returned to pots or other containers so that they can be overwintered in a protected place. Most will survive, provided they do not freeze, but the further the temperature falls below 13°C (55°F) the more likely are they to suffer from decay caused by the grey mould fungus, *Botrytis cinerea*. Occasional dusting with sulphur or spraying with benomyl will help to prevent this.

Regal pelargonium 'Aztec' – mainly for the greenhouse.

Fuchsias

Few shrubs can rival fuchsias for continuous flowering from spring until autumn. In gardens, these South American species have been almost completely supplanted by man-made hybrids which grow in similar temperatures but offer a vastly increased range of flower sizes, shapes and colours, ranging from tiny bushes barely 30cm (1ft) high to large shrubs, some erect, some wide-spreading and some cascading.

For gardeners, fuchsias fall into two main groups. In the first are the hardy fuchsias, suitable for planting permanently out of doors in the milder, and particularly the maritime, parts of Britain. The others can be grown as pot or basket plants in cool greenhouses or outdoors from about late May to late October. In winter most of these will survive provided they do not freeze, but if the temperature drops below about 10°C (50°F) they will lose all or most of their leaves whereas at higher temperatures they will retain many of them or produce new ones so that they are ready to make a quicker start in the spring.

A fuchsia flower consists of a tube, a calyx, a corolla, anthers and pistil, all of which may differ in size, shape and colour. Though the colour range is fairly limited, from white, palest pink, mauve and lavender to orange, scarlet, crimson and deep violet-purple, this still gives you the choice of a vast number of combinations which have been exploited to the full by fuchsia fanciers who have produced hundreds of varieties.

There are also differences in habit, some growing erect and in time becoming quite tall, many well branched and bushy, some arching and some pendulous. Fuchsias can also be readily trained by tying their stems to canes or other supports and pinching out the tips of young shoots to make them branch. By these means it is possible to grow fuschias in pots, hanging baskets and window boxes, or to train them against walls, fences or beneath the rafters of a greenhouse.

The flowering season is long, from spring to autumn under glass and usually from about July to late October outdoors, but varieties vary greatly. To some extent fuchsias are 'long-day plants', that is, they usually flower when days are longer than nights, but hybridization and selection have somewhat confused this natural characteristic.

Fuchsias will grow in all reasonably fertile soils in sun or partial shade, but they flower most freely in good light. Under glass they may benefit from a little shading in summer but require none at other times of the year. They can be grown in soil-based or peat-based potting mixture, should be watered fairly freely in spring and summer, but rather sparingly in winter or scarcely at all if conditions are so cold that they lose all their leaves.

Selected varieties are increased by cuttings which root quite readily at any time in spring or summer in a propagator or a pot placed inside a polythene bag.

Diseases are rare and the most troublesome pests are capsid bugs, which deform the leaves, and white fly which weakens the plants and disfigures them by encouraging sooty mould. Capsid bugs can be killed by spraying with HCH or diazinon, white fly with pirimiphos methyl or permethrin.

A H

Fuchsias come in hundreds of varieties, the complex pendulous flowers combining in an array of colours.

THE GOOD COMPANIONS

One of the biggest changes in twentieth-century garden-making has come about through our increased awareness of how important it is to group plants that go together well. In the right company the beauty and effectiveness of a plant can be greatly enhanced; with the wrong companions the reverse can happen.

At one time it was thought that good plant association (the gardeners' term) meant keeping plants of a kind together – hardy perennials in herbaceous borders, shrubs in shrubberies, trees in arboretums, roses in rose gardens, and so on. Two factors have destroyed that notion: one the decreasing size of gardens, which has made it physically impossible to segregate plants in this way, the other a growing realization that the contrasts between plants of totally different character can be used positively to devise effective arrangements.

So the idea of the mixed border was born and prospered exceedingly. Shrubs form the permanent framework, herbaceous plants provide variety of form and colour, and roses and bedding plants help to maintain colour much more continuously and for a longer period than would be possible without them.

A patchwork of brilliant colours made with annual plants. The purple centrepiece of *Verbena venosa* is backed with pink lavatera and deep coppery-red Helichrysum 'Hot Bikini', with bronze and gold marigolds in the foreground and a cooling group of pearl grass, *Briza maxima*, which can be dried for winter decoration.

MIXING COLOURS AND FORMS

In all plant associations there are two major factors to be considered: colour and form. Colour is a particularly emotive subject and people react to it in highly personal ways. Some cannot stand white, often explaining that it reminds them of funerals. Many are irritated by bright yellow or orange, depressed by blues and purples or find reds vulgar and dominating. How is it that colours can exert such a range of impressions?

All the colours that we see can be made by mixing three primary colours, red, yellow and blue. At full saturation these colours, in association, produce the strongest contrasts, but their effect can be diminished either by lowering or increasing their luminosity, the one making them appear much duller and blacker, the other much lighter or closer to white. Mixtures of any two of the primaries will produce intermediate colours –

orange when red is mixed with yellow, green from yellow and blue, and purple from blue and red. Mix all three primaries and you get the endless varieties of muted shades which eventually lead, by way of the browns and greys, to black.

We can see something of how this works by making a colour clock. Red occupies a segment at 12 o'clock; pure blue is at 4 and pure yellow at 8. At 1 is violet-red, at 2 violet, 3 blue-violet, 5 blue-green, 6 green, 7 yellow-green, 9 yellow-orange, 10 orange, 11 orange-red. The clock shows which colours will produce contrasts and which harmonies, and just how strong or soft those contrasts or harmonies will be. The nearer together the colours are on the clock, the softer the harmonies they produce; the effect can be further softened by diluting the colours.

Colours known as 'complementary' face each

other across the clock-face – orange-red and blue-green, for example, or pure yellow and violet. If you look at a strong colour for a while and then switch your eyes to white or a neutral colour, the complementary colour will then appear for a few seconds. Gertrude Jekyll, who in the early years of this century wrote the best book about the use of colour in the garden, believed that this apparition represented a natural longing for a totally different colour and she made great use of complementary colour associations in the flower borders she planned so skilfully. She also used contrasts when she wanted to please; the principles of colour association have not altered since her day.

However, though it is correct to regard harmonies as restful by comparison with contrasts, they vary a great deal among themselves. Harmonies based on the red, orange and yellow section of the colour circle can be very bright and exhilarating, whereas those in the red, violet to blue section are much quieter and those in the blue-green section are the most sober of all.

Green is a basic garden colour which can be associated with any of the others. But proceed with caution: leaf greens are much more varied,

A little garden of herbs, enlivened by royal lilies (*Lilium regale*), which enjoy the shade provided for their roots but are able to push up their leaves and flowers into the sunshine. The herbs include borage, with blue flowers, fennel, with very finely divided leaves, parsley running to seed and the old-fashioned pot marigold or calendula.

Below: Steely blues and golds, ideal for a warm, sunny place and well-drained soil. In the foreground is *Eryngium giganteum*, a vigorous biennial sea holly, which produces plenty of seed to ensure its survival. The background plant is the golden marguerite, *Anthemis tinctoria*, a perennial which flowers most of the summer.

It would be difficult to conceive a more striking contrast than this: the brash modernity of the new scarlet 'montbretia', *Crocosmia lucifer*, and the primly discreet *Astrantia major*, each pink and white flower looking like a tiny Victorian posy. Both plants are perennial and the astrantia is easily grown from seed.

both in composition and in luminosity, than is generally realized. The very brightest greens tend, by competition, to tone down other luminous colours such as scarlet, yellow and orange whereas dark greens, such as those of yew and cherry laurel, tend to enhance the tones of contrasting colours.

You can also use colours in the garden to create illusions of distance. Very luminous colours, such as white and yellow, stand out so clearly, even when a long way off, that they often appear to be closer than they really are. Dark colours, and those of low luminosity in the purple and violet range, do the opposite, and exaggerate the distance between themselves and the viewer. Some colours are so alien to all the others that it is nearly impossible to assimilate them. This is one reason for using very bright reds with caution in Britain. Someone once referred to them as 'burning holes in the landscape'.

Contrasts and harmonies of form are just as important as those of colour, but it is more difficult to codify them simply. Leaves may be large or small, rigid or soft, smooth-edged, jagged, lobed, fingered or composed of numerous separate leaflets arranged along a central mid-rib, a form botanists term pinnate. They can also differ enormously in surface texture.

Not only are there many different greens in leaves, as well as blue-greys, silvery greys, purples, coppers and bronzes, there is an immense range of variegations, with white, cream, yellow and pink arranged in all manner of ways – speckled, blotched, veined and feathered.

Trees and shrubs vary enormously in habit, from spreading to narrowly erect, densely branched, open branched, angularly branched or 'weeping'.

MODEL LAYOUTS

The best way to learn about plant associations is by observing them in well planned gardens and for this purpose there are few better 'schools' than Sissinghurst Castle, Kent; Great Dixter, Northiam, East Sussex; Cranborne, Dorset; Hidcote Manor, near Chipping Campden, Gloucestershire; Knightshayes Court, near Tiverton, Devon; and Crathes Castle, Banchory, Grampian.

Wherever you go you can pick up ideas, even from the simplest cottage or suburban garden. Genius in these matters is not confined to the great and in any case the most felicitous results are often more the result of luck than good management. Even when you know fairly precisely what you want, it is often difficult to get it quite right at the first attempt and adjustments may be necessary later in the light of what actually happens on the ground.   A H

This richly-coloured carpet of ground-hugging plants is composed mainly of heathers, some chosen for their contrasting flower colours, others for the lemon or bronzy-yellow colour of their leaves. A single plant of silver-leaved *Euryops acraeus* intensifies the heather colours and is happily in scale with them.

DAZZLING TRUMPETS

Lilies were a very varied lot long before man came on the scene and began to take a hand in their diversification. Over eight hundred species have been recorded growing in the wild and a number of these are cultivated in gardens, though in recent years they have tended to be supplanted by man-made hybrids. Whether this is entirely a good thing is open to doubt. The hybrids have certainly produced new colours and forms and some magnificent plants, and some of them are easy to grow. But few actually surpass the best species either in beauty or in vigour and it would be a great loss if over-preoccupation with the hybrids led to neglect of the species.

Lilies flower in four basic forms: trumpet, bowl, turk's cap and cup-shaped. The trumpet is the classical lily shape and varies from very long and slender, as in *Lilium formosanum*, to broad and fairly short, as in the ever-popular *L. regale*. The bowl shape is best exemplified by the magnificent *L. auratum*, which when fully open can have almost flat flowers 20–25cm (8–10in) across. The turk's cap, or reflexed, is a widespread and familiar form with the flowers usually hanging downwards and the petals always swept back at the tips, as in *L. martagon*, *L. tigrinum* and *L. chalcedonicum*. The flowers of cup-shaped lilies are usually carried in upward-facing clusters; examples are *L. bulbiferum*, *L. hollandicum* and *L. maculatum*.

All lilies make bulbs but these do not have an extended resting season and do not like being out of the soil for long at any time of the year. Once established in the garden, lilies are best treated like herbaceous perennials, to be lifted, divided and replanted as quickly as possible – and only when this becomes necessary because they are over-crowded or for some other reason. The best time to do this is as soon as the leaves have withered, which for early-ripening kinds, such as the Madonna lily, *L. candidum*, and its apricot-yellow hybrid *L. testaceum*, is usually in July or the first fortnight in August, and for late-growing kinds, such as *L. speciosum* and *L. auratum*, not until late October or early November.

Bulbs from distant places such as western North America and Japan may not be available on the market until midwinter and it is a very chancy matter planting them directly out of doors. Usually it is wise to pot them singly in 10–15cm (4–6in) pots according to the size of the bulbs. Use a peat-based potting compost (lime-free for lime-hating kinds) and keep them in a frame, cool greenhouse or other light but protected place until they are growing freely in the spring and can be planted out with roots and compost intact. If lily bulbs home-grown in Britain are available, it may be possible to obtain delivery much earlier and then it is usually best to plant them at once where they are to flower.

All lilies like porous yet fertile soil, moist in spring and summer when they are making their growth but for most (there are exceptions) not waterlogged in winter. They like humus in plenty because it helps to maintain these conditions and a good many lilies dislike lime in the soil, preferring it to be moderately acid. Again there are exceptions, and plenty of lilies will grow perfectly well in neutral or even moderately alkaline soils.

Another difference between lilies is in the way they form their roots. Some make all root growth from the base of the bulb and some have a second root system growing from the base of the stems above the bulbs. Clearly it is better if these stem-

Turk's cap lily.

Lilium regale.

Lilium candidum.

rooting kinds are planted sufficiently deep to give scope for this upper root system to be developed; but since nearly all lilies, stem rooting or otherwise, grow well when covered with 10cm (4in) of soil, the distinction is not quite so important as is sometimes suggested. The two principal excep-tions are *L. candidum* and *L. testaceum*, both of which like to grow virtually on the surface with the tops of their bulbs exposed.

Lilies grow well in open places provided they do not become dry and sun-baked in summer. They often grow even better in dappled or intermittent shade or when planted among low-growing shrubs and leafy perennials (evergreen azaleas and herbaceous peonies are excellent), which will shade the soil, keeping it cool and moist, but will allow the lily stems to grow up into the sunshine.

When planting lilies, it helps to surround the bulbs with a mixture of equal parts soil, peat (or leafmould) and sharp sand (or perlite) to which a light peppering of bonemeal or John Innes base fertilizer has been added. This same mixture is ideal for lilies that are to be started in pots and planted out later on. All lilies can also be grown throughout in pots in unheated or very slightly heated greenhouses or in other shelter provided they get a reasonable amount of light. Pots should be big enough to give the lilies plenty of rooting space.

Some lilies are very sensitive to virus infections which rapidly debilitate them and render them useless. Other kinds seem able to survive such attacks with little outward sign of harm and this, though satisfactory in one way, can be dangerous in another since the virus-tolerant lilies can become unsuspected sources of infection for the virus-sensitive kinds. *L. tigrinum* is a notorious virus carrier and is best kept out of the garden if virus-prone lilies, such as *L. auratum* and *L. speciosum*, are to be grown. There is no easy remedy for virus diseases but they are spread mainly by greenflies, so periodic spraying with aphicides will help reduce the risk of infection.

The other principal disease of lilies is grey mould caused by the fungus *Botrytis cinerea*, and this can be particularly troublesome with *L. candidum*, the leaves of which can be severely disfigured by the time the flowers open. Grey mould is difficult to cure but infection can be prevented by occasional spraying in spring and summer with benomyl, thiram or a copper fungicide.

Many lilies can be raised from seed and some, notably *L. regale*, *L. longiflorum* and *L. formosanum*, grow so rapidly that seedlings will flower the first year and quite a high percentage can be expected to flower the second year. Seed can either be sown in late summer or autumn, as soon as it is ripe, or the following spring. It is best sown in pans in a compost of equal parts soil, peat and either sand or perlite, and germinated in a greenhouse or frame without artificial heat. The seedlings are best left undisturbed for the first summer, but in the autumn they can be potted in 7cm (3in) pots and by the end of the second year most should be sufficiently large to be planted outdoors.

Flowers of 'Enchantment'.

Lilies can also be increased by splitting up the bulb clusters. This is done at the normal planting season for the species or hybrids. Lilies can also be increased by detaching scales from the bulbs and pressing these to half their depth in a mixture of equal parts peat and either sand or perlite. If kept moist in a frame or cool greenhouse most of the scales will soon form little bulbils at the base and after three or four years these can be grown on to flowering size. Scale propagation is a useful means of increasing, fairly rapidly, stocks of hybrids and garden varieties which do not breed entirely true from seed. Species, which do grow true to type from seed, are better increased in that way since seedlings will start life virus-free whereas scales will be infected by whatever viruses their parent plants were carrying.

Some lilies, including *L. tigrinum* and *L. bulbiferum*, carry little bulbils in the axils of the leaves up the flowering stems and these can be detached and grown on into flowering-sized bulbs. This is a very easy means of increase and the bulbils produce plants exactly resembling their parents.   A H

BULB BONANZA

Bulbs planted in autumn provide many of the gayest flowers of spring. They include the stately tulips, favourites for four centuries and still being further developed and improved; the daffodils so easy to grow that they are often 'naturalized' in rough-mown grass and left to fend for themselves for years; the sturdy hyacinths richly scented and ideal for formal settings or planting in containers; crocuses and muscaris to make carpets of colour or to be used as edgings to beds; bluebells for woodlands, scillas and chionodoxas for rock gardens, alliums to grow among the herbaceous plants and many more.

Plant bulbs in different places and in different ways. Tulips and hyacinths, for example, can be arranged regularly in straight rows or circles since this fits well with their role as bedding plants either on their own or with a groundwork of forget-me-nots, polyanthuses, primroses, double daisies or wallflowers. In contrast, daffodils, especially when naturalized, are planted to look as natural as possible, either in long, curving drifts, or in narrower, winding trails rather like golden streams, perhaps ending in a larger splash of colour.

Random planting suits many of the smaller bulbs but when you grow bluebells, snowdrops, fritillarias, winter aconites and so on in woodland or wild gardens, try to get a complete cover of the ground just as bluebells do when they grow wild in the woods. In borders, it is effective to keep bulbs in fairly compact groups so that they make clumps of colour when in flower, and can be identified and cared for according to their needs.

Some gardeners object to what they consider the untidiness of bulb foliage after the flowers have faded. If the bulbs have been used in formal

Daffodils at Sutton Place.

displays, they will probably be carefully dug up and replanted close together in some out of the way place where they can complete their growth before they are stored ready for replanting. If bulbs are used more permanently in association with other plants, these can be chosen and grouped so that they grow up around the bulbs as they fade and help conceal them. You can cut off the bulb leaves when they start to wither as they will then have completed their useful function in feeding and fattening the bulbs.

Bulbs look good in containers of many kinds. For window boxes, it is the shorter ones such as the early-flowering tulips, miniature daffodils, crocuses, scillas, chionodoxas and muscaris that are most suitable; plant them in association with low-growing spring flowers such as aubrieta, arabis, primroses, polyanthuses and double daisies. If you use urns and ornamental containers on terraces and patios, you can choose from a wider selection, like the tall May-flowering tulips, large daffodils and hyacinths, possibly with wallflowers and forget-me-nots.

Most bulbs like open, sunny places but some, including bluebells, snowdrops and winter aconites (*Eranthis*) will grow in shade provided it is not too dense. All like fertile, rather porous soils that do not dry out badly while making their growth.

Bulbs are really herbaceous perennials, which differ from others by possessing special storage organs. They can be increased by lifting and dividing the bulb clusters. This is best done when they are dormant, which is usually in the summer. Hardy bulbs do not need to be lifted and replanted every year unless you are using them in bedding-out schemes; they can be left to grow undisturbed until they become overcrowded and the number or quality of the flowers deteriorates.

Some bulbs grow well planted in grass. The neatest and quickest way to do this is with a special tool with a handle like a spade and a small circular blade which cuts and withdraws a plug or turf. This can be replaced neatly when a bulb has been dropped into the hole. After flowering, do not cut down the leaves until at least six weeks after the last flowers have faded. (This, of course, will restrict the amount of mowing that can be done.) If leaves are cut off too early the bulbs will be starved, and over the years may become so weakened that they are unable to flower.

Right: *Erythronium revoltum* thrives in semi-shade.

BULB TYPES

Crocus   There are spring-, autumn- and winter-flowering kinds; the first group is by far the most popular and generally useful. All crocuses form corms which need to be planted 3–6cm (1½–2½in) deep, the winter- and spring-flowering kinds in September but the autumn-flowering kinds in August. All like reasonably fertile soil and open, preferably sunny places. The species, including the many colour forms of *Crocus chrysanthus*, make good rock-garden plants, but the large-flowered hybrids are usually grown in beds or in short grass, which should not be cut until all the crocus leaves have withered.

Chionodoxa   Often known as Glory of the Snow, these are charming little bulbs for rock gardens and for edging borders. They have short sprays of starry blue or blue and white flowers in March and April. Plant 5–7cm (2–3in) deep in good soil and in an open, preferably sunny place and leave undisturbed until overcrowded.

Below: *Crocus chrysanthus* 'Nanette'.

Above: Tulips arrived in Britain in the sixteenth century.

Eranthis The winter aconites look rather like celandines, with a green ruff around each short-stemmed, golden yellow flower. They will grow in sun or semi-shade and can be in flower by January if the weather is favourable. Plant 4–5cm (1½–2in) deep and leave undisturbed until overcrowded.

Erythronium One kind is commonly known as dog's tooth violet and another as trout lily. They are charming small bulbs with white, pink, purple or yellow flowers, a little like those of cyclamen. All thrive in semi-shade in rather moist soil containing plenty of peat or leaf mould. Plant 5cm (2in) deep and leave undisturbed until overcrowded. The leaves of the variety *Erythronium dens-canis* are attractively mottled.

Fritillaria This is a very big genus containing a lot of unusual-looking plants some of which are quite difficult to grow. One of the most popular is *F. meleagris*, the snake's head fritillary, with bell-shaped flowers on slender stems in March-April. They may be all white or chequered white and maroon. This plant likes fairly rich, moist soil and can be naturalized in grass if it is not cut until all the fritillary leaves have died. Very different in character is *F. imperialis*, the crown imperial, a big plant with stout stems each bearing in spring a cluster of bell-shaped yellow or reddish-orange flowers. It likes rich well-cultivated soil and is prone to grey mould disease which can be attacked with a fungicide in spring. Cover bulbs of *F. meleagris* to a depth of 5cm (2in), those of *F. imperialis*, 8–10cm (3–4in).

Galanthus These are the snowdrops, in flower during February and early March. The British species, *G. nivalis*, and the varieties derived from it will all grow in sun or shade and are good woodland plants; but the Mediterranean species, with large flowers and broader leaves, succeed best in full sun.

Hyacinth By far the most popular hyacinths are the large-flowered or Dutch varieties, grown formally, mainly in pots, bowls, window boxes. However, there are other types, called Roman, Cynthella and multi-flowering, which have smaller more loosely formed sprays of bloom – these are better for informal groupings with other spring bulbs in borders and rock gardens.

All hyacinths like fertile, porous soil with plenty of moisture while they are making their growth in spring, but warmth and sunshine to

Fritillaria meleagris looks good in grass.

ripen the bulbs in summer. They do not mind being lifted annually but this should not be done until the leaves have withered in June or July. They can be stored until October as they have a fairly long resting period. When planted outdoors, the bulbs should be covered with 6–8cm (2½–3in) of soil, but in pots, bowls and other containers leave the tips of the bulbs to peep through the soil. Make sure that container-grown hyacinths have at least eight

weeks in a cool place before they are brought into warmer surroundings, where an average temperature of about 18°C (65°F) is maintained. If you hurry growth unduly at the outset, without the period of relative cold, the flower spikes will be poor.

Iris The bulbous-rooted irises include some small, very early-flowering species such as light

Bulbs are pretty versatile, but they only look good if enough are planted to make a convincing display.

blue *Iris histrioides*, violet-purple *I. reticulata* and yellow *I. danfordiae*, and also the much taller, May- to June-flowering hybrids known as Spanish, English and Dutch irises. The first group are plants for rock gardens, raised rock beds and pots in an unheated greenhouse, the second are good border plants and cut flowers. All like porous, fertile soils and sunny places and need only be disturbed when overcrowded.

Leucojum   The snowflakes, which look a little like snowdrops though some, such as *Leucojum aestivum* which flowers in April and May, are much taller. They will grow in sunny or lightly shaded places and can be left undisturbed for years.

Muscari   The grape hyacinths, with small spikes of blue or white flowers, do look rather like tiny hyacinths. They are easy, fast-spreading bulbs excellent for carpeting beneath deciduous trees or for growing in rock gardens and at the front of flower borders. All can be left undisturbed for years and will spread by self-sown seedlings. *Muscari comosum plumosum* is a larger plant with sprawling plumy spikes of violet-blue flowers. All flower in spring.

Narcissus   This is the botanical name for the daffodils and they have become one of the most highly developed of all the hardy bulbs. With the exception of some very early multi-flowered varieties such as 'Scilly White' and 'Soleil d'Or', they are all completely hardy. There are a number of different species ranging from very small plants, such as *Narcissus bulbocodium* and *N. cyclamineus*, to much larger ones, such as *N. pseudo-narcissus* and *N. poeticus*, but it is the innumerable hybrids between the species which have made daffodils such valuable plants both for gardens and as cut flowers. The flowering season is from January until May with the peak in April. They are among the best bulbs for naturalizing, especially some of the vigorous trumpet and large-cupped varieties.

Daffodil bulbs are best planted in August or September and should be covered with 5–6cm (2–2½in) of soil and left undisturbed until they show signs of becoming overcrowded.

Scilla   Most bulb growers include the bluebells as well as the small squills under this name, but botanists separate the bluebells in another genus called *Endymion*. The popular squills, such as *Scilla sibirica* and *S. tubergeniana*, are all small plants with starry blue flowers in spring, excellent for carpeting in the same way as muscari. The common bluebell is useful for naturalizing in woodland, but the larger-flowered Spanish bluebell, *Scilla (Endymion) campanulata*, is also a good border plant for open or semi-shady places. It carries its bell-shaped blue, pink or white flowers on 30cm (12in) stems in May.

Tulips   These were the first bulbs really to capture the imagination of gardeners. In general, they have a greater need than daffodils for sunshine, warmth and good drainage, combined with a fairly rich soil that does not become dry during the period of peak growth from March to May. They rest from late June until mid-October and actually seem to derive some benefit from being lifted in July and stored in a dry place at a temperature around 18°C (65°F) until early October when they can be replanted, preferably in fresh, well-cultivated ground. Alternatively, they can be left undisturbed for many years, especially some of the species, and in some places they can even be naturalized though they lack the vigour and adaptability of daffodils. The greatest use of the large-flowered garden varieties is as spring bedding plants and cut flowers, but some of the smaller-flowered varieties and species are often planted in rock gardens.

Garden varieties of tulips are classified in groups according to their time of flowering and type of flower. The main groups are early single and early double, both flowering in April; *kaufmanniana* and *greigii* hybrids, also April flowering and often confused with one another since they have been interbred; *fosteriana* hybrids flowering late in April and with very large flowers; the May-flowering Darwin and Lily-flowered, which differ mainly in flower form – the blooms are less rounded in the Darwins and the petals more pointed and reflexed in the Lily-flowered group. There are also smaller classes including one, called multi-flowered, which carries several flowers per stem and another 'Viridiflora' which has a partly green flower. Parrot tulips have large flowers in May, usually with twisted or curled petals, and two or more colours curiously streaked and blotched. Late double tulips flower in May and have big double flowers rather like peonies, and Rembrandt tulips resemble the May-flowering varieties except that the colours are 'broken', which means that the flower colour, instead of being more or less the same all over, or divided into two or more large and clearly defined zones, is flaked or feathered, sometimes forming beautiful patterns. For several centuries these 'broken' flowers were prized by tulip fanciers who were prepared to pay high prices for well-defined or unusual patterns and colourings.

A H

IN DEEP
AND
SHALLOW
WATERS

Water can be used as a medium in which to grow a quite different range of plants: aquatics actually in it, and bog plants in the wet soil immediately around it. They are not incompatible with the mirror effect provided they are not permitted to cover the whole surface, but they are incompatible with crystal-clear water which can only be maintained by constantly changing the water in the pool or by treating it with chemicals to prevent algae living in it and clouding it.

Lysichitum americanus: large flowers, larger leaves.

Really you need to make a broad choice at the outset between pools with plants and pools without them, water that is still and water that is in movement.

You can also use water in formal or informal stretches – in regularly shaped basins, canals or rills, which are often very suitable near the house, on a terrace or in a rose garden, or in irregularly curving pools that appear to belong naturally to the site. Informal pools are often associated with rock gardens, and they can be used just as effectively in wild or woodland gardens or indeed in any setting that is not itself regular and geometric. If water lilies are to be grown, place your pool where it gets sunshine for much of the day; without it the flowers will not open.

In small gardens, streams are often more of a problem than pools since they do need to appear natural and that rather presupposes that they will follow the correct contours of the land, which is not always where they are wanted. Yet to confine streams too obviously to the higher ground where they have to be retained by embankments can look silly.

Plastic (PVC) or butyl rubber liners have almost entirely replaced concrete or puddled clay as a means of making pools watertight. Liners should be obtained sufficiently large to cover both bottom and sides and overlap sufficiently to be tucked into the soil or hidden beneath turf, rocks or paving slabs.

A more expensive alternative is to use fibreglass, a far more rigid material which must be pre-formed to the required shape. Fibreglass pools of many sizes and designs are offered by specialist water-feature firms and by many garden centres. They are the simplest way to make a pool since all you need to do is choose your pool and then dig a hole large enough to accommodate it.

With plastic or rubber liners you determine the form of the pool yourself and excavate the soil to this design. Formal pools often have vertical or very steep sides but for informal pools it is preferable to prepare a dish-shaped hole with shallowly sloping sides. This is partly because it is a very trouble-free shape, with the weight of the water holding the liner firmly down, and partly because it is a natural shape which looks right and gives plenty of scope for planting in different depths of water according to the needs of the plants. As a rule a depth of 60cm (2ft) in the middle of the pool is ample and 45cm (1½ft) will suffice for most aquatics. Marginal plants vary in their preferences from water about 8cm (3in) deep to none at all, simply wet soil for their roots.

Primula beesiana has flowers in whorls up the stem.

The surface on which the waterproof sheet is to lie should be smooth and free of sharp stones or other rough objects which might damage it. Rake the soil or flatten it with the back of a spade or spread some sand over it. When the sheet has been roughly laid in position (or PVC, which is very flexible, stretched across the pool like a limp drum cover) lay a few stones or turves around the edges to hold it in position, and run in some water. Its weight will stretch and settle the sheet securely on the bottom and sides of the pool. Once the liner has settled, you can cover the edges with soil, turves, rocks or paving slabs. Streams can be lined in a similar way but if they wind and twist and tumble over cascades or waterfalls they are liable to tear, and it may be easier and more satisfactory to line them in the old-fashioned way with concrete. Preformed fibreglass sections for streams and cascades are available but it is difficult to disguise them satisfactorily and some parts tend to protrude awkwardly when the job is done. Concrete can be spread easily where it is required, with rocks

actually bedded into it where this seems desirable.

When you come to prepare the bottom of your pool for planting, you can spread soil all over the liner or concentrate it in mounds here and there. Easier still is to plant in plastic baskets which can be purchased from any dealer in aquatics. The procedure is exactly as if you were potting the plants, and you can do it comfortably indoors, after which you just sink the baskets in the pool wherever you want them. When the plants grow too big or are otherwise in need of attention, the baskets can be fished up, and the soil in them renewed if necessary, and they can go back with a minimum of fuss.

Mid-April to mid-June is the best season for planting aquatics, but when they are sold in containers, as many are nowadays, they can be moved like other container-grown plants at almost any time provided their roots are not unduly disturbed. Some kinds float freely in the water and require little or no soil. They can be planted by simply dropping them into the pool. These submerged aquatics are useful as protection for fish and to supply oxygen to the water which, on warm days, can be seen rising in bubbles from their leaves.

Fish are not really an appropriate topic here, but it is important that they are not introduced until plants are growing freely in the water.

If the garden has a natural stream or spring, no other form of circulation need be considered, and if the stream has sufficient flow it may even be possible to make it operate a ram to raise water to a higher level from which it can flow into fountains or over waterfalls and cascades. Most gardeners possess no such facilities and if they want moving water at all must seek other means to obtain it, either from a mains supply, which is expensive and bad for plants, or by recirculating it with a pump. Small submersible electric pumps are available for this purpose and usually provide the best solution.

WATERY PLANTS

Aruncus sylvester Goat's beard. Creamy plumes appear in early summer. A variety named 'Kneiffii has finely divided leaves. For boggy soil.

Astilbe False goat's beard. Shorter than aruncus and with more cone-shaped plumes of white, pink or crimson flowers. Also suitable for damp soil but not actually for growing in water.

Caltha Marsh marigold, kingcup. The commonest species, *C. palustris*, grows wild in Britain and has flowers like huge buttercups. There is a double-flowered variety named 'Flore-pleno' which is even more effective. Another species from the Caucasus has even larger flowers and is called *C. polypetala*. All like the very damp soil at the edges of pools and streams.

Filipendula Spiraea-like plants of which one species, *F. ulmaria*, is the British meadowsweet with plumes of creamy flowers in summer. There is a yellow-leaved variety named 'Aurea' and another with double flowers named 'Floreplena'. Other species are *F. palmata*, pale pink; *F. purpurea*, rosy-purple and *F. rubra*, pink. All are for damp soil.

Iris There are numerous kinds including all the varieties of *I. sibirica* and *I. kaempferi* as well as the common yellow flag, *I. pseudocorus*, in both its green and white variegated forms and the tall creamy white *I. ochroleuca*, all of which can be grown in damp soil beside pools. *I. laevigata* prefers to grow in shallow water and is available in light blue, dark blue, pink and white varieties.

Above: The candelabra primula.

Nymphea (water lily), long-lived and easy to grow.

Lysichitum Skunk cabbage. The popular name refers to the very large leaves and the rather heavy smell of this handsome plant with arum-lily flowers in spring. These are yellow in *L. americanus*, the most vigorous kind, and white in *L. camtschatcensis*. Both are for wet soil or very shallow water.

Lysimachia Yellow loosestrife, creeping jenny. The two popular names distinguish plants of very different character. The yellow loosestrife, typified by *L. punctata* and *L. vulgaris*, make big clumps of erect stems bearing yellow flowers in summer. The creeping jenny, *L. nummularia*, trails flat on the ground and also has yellow flowers and an attractive yellow-leaved variety named 'Aurea'. All are for moist soil.

Lythrum Purple loosestrife. Two kinds, *L. salicaria* and *L. virgatum*, both have slender spikes of magenta flowers. They like moist soil.

Mimulus Monkey flower, musk. Several kinds, including *M. cupreus*, yellow and brown; *M. cardinalis*, scarlet; *M. luteus*, yellow spotted with pink, and *M. tigrinus*, yellow, pink and crimson, all grow well in wet soil.

Nymphaea Water lily. There are many species and hybrids, differing in vigour and colour, from white, pale yellow and pink to crimson. All have heart-shaped, floating leaves with the flowers seeming to rest on them. The flowers are only open during the middle part of the day. Their depth of water requirement varies from 8cm (3in) for small kinds, such as *N. pygmaea* and its varieties, to a minimum of 30cm (12in) for big kinds, such as 'Escarboucle', 'James Brydon' and the varieties of *N. laydekeri* and *N. marliacea*.

Osmunda regalis Royal fern. Upstanding yellowish green fronds. Likes wet soil.

Pontederia cordata Pickerel weed. Broadly lance-shaped leaves on long stalks and spikes of blue flowers in July and August. Likes shallow water.

Primula Primrose. A number of primulas thrive in moist soil. These include all the 'candelabra' species, so-called because they carry their flowers in successive tiers of diminishing size. Examples are *P. aurantiaca*, *P. japonica*, *P. pulverulenta*, *P. helodoxa*, *P. beesiana*, *P. bulleyana* and *P. cockburniana*. Also suitable are *P. sikkimensis* and *P. florindae*, with heads of dangling yellow flowers, and cluster-flowered species such as *P. denticulata*, *P. capitata* and *P. vialii*.

Rheum palmatum An ornamental rhubarb with large, red-tinted leaves and crimson flowers. Likes moist soil.

Rodgersia Several kinds are available, including *R. aesculifolia*, *R. pinnata*, *R. podophylla* and *R. tabularis*. All like moist soil. They have large, umbrella-like or deeply divided, bronzy-green leaves and branched clusters of small pink or white, spiraea-like flowers.

Sagittaria sagittifolia Arrowhead. The popular name refers to the shape of the leaves. The white flowers are borne in spikes and are double in a variety named 'Flore Pleno'. Likes to grow in shallow water.

Scirpus tabernaemontani 'Zebrinus' Porcupine quill rush, zebra rush. The popular names well describe this striking foliage plant which has long quill-like leaves banded with green and white. It likes to grow in shallow water.

A H

CHRISTMAS AND LENTEN ROSES

Christmas and Lenten roses are closely allied plants belonging to the genus *Helleborus*. They have no connection of any kind with true roses and get their popular name solely because of the very superficial resemblance of their flowers to single roses. All are hardy herbaceous perennials.

Christmas roses are all varieties of *Helleborus niger*. They have large evergreen leaves composed of numerous leaflets arranged like the claws of a bird's foot. The flowers are white, often tinged or spotted with rose, carried singly or up to three in a cluster on bare stems 15–30cm (6–12in) long. Some forms start to flower in November or December, others not until January, February or even March.

Lenten roses are forms and hybrids of *Helleborus orientalis* and other allied species. Their leaves are similar to those of *H. niger* but larger and longer stemmed and so are the flowers, of which there may be up to four on each 40–60cm (16–24in) stem. Colours are also more varied, from white to deep plum purple with many intermediate shades of purplish-pink, spotted and flushed and very beautiful. Though they are at their peak in March some may start to open in January and there may still be Lenten roses around in May.

In addition there are several other beautiful hellebores worth growing for both foliage and flower. Two of the best are *H. foetidus* with very dark green leaves and big sprays of apple-green flowers edged with purple, the whole plant no more than 45cm (18in) high, and *H. corsicus*, twice this height with large lighter green, saw-edged leaves and large upstanding clusters of light green flowers. Both kinds start to flower in January and continue well into the spring.

All hellebores will grow in shade but *H. corsicus* does just as well in full sun. All like cool, rather moist, humusy soil with plenty of leafmould or peat and all like to be left alone to grow into large clumps and colonies. They will often spread freely by self-sown seedlings and this is particularly characteristic of the Lenten roses and of *H. corsicus*.   A H

Above: Lenten roses (*Helleborus orientalis*).

Left: The Christmas rose (*Helleborus niger*).

LAWNS, TREES
AND
SHRUBS

A well-kept lawn surrounded by mature trees and shrubs sets off a bed of heathers.

CARPETS OF GREEN

Most people want a lawn – an expanse of mown grass – in their garden for one or two quite different purposes. One is to make a smooth green carpet on and beside which trees, shrubs and flower beds can be effectively displayed. That is the appearance motive. Some, but fewer, private owners seek a true grass surface for playing such games as tennis, bowls and croquet. These require the finest grasses, cut to 8mm ($\frac{1}{3}$in) or less and intensively maintained.

Lawns for appearance are our main concern here, and they, by contrast, can be created just as well from a very different breed of stronger-growing grasses. What is odd is that much of the publicity from seed firms presses the virtues of fine grasses for all purposes. Partly, perhaps, this has come about because fine grasses fit the traditional idea of an English lawn; but also, I suspect, it is because they are more profitable in the long run since fine-grass lawns demand so much more maintenance and expenditure on fertilizers, herbicides, etc.

The main lawn grasses on the market are fescues and bent grasses of the *Agrostis* species, rye grasses and smooth-stemmed meadow grasses. Occasionally other species are used for special purposes, such as wood meadow grass (*Poa nemoralis*) for shady places and rough-stalked meadow grass (*Poa trivialis*) where the soil is damp. Unfortunately neither makes a really good sward and it is really better to correct the unsatisfactory conditions or use something other than grass to surface these awkward places.

Fescues and bent grasses have narrow leaves, stand mowing well and are the main grasses used to create very close smooth turf. They are generally used in mixtures, the bent grasses being

Japanese shrubs and potted plants frame a compact London lawn – enlivened by stone carvings and a wooden tree-seat.

Making a Lawn

From Seed. Make sure the ground has been broken down, levelled and cleared of weeds before sowing. Divide the sowing area into strips and sow the seed broadcast. Rake in gently to a depth of 3–6mm ($\frac{1}{10}$–$\frac{1}{5}$in) or cover with sifted soil. Rye and meadow grass take about 14 days to germinate, while finer grasses take up to 4 weeks.

 From Turf. Turves also need a level weed-free surface before laying. Stand on a piece of board to avoid disrupting the laying surface with boot-prints. With conventional turves (not the carpet-roll type), lay them in straight rows staggered like bricks in a wall. After laying (*inset*) sprinkle a little sifted peat and sand and brush in to seal.

more creeping than the fescues and so helping to bind the turf together. They require good drainage and aeration, are not very resistant to weed invasion and must be well cared for.

 Perennial rye grass (*Lolium perenne*) and smooth-stalked meadow grass (*Poa pratensis*) are much stronger-growing species used a great deal in agriculture; shorter-growing, more freely branching forms have been selected for garden use. They are hard-wearing and have a good green colour but they die out if persistently mown very hard. Both are excellent for lawns, often mixed with *Agrostis tenuis*. Good selected forms of perennial rye grass are Aberystwyth S23, Aberystwyth S321, Kent Indigenous, Hunter, Manhattan, Pelo and Sprin-

ter. Recommended forms of smooth-stalked meadow grass are Bensun, Delft and Merion.

WHEN TO SOW AND HOW

Late March to late April and mid-August to late September are the best periods for sowing. Earlier than this the soil is rarely warm enough for germination, while seedling grass from later autumn sowings can be severely damaged by weather, and summer sowings may be held back by dryness, though this can be overcome by watering. Sowing rates are 20–40g per m^3 ($\frac{3}{4}$–$1\frac{1}{2}$oz per sq yd) according to the speed with which complete grass cover is required.

All seed should be sown on soil that has been well broken up and cleared of weeds, if necessary by leaving it fallow for two or three weeks so that weed seeds can germinate and then killing the seedlings with a herbicide such as paraquat (Weedol) or glyphosate (Tumbleweed) which leaves no harmful residue in the soil.

Seedling grass, whether fine or coarse, should not be cut intil it is at least 50mm (2in) high and then only to 25mm (1in). Later, when it has started to tiller (produce side growths), cutting can become progressively more severe. It is best not to use selective weedkillers on young grass and in any case all the annual weeds that may appear will automatically disappear with regular mowing. More persistent weeds can be removed by hand or dealt with later. However, if it is decided that some chemical treatment is necessary earlier, ioxynil (Actrilawn) will prove the safest herbicide to use.

A Nice Piece of Turf

The conventional way to make lawns from turf is to purchase turves cut from a meadow or from a field in which grass has been specially cultivated for this purpose. The traditional method is to cut strips 90cm (3ft) long, 30cm (1ft) wide and 4–5cm (1½–2in) thick. These long turves are rolled up for transport and convenient stacking on arrival. For some purposes turves 30cm (1ft) square are preferred and these are handled flat.

A fairly new and quite different approach is to sow grass seed on a thin layer (about 20mm/¾in) of moist peat spread over fine nylon netting backed by an impermeable sheet which prevents the grass roots growing through into the soil beneath. They do, however, grow through the netting, becoming so firmly enmeshed with it that in a few weeks the turf can be rolled up like a carpet with all the roots intact. As it is being relaid, the backing sheet is stripped off so that the grass can proceed to grow normally into the soil. This kind of turf is much lighter than conventional, soil-grown turf and can be supplied in much larger sizes so that laying time is reduced and there are fewer joins between turves to fill up and knit together. Since it is grown from seed, this can be specially selected for various purposes and the turf should be weed-free.

The best seasons for turfing are the same as those for sowing except that it is more difficult to turf than it is to seed in summer or at any period when the weather is warm and dry. Conventional turves are laid in straight rows with the turves in alternate rows staggered like the bricks in a wall so that they bond together more firmly. The edges of lawns are always laid with full-sized turves; any cutting-down to obtain a perfect fit is done in one of the inner rows.

Sturdy country lawns (above and right) make welcoming surfaces for croquet, with borders to admire or a summerhouse for contemplation.

Mowing and Maintenance

The way you look after a turf lawn is just as important as if you had raised it from seed. The methods are the same whatever the origin of the grass but they may need to be more intensively applied for the first year or so if you are using existing or site turf or turf imported from a meadow not specially sown for the purpose.

First there is mowing, which can determine whether it is the coarser or the finer grasses that survive. Coarse grasses like to have 2–3cm ($\frac{3}{4}$–$1\frac{1}{4}$in) of growth and, given this, can smother many of the fine-bladed, short-growing grasses. These come into their own when turf is constantly kept at around 5mm ($\frac{1}{5}$in) which destroys most of the coarse grasses.

However, close mowing brings problems of its own. There are many prostrate weeds, including clover, medicks and pearlwort, that are unaffected by close mowing which can encourage moss by weakening the grass. In summer it can leave roots dangerously exposed to scorching by the sun and drying by both sun and wind. Heavily mown lawns are more subject to disease and also more liable to change quickly in their composition so that, where one month there was a beautiful green sward of fine fescues and bent grasses the next there is a patchy mixture of weeds and grasses of many kinds. It takes skill and perseverance to maintain a really close-mown lawn throughout the year whereas anyone with a little common-sense who is prepared to spend an hour or so in the garden every week can have a very presentable lawn of rye or smooth-stemmed meadow grass.

The type of mow affects the kind of cutting machinery that is appropriate. Fine lawns need to be cut with multi-bladed cylinder mowers or, if rotary mowers are used, they must be of a type capable of giving a very clean, level, close cut. By contrast the coarser lawn grasses are best cut with rotaries which handle them effortlessly, even if they get a bit out of hand if you have left them for a fortnight or so to go on holiday.

For a lawn made from site grass, the happy medium is to keep it constantly mown, twice a week when the weather is warm and damp and it is growing fast, to a height of 15–20mm ($\frac{1}{2}$–$\frac{3}{4}$in). Later on, when rough grasses and weeds have been brought under control, this can be raised a little to 20–25mm ($\frac{3}{4}$–1in) if the lawn is required solely for good appearance combined with low maintenance. If a more formal, closely trimmed lawn is preferred, the cutting blades can be lowered to 10mm ($\frac{2}{5}$in).

War on Weeds

Weed control by chemical as opposed to mechanical means is the next essential if a really weed-free lawn is required. It is certainly the ideal of most lawn owners but not of all. I know plenty of people who delight in seeing white daisies peppering the green grass and in the rougher parts of my own garden I am very content to have the blue haze of a little speedwell from Asia Minor (*Veronica filiformis*) which flowers at exactly the right time to make a perfect foil for golden daffodils.

But if all weeds are taboo it will be necessary to use a mixture of herbicides as no single chemical will account for all the weeds likely to be present. Mixtures of 2,4-D and mecoprop (Verdone, Lornox Pus, Supertox, Geigy Special Turf Weedkiller), 2,4-D and fenoprop (Clovercide, 4-50 Selective Weedkiller), 2,4-D, bromofenoxin and CMPP (Gesal New Lawn Weedkiller), and MCPA and mecoprop (PBI Lawn Weedkiller) are available. All will give good results and it is not a bad idea to ring the changes on different mixtures to cover as wide a spectrum of weeds as possible.

At first it will almost certainly be necessary to treat the whole area but as the weeds disappear it will be possible to concentrate progressively on the remaining bad areas until finally spot treatment of individual weeds is sufficient. The best time for weed killing is when the weeds are growing actively in spring and summer. It should be done a day or so before cutting, so that the weed leaves have adequate time to absorb the chemical, and when the leaves are dry and there is no immediate prospect of rain. The most economical method of application is with a spraying machine which should have a hood over the nozzle to prevent drift. Some manufacturers supply machines ready-equipped with efficient hoods; otherwise, a hood can be made from half a large plastic bottle or a plastic funnel with the stem shortened and slipped over the spray nozzle. The alternative to spraying is to apply the selective herbicide from a special applicator fitted with a fairly long (22cm/9in) sprinkle bar. This is quick and safe, as there is little risk of drift even in windy weather, but it is not as economical as spraying.

Fertilizers and Feeding

Feeding is as important as weed control: to strengthen the grass and enable it to smother moss and pearlwort. Nitrogen is the most required element but it needs to be balanced with phosphorus and potassium. A mixture containing approximately twice as much nitrogen as phosphate and potash will do well for spring and summer use up to mid-August, after which no further nitrogen should be given for fear of encouraging soft growth which might be harmful in the winter months. However, the very readily available and relatively cheap National Growmore Formula, 7:7:7, is satisfactory for lawns in spring and summer, as it is for most garden plants, and so is often the best as well as the most convenient buy. It is advisable that the nitrogen should be largely supplied as sulphate of ammonia, except on very acid soils, as this fertilizer has the effect of reducing the amount of calcium carbonate in the soil and making it more acid. This suits the finer grasses and discourages some weeds.

These fertilizers are all quick-acting and relatively quickly exhausted, particularly in their nitrogen content. The grass can be seen to turn a richer green within a few days of application but is likely to start paling off after five or six weeks unless more is given. However, too much fertilizer will scorch the grass by increasing the salt concentration in the soil water to unacceptable levels.

There is a correct system: this is to apply fertilizer in small quantities fairly frequently, first in April, again in late May or early June and a third time in late July or early August. How much should be given at each application will depend on the concentration of chemicals in the fertilizer mixture, but for National Growmore, 100g per m^2 (3½oz per sq yd) is all right for the spring application and 50g per m^2 (1¾oz per sq yd) for each of the summer applications. With concentrated fertilizers it is important to distribute them evenly as local concentration can cause damage.

Lawns made of fine grasses may require a fourth feeding in September, when the mixture should contain little or no nitrogen but a higher ratio of potash to fortify the grass against attack by fungi.

Raking and Rolling

Raking performs a useful service by dragging out the dead grass that inevitably collects beneath the surface. Where this builds up to the density and thickness which groundsmen expressively describe as 'mat' or 'thatch', more drastic action is required. It may be necessary to slit the turf to a depth of a few centimetres to cut up the thatch and allow it to be dragged out more readily. Special equipment is available for this, some hand-operated, some mechanically powered. All this can be expensive and time-consuming but it is only likely to be required on lawns formed of fine grasses. This is not to say that thatch does not form under coarser grasses but it causes far less damage and can usually be ignored. However, it is worth noting that air-cushion mowers tend to ride on the thatch, and as this thickens they gradually cut higher and higher above soil level. This may well require rectification from time to time.

Rolling plays no part in the maintenance of ordinary lawns and only adds unnecessarily to work and problems by over-compacting the soil. It is necessary for sports turf where a very true playing surface is required but even here should always be kept to the minimum weight and frequency.

Aeration may be necessary occasionally for lawns that are much rolled or receive a lot of wear. Soil, particularly if it contains a fair amount of clay, may become so compacted that grass roots can no longer breathe, useful bacteria are replaced by harmful ones and all manner of things start to go wrong. Over-compaction can be prevented or delayed by good initial preparation of the soil and generous additions of humus-forming materials such as peat or compost, plus twice-yearly top dressings of finely milled peat, one in early spring, the second in early autumn, raked or brushed down into the sward. Each dressing can be as generous as possible without actually covering the grass.

Even with these precautions some extra aeration may be necessary. The simplest but crudest method is with a fork thrust 6–7cm (2¼–2¾in) into the soil and then gently heaved back so that the soil is slightly raised. This must be done every 10–15cm (4–6in) all over the compacted area and is a slow job. Aeration equipment of many kinds is available, some of it hand- and some power-operated. The most effective punches out little holes in the turf which can then be filled with fine peat and/or grit scattered over the surface and brushed in. Aeration is usually carried out in autumn but can be done at any time when the turf is sufficiently moist to be penetrated easily.

Watering is necessary in dry weather, in late spring and summer, particularly for lawns that are closely cut and so give the soil less protection from sun and wind. Overwatering or watering too fast can do serious damage to soil texture. The ideal is to water through a sprinkler that delivers no more than 1cm (½in) of water per hour, to keep it operating for at least an hour each time it is used, and to use it only when the soil shows definite signs of becoming dry.   A H

HEIGHT NO LIMIT

Trees are the largest plants in the garden, the most permanent and the most dominating. Well chosen and placed, they can give it character and provide striking focal points. Badly chosen or overcrowded, they can become oppressive and make it difficult for other plants to grow.

In small gardens trees must nearly always be used as single specimens or in very small groups. In larger gardens it may be possible to use them to form coppices or woodlands, but if you decide to underplant with shade-loving shrubs, such as rhododendrons and camellias, the trees must be fairly widely spaced so that the shade is not too dense and the soil not too impoverished by their roots. Dappled shade is the ideal to aim for, with sunshine filtering through the canopy of leaves.

Trees vary enormously not only in their ultimate size, which may be anything from 4–40m (13–130ft) under British conditions, but also in habit. They can also be deciduous or evergreen and many of the evergreens belong to the great conifer family characterized by narrow, often needle-like leaves, for which reason a distinction is often made between broad-leaved trees and conifers. Trees also vary greatly in shape and branch pattern. Most native British trees are deciduous and rather billowy in outline. By contrast most conifers are evergreen and conical, creating a rather spiky effect very different from that of the oaks, beeches, elms and limes.

Some trees spread their branches widely and some hold them erect, and there are also erect varieties of normally spreading trees. These are known as fastigiate. One form of the common oak makes a splendid upstanding specimen only 4–5m (13–16ft) wide, even when old, and there are similar erect forms of the black poplar, the common beech, the hornbeam, the tulip tree (liriodendron), the maidenhair tree (ginko), some of the ornamental cherries and many more. There are also fastigiate conifers, including several cypresses and junipers. Such trees give you height in the garden without corresponding spread. Even so, some spread their roots widely and limit what you can plant nearby. Elms and poplars are notable offenders; elms also produce suckers freely, often far removed from the parent tree, and these can be a great nuisance.

As well as rounded, spiky and columnar trees there are some with a graceful weeping habit. Popular weepers include the weeping ash, beech, birch, elm and willow.

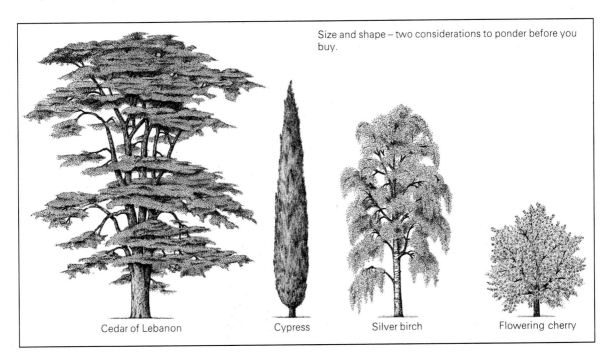

Size and shape – two considerations to ponder before you buy.

Cedar of Lebanon   Cypress   Silver birch   Flowering cherry

The Japanese maple (*Acer palmatum*) has superb autumn colouring.

Acer palmatum, a maple, glows red behind the evergreen shrub *Cordyline indivisa*, hardy in mild areas.

Some trees are grown primarily for their flowers and some have yellow, copper, purple or variegated leaves which can also be usefully employed to enrich and extend the colour combinations in the garden. Some also have attractively coloured bark: notable among these are the numerous birches which have white bark; *Acer griseum*, in which the bark is cinnamon-coloured and peeling; the snake-bark maples, in which it is green striped with white, and *Prunus serrula*, in which the bark is a shining mahogany-red.

Planting and Caring

Installing a new tree has become more flexible now that you can buy them – and shrubs as well – in containers from which they can be planted at almost any time of the year. The traditional method – lifting them from the open ground – can only be done with safety when they are dormant, or nearly so, between mid-October and late March. There is still much to be said for this way of planting, especially with large-rooting trees which do not fit easily into containers, however large. 'Open-ground' plants are also available in greater variety and often in larger sizes, and provided they are carefully handled and replanted quickly before their roots become dry, they often establish themselves more rapidly and satifactorily than container-grown plants. If there has to be an interval between acquiring and planting your new tree, heel it in temporarily in a suitable hole in moist ground.

For planting in the final site, dig a hole with plenty of width to spare. Usually the soil mark on the trunk will indicate the depth at which the tree was growing in the nursery, and you should also allow for this when preparing the site. If no soil mark is visible, the uppermost roots should be covered with 5–8cm (2–3in) of soil.

Ground for trees should be well prepared by digging. Remove all weeds and enrich the soil with manure or compost, plus a sprinkling of slow-acting fertilizer such as bonemeal. It helps to prepare a planting mix of garden soil plus half its bulk of peat or leafmould, a similar quantity of sand and a peppering of bonemeal. Work two or three spadefuls of this around the roots of each tree before the soil removed from the hole is returned.

Trees almost always require secure staking for the first few years and, to prevent injury to the roots, the stakes are best driven in before the trees are planted. This has the added advantage that the tree can be immediately secured to the stake, leaving your hands free to shovel in the soil which should then be trodden down firmly around and over the roots.

Little pruning should be necessary for a few years except to remove young stems from the main trunks if these are to be kept bare, and to thin out

The magnolia is famed for its cupped flowers which bloom in spring.

branches a little if too much growth threatens to spoil the natural shape of the tree. Later on, as trees become mature and some branches die or become injured, pruning should always be done in such a way as to preserve, so far as possible, the distinctive shape and branch pattern of the tree.

Almost invariably this is best done either by removing branches completely or by cutting each back to a point at which another branch grows from it. The worst method of pruning trees is to shorten branches equally all over, leaving a mophead of stumps likely to produce a thicket of young stems, like a pollarded willow. The work can be done at almost any time of year except in March-April when the sap is rising strongly and there is a danger that some wounds will 'bleed'. However, the safest time for pruning deciduous trees is November-February, and for evergreen May-June.

RECOMMENDED TREES

Acer The maples, of which there are a great many, ranging in size from mere bushes in some forms of *A. palmatum* to large trees. All are deciduous. All forms of *A. palmatum* are suitable for garden planting, most colour brilliantly in autumn and some have finely divided leaves. Also good are *A. griseum*, with peeling cinnamon-coloured bark; *A. pensylvanicum*, with smooth green bark striped with white; *A. negundo* in two varieties, 'Aureum' with yellow leaves and 'Variegatum' with light green and white leaves; *A. platanoides* 'Crimson King', fast-growing with beetroot-red leaves, and *A. pseudoplatanus* 'Brilliantissimum', a very slow-growing sycamore with pink, cream and light green leaves.

A weeping willow-leaved pear, backed by a magnolia and a semi-weeping Lawson Cypress 'Intertexta'.

Betula The birches. Our native birch, *B. pendula*, has fine weeping varieties such as 'Trisitis', 'Youngii' and 'Dalecarlica', the last with deeply cut leaves. Good white-stemmed kinds are *B. ermanii* and *B. utilis*.

Carpinus betulus The hornbeam, which looks like beech and is best planted in its pyramidal variety, 'Fastigiata'.

Cypress Three genera, *Chamaecyparis*, *Cupressus* and *Cupressocyparis*, contribute to this very large and valuable group of evergreen coniferous trees. It is the columnar and coloured-leaved (yellow, grey, and blue-green) varieties that are most worthwhile. Good forms of *Chamaecyparis lawsoniana* are 'Allumii Aurea', 'Columnaris', 'Ellwoodii', 'Erecta', 'Kilmacurragh', 'Lanei Aurea' and 'Winston Churchill'. Good forms of *Cupressus macrocarpa*, which grows faster but is not so hardy, are 'Donard Gold' and 'Goldcrest'. *C. glabra* 'Pyramidalis' is tall, narrow and grey-green. Yellow forms of *Cupressocyparis leylandii*, which

Garrya elliptica (left) and *Daphniphyllum macropodum* emerge from the mist of a March day at Great Dixter.

are fully hardy and very fast growing, are 'Castlewellan' and 'Robinson's Gold'.

Laburnum vossii Long trails of yellow flowers in May-June.

Magnolia The best tree magnolias for general planting are the various forms of *M. soulangiana*. All make wide, multi-branched plants. Their cupped flowers vary from pure white in 'Alba Superba' to wine red in 'Rustica Rubra' and 'Lennei'.

Malus The crab-apples, of which there are a great many excellent kinds, some grown mainly for their flowers in spring, some for their coloured fruits in autumn. *M. floribunda* has pink and rose flowers, 'Profusion' is dark red, 'Eleyi' is similar with purple leaves, 'Golden Hornet' has yellow crab-apples, and 'John Downie' red and yellow fruits excellent for jelly-making.

Prunus This huge genus includes all the almonds, peaches, cherries and plums, some of which are highly ornamental trees grown mainly for their flowers in spring, some also for their purple foliage. A fine pink-flowered almond is 'Pollardii'. A good double-flowered pink peach is 'Clara Meyer'. *P. cerasifera* 'Pissardii' is the purple-leaved plum with small pinkish-white flowers. *P. subhirtella* 'Autumnalis' has small white flowers in November and December; the variety 'Autumnalis Rosea' has pink flowers. Good spring-flowering ornamental cherries are 'Ama-no-Gawa', pink and narrowly erect, 'Kanzan', 'Pink Perfection' and 'Shirofugen', deeper pink and wide-spreading, 'Tai-Haku', white, and 'Ukon', pale yellow.

Robinia pseudoacacia The false acacia, a tree with feathery leaves best planted in its yellow-leaved variety 'Frisia'.

SHRUBS

Shrubs, like trees, may be evergreen or deciduous. Many of the evergreens are conifers with very small, narrow, awl-shaped or ferny leaves. Some are grown primarily as flowering plants and some for their foliage, and it is important to get a good balance between both since the flowers are usually only out for a few weeks each year whereas the foliage is there for months, even the whole year.

Shrubs attain maturity more rapidly than most trees and are not usually quite so difficult to move. Some kinds transplant much better when old than others: rhododendrons and azaleas are notably good and hollies generally rather bad.

Mauve and white hydrangeas in a woodland setting: useful shrubs for a flower display after midsummer.

Prepare the soil and plant as for trees. Support is not usually necessary for small plants, but taller ones should be tied to a stake for the first year, especially if they are planted from containers and so have not developed roots to anchor them.

Pruning tends to be rather more complicated, largely because so many shrubs are grown primarily for their flowers and/or fruits and the art is to disturb their emergence as little as possible. Three main methods of pruning may be used: thinning, on much the same lines as advised for trees; hard cutting back, and summer pruning.

Thinning is the method commonly used for shrubs that have completed their flowering by midsummer and is done directly the flowers fade. Often it is sufficient to cut out all, or most of, the stems or branches that have just flowered and to retain all the young growth that will flower another year. Thinning may also be used for later-flowering shrubs or those that are grown primarily for their foliage; it is then often done in autumn, or in February-March before growth recommences.

Flower buds of the male *Skimmia japonica*: its spring flowers are white and scented.

Evergreens do not respond so well to autumn pruning and, if they need much thinning out, are generally dealt with in May-June, or immediately after flowering if they are in bloom then.

Hard cutting back is usually done in winter or very early spring and is most frequently used for shrubs that flower in late summer or autumn or are deciduous and grown primarily for their leaves and/or the colour of their young bark. All growth may be cut down quite close to ground level.

Summer pruning is most useful for shrubs that are wall-trained, and so need a permanent framework of branches but must be kept neat and tidy. All young side-growths from these main branches are shortened in summer, not necessarily all at once, but little by little so the plant is not denuded while it is in full growth.

Shrubs respond to good cultivation but the soil around them should never be deeply disturbed because it is likely to be full of their roots.

RECOMMENDED SHRUBS

Berberis The great barberry family, which includes both deciduous and evergreen kinds. The former are very dense and spiny with yellow flowers followed by red berries. *B. aggregata* and *B. thunbergii* are typical, the latter with several fine-coloured leaf varieties including 'Atropurpurea', purple, and 'Rose Glow', purple and pink. The evergreen kinds also have yellow or orange flowers usually followed by blue-black berries. Two of the best are *B. darwinii*, with small holly-like leaves and orange flowers in spring, and *B. stenophylla*, thicket-forming and narrow-leaved with yellow sweetly scented flowers in spring.

Buddleia The most popular kind is *B. davidii*, the butterfly bush, with long, conical spikes of small, sweetly scented purple flowers in late summer. There are numerous varieties differing in depth of colour; some are white. All can be pruned hard each March if desired.

Ceanothus There are both evergreen and deciduous kinds, the former flowering mainly in spring, the latter in summer. Most are a little tender and are often trained against sunny walls, the evergreens summer-pruned, the deciduous kinds thinned or cut back in March. Good evergreen kinds with thimble-like clusters of small blue flowers are *C. impressus* and *C. burkwoodii*, the latter with an extended flowering season. Recommended deciduous kinds are 'Gloire de Versailles', light blue, and 'Topaz', dark blue.

Chaenomeles These are the spring-flowering shrubs most people call japonica or Japanese quince. They are deciduous and thicket-forming, but are frequently trained against walls where they need to be summer-pruned. The species has scarlet flowers but there are varieties and hybrids in many shades from white to crimson.

Cornus The dogwoods, some of which are classified as trees. The varieties of *C. alba* are all thicket-forming shrubs with coloured stems and good foliage. Recommended varieties are 'Elegantissima', which has red stems and light green and white leaves, and 'Spaethii', similar but with light yellow leaves.

Cotoneaster A big genus of evergreen and deciduous shrubs ranging from completely prostrate kinds such as *C. dammeri* to almost tree-like plants such as *C. frigidus* and the 'Cornubia' variety. All have white flowers followed by red or yellow berries.

Cytisus The brooms, many of which have slender

green stems and very small leaves. An exception is *C. battandieri* with trifoliate leaves covered in grey down and clusters of yellow, scented flowers in summer. The hybrids of *C. scoparius* flower earlier, in May and June, and are cream, yellow, yellow and red, crimson or pink according to variety. *C. kewensis* is pale yellow, early-flowering and short but wide-spreading. *C. multiflorus* is taller than most, slender-stemmed and white-flowered. All like sun and good drainage and can be lightly pruned after flowering.

Deutzia Useful free-flowering deciduous shrub of medium to large size. Many are hybrids sold under garden names such as 'Magician', white and purple, and 'Mount Rose', purplish-pink. All flower in late spring or early summer and can be thinned after flowering.

Elaeagnus Evergreens grown for their foliage. The best is *E. pungens* 'Maculata' with a large yellow blotch in the centre of each green leaf.

Erica The heathers, a big genus with numerous species and a much larger number of garden varieties. Many are ground-hugging plants but some are much taller bushes. Most prefer acid soils but some, including *E. carnea. E. darleyensis, E. medditerranea* and *E. terminalis*, are tolerant of lime. There are also great differences in when they flower. *E. darleyensis* flowers in winter and early spring; *E. carnea* mainly in spring though some varieties are earlier; *E. arborea* (a tall heather) in early spring; *E. cinerea* mainly in summer; *E. terminalis* (another bushy kind) in late summer, and *E. ciliaris* and *E. vagans* in late summer and autumn.

Escallonia Mainly evergreen shrubs of medium to large size with clusters of small flowers in summer. Good garden varieties are 'Edinensis', pink; 'Apple Blossom', pink and white; 'Iveyi', white, and 'Crimson Spire', which is a light crimson colour.

Forsythia Among the first shrubs to make a big display in spring with their yellow flowers. 'Lynwood' is one of the best varieties. All are deciduous and large but can be thinned drastically after flowering.

Hebe The shrubby veronicas, all evergreen and mostly carrying their small flowers in short well-packed spikes. Among the many good varieties are 'Autumn Glory', compact, violet blue; 'Carl Teschner', smaller with dark leaves and violet and white flowers; *H. franciscana*, compact, blue; 'Great Orme', compact, pink; *H. pinguifolia*

The yellow flowers of the Far Eastern shrub *Corylopsis pauciflora* are set off by the red stems of the deciduous shrub *Cornus alba* 'Sibirica', commonly known as dogwood.

'Pagei', low-growing with grey leaves and white flowers, and *H. salicifolia*, a large bush with white flowers.

Hydrangea The shrubs that make the most solid flower display after midsummer. The hardiest is *H. paniculata*, with large conical clusters of creamy white flowers becoming tinged with pink as they grow older; it can be pruned hard each March. For colour the best are the numerous varieties of *H. macrophylla*, some with large globular heads of flower (the Hortensias or Mopheads), some with flat heads (the Lacecaps). Good varieties of the former type are 'Generale Vicomtesse de Vibraye', 'Hamburg' and 'Madame Emile Mouilliere', all white. Good Lacecap varieties are 'Blue Wave', 'Mariesii' and 'White Wave'. In acid soils the coloured varieties will be blue or violet-purple, in alkaline pink, rose, crimson.

Hypericum A big genus of shrubs all with yellow flowers. Two of the best are 'Hidcote', medium-sized and with nearly evergreen leaves, and *H. inodorum* 'Elstead', a smaller shrub with small flowers followed by shining chestnut-red fruits.

Kolkwitzia amabilis A fairly big deciduous shrub with pink flowers in May-June.

Lavandula The lavenders, with grey aromatic leaves and spikes of light blue to violet purple flowers in summer. All like sunny places and lime in the soil.

Magnolia stellata A large but slow-growing bush with starry white or pink flowers.

Mahonia Evergreens with rather holly-like leaves. All have yellow flowers. *M. aquifolium* is medium-sized, flowers in spring and usually bears good

Hypericum inodorum 'Elstead' – one of the smaller varieties, with its yellow flowers and shiny red fruits.

Virbinum tinus, a large evergreen whose white flower clusters are replaced by deep blue, and later, black fruits.

crops of grape-purple fruits. *M. japonica* makes a large spreading bush and has scented flowers in winter. 'Charity' is also winter-flowering, taller, and deeper yellow.

Olearia Evergreens with small daisy-type flowers. Most are a little tender. The hardiest is *O. haastii*, flowering in July-August. One of the most spectacular is *O. scilloniensis* with grey leaves and abundant white flowers in May-June.

Philadelphus The mock-oranges, nearly all sweetly scented and all deciduous. They differ considerably in size. 'Sybille' and 'Erectus' are small, the first white and purple, the second all white. *P. intectus* is very tall and white. Intermediate in size are 'Beauclerk', 'Belle Etoile' and 'Virginal', the last with double flowers.

Potentilla Small deciduous shrubs with divided leaves and round flowers produced all summer. Good kinds are 'Abbotswood', white; 'Elizabeth', primrose; 'Goldfinger', yellow, and 'Red Ace', orange-red.

Pyracantha Fairly large evergreens with clusters of white flowers in summer followed by red, orange or yellow berries in autumn. Good kinds are *P. rogersiana*, with red berries; 'Mohave', orange berries, and 'Golden Charmer', yellow berries.

Senecio 'Sunshine' A medium-sized shrub with grey leaves and clusters of yellow daisy-type flowers in summer.

Skimmia japonica A small- to medium-sized evergreen with short spikes of white, or pink-tinged, scented flowers in spring followed by red berries on female bushes – provided a male is nearby for pollination.

Spiraea A big and varied genus of deciduous shrubs. Good kinds are *S. arguta*, fairly small with slender sprays of small white flowers in spring; *S. bumalda* 'Anthony Waterer', small with flat heads of carmine flowers in summer; *S. bumalda* 'Goldflame', like the last but with golden young leaves; *S. prunifolia*, fairly large with arching stems and double white flowers in May, and *S. vanhouttei*, with single white flowers.

Syringa The lilacs are mostly very large shrubs though there are some quite small kinds, such as *S. velutina*, a compact bush with small leaves and little spikes of sweetly scented lilac flowers in May-June. There are numerous varieties of the common lilac, some with single flowers such as 'Souvenir de Louis Späth', reddish purple; 'Maud Notcutt, white, and 'Primrose', pale yellow. Doubles include 'Charles Joly', purplish-red; 'Katherine Havemeyer', lavender-purple; 'Michael Buchner', pale pink, and 'Madame Lemoine', white.

Viburnum A big and very varied genus. *V. fragrans*, pale pink, and *V. bodnantense*, rose-pink, are large, deciduous, sweetly scented and winter-flowering. *V. carlesii* is medium-sized, white, scented, deciduous and spring-flowering, and *V. burkwoodii* is much like it but evergreen. *V. davidii* is short but wide-spreading, with handsome evergreen leaves. *V. opulus sterile* is the Snowball Tree, so-called because of its globular clusters of white flowers in June. It is deciduous. *V. tinus* is the Laurustinus, a large evergreen with clusters of white flowers from autumn until spring.

Weigela Medium-sized deciduous shrubs with pink or red funnel flowers in May-June. 'Bristol Ruby' is a good deep red variety, 'Foliis Purpureus' has pink flowers and purple leaves, and 'Variegata' pink flowers and white-edged leaves.

A H

FILTERING THE WIND

In very exposed gardens, and especially near the sea where salt-laden wind can be a problem, it may be impossible to make a garden without providing a windbreak. The most effective is a belt of evergreen trees which absorbs the wind gradually rather than checking it suddenly and causing great turbulence.

The alternative is a tall hedge, preferably evergreen. This can give some protection on the leeward side up to thirty times its height. In most gardens, hedges serve rather different purposes, partly as barriers to mark boundary lines and keep out intruders but also as ornamental features and to create divisions within the garden.

The requirements for these wind-taming devices are naturally different. Windbreaks must be fast growing yet sturdy, well anchored in the soil and able to survive intense exposure. Outer hedges also need to be strong, well branched and impenetrable. Within the garden, however, appearance becomes the dominant qualification. Here there is even a place for miniature hedges formed of low-growing plants such as lavender, rosemary and santolina.

For all hedges the ground should be well prepared by digging and enriched with manure and fertilizer to a width of at least one metre for the entire length of the hedge.

The best time to plant evergreen hedges is in spring or autumn, deciduous hedges in autumn or winter. The simplest and most effective method of planting is usually to open up a trench about 30cm (1ft) wide and deep (more for very big plants) the whole length of the hedge, space out the plants in this at the correct distance apart and then return the soil and tread it in firmly. In exposed places it will be wise to drive in posts every 2–3m (6–10ft), strain one or two wires between them and tie the plants to these so that there is no risk of their being rocked or blown out by wind.

A sweeping shelter hedge.

Below left: Prunus in purple
and green makes a splendid
boundary hedge.

Below: Magnificent yews at
Sissinghurst.

Initial pruning depends on the type of hedge
plant used and the purpose for which it is required.
Windbreaks, often formed of some variety of
cypress, are best left to grow up as rapidly as
possible with their leading growths unpruned.
Privet and hawthorn, by contrast, used as outer
barriers and therefore needing to be well branched
right from the base, should be beheaded as soon as
they are planted to encourage branching from low
down. Subsequently, evergreen hedges are trimmed between May and August, with any hard
cutting necessary done as early as possible in that
period. Deciduous hedges are pruned in winter
with no more than light thinning in summer.

Flowering hedges must be pruned so as to
interfere as little as possible with their flowering.
This means doing it immediately after flowering, if
flowering is over by June, or doing it in spring if the
shrubs flower after midsummer. Berry-bearing
shrubs, such as pyracanthas, are best pruned in
summer when it can be seen where the berries are
and care can be taken to retain as many as
possible.

Clipping of all small-leaved hedges can be done
with hand shears or mechanical trimmers. Large-
leaved hedges, and also flowering and berry-
bearing hedges, can be thinned in the same way,
but a better though slower job is achieved using
secateurs.

RECOMMENDED HEDGES

Aucuba japonica   Evergreen with large laurel-like leaves, light green or yellow spotted. Grows well in shade. Plant 60–90cm (2–3ft) apart. Grows to 2m (6½ft) high. (*Boundary hedge*)

Beech   Deciduous but retaining its russet brown, dead leaves in winter when clipped as a hedge. Excellent for a thin yet rigid hedge. Plant 45cm (18in) apart. To 6m (20ft) high. (*Windbreak*)

Berberis darwinii and *B. stenophylla*   Evergreen, small-leaved, spiny and impenetrable with small orange or yellow flowers in spring. Plant 60cm (2ft) apart. To 2m (6½ft) high (*Flowering*)

Box (*Buxus sempervirens*)   Small-leaved evergreen available in green and yellow-leaved ('Aureo variegata') varieties. Plant normal kinds 30cm (12in) apart, 'Suffruticosa' 15cm (6in) apart. To 2m (6½ft) high. (*Formal*)

Cotoneaster simonsii   Small semi-evergreen leaves and scarlet berries. Excellent on its own or with other shrubs. Plant 45cm (18in) apart. To 1.4m (5ft) high. (*Berry-bearing*)

Cypress   Evergreen belonging to three different botanical genera, *Chamaecyparis*, *Cupressocyparis* and *Cupressus*. All these plants have very small leaves in feathery sprays and stand clipping well. Tallest and fastest growing is the Leyland cypress (*Cupressocyparis leylandii*) available in green- and yellow-leaved ('Castlewellen' and 'Robinson's Gold') varieties. To 10m (33ft) high. Next fastest is the Monterey Cypress (*Cupressus macrocarpa*) also available in green- and yellow-leaved varieties. It is less hardy, more liable to blow out and inclined to die as it ages when clipped. To 6m (20ft) high. Slowest is the Lawson cypress (*Chamaecyparis lawsoniana*) but still capable of growing 60–80cm (24–32in) annually. Available in numerous varieties : dark green, light green, blue-grey and yellow. Very hardy. To 6m (20ft) high. Plant cypresses 80–100cm (32–40in) apart. (*Windbreak*)

Escallonia   Evergreens with small leaves and white, pink or red flowers in summer. Excellent near the sea and in warm inland gardens. Plant 75cm (2½ft) apart. To 2m (6½ft) high. (*Seaside*)

Euonymus japonicus   Evergreen with medium-size leaves, either shining dark green or yellow variegated. Excellent near the sea. Plant 45cm (18in) apart. To 2.5m (8½ft) high. (*Seaside*)

Griselinia littoralis   Evergreen with fairly large, rounded light green or yellow variegated leaves.

Above: *Hydrangea macrophylla*.

Below: A dense hedge of berry-forming *Cotoneaster lacteus*.

Excellent near the sea. Plant 60cm (24in) apart. To 2.5m (8½ft) high. (*Seaside*)

Holly (*Ilex aquifolium*) Spiny-leaved evergreen making an impenetrable hedge. Available in dark green, white and yellow variegated varieties. Plant 45–60cm (18–24in) apart. To 4m (13ft) high. (*Boundary*)

Holm oak (*Quercus ilex*) Evergreen with small to medium-size leaves. Excellent by the sea. Plant 60cm (24in) apart. To 6m (20ft) high. (*Seaside*)

Hornbeam (*Carpinus betulus*) Like beech in appearance but grows better on heavy, poorly drained soil. Plant 45cm (18in) apart. To 6m (20ft) high. (*Windbreak*)

Laurel Two kinds are suitable for hedge making, both evergreen, the cherry laurel (*Prunus laurocerasus*) with large, shining, bright green leaves and the Portugal laurel (*Prunus lusitanica*) with smaller, darker green leaves. Plant 60–90cm (2–3ft) apart. To 3m (10ft) high. (*Boundary*)

Laurustinus (*Viburnum tinus*) Laurel-like ever-green with clusters of white flowers in winter and spring. Excellent near the sea or in mild inland districts. Plant 60–80cm (24–32in) apart. To 2.5m (8½ft) high. (*Seaside*)

Lavender (*Lavandula*) Aromatic grey-leaved evergreens with blue flowers excellent for small hedges or dividing lines. Plant 30–35cm (12–14in) apart. To 60cm (2ft) high. (*Flowering*)

Lonicera nitida Small-leaved evergreen available in green and yellow ('Baggessen's Gold') varieties. Stems not very strong but excellent for hedges to 1.5m (5ft) high. Plant 30–40cm (12–16in) apart. (*Formal*)

Myrobalan plum (*Prunus cerasifera*) Deciduous, spiny and impenetrable when clipped. Available in green- and purple-leaved ('Atropurpurea') varieties which are attractive intermingled. Plant 60cm (2ft) apart. To 3m (10ft) high. (*Boundary*)

Privet (*Ligustrum ovalifolium*) Semi-evergreen available in green- and yellow-leaved varieties.

Box hedge used for edging.

Above: Peacocks at Great Dixter, Sussex.

Giraffes in Gloucestershire.

Above: Monkey in Norfolk.

Below: Geometric topiary in Mappowder, Dorset.

Large bird in Dorset cottage garden.

Plant 30cm (12in) apart. To 2m (6½ft) high. (*Formal*)

Prunus cistena Similar to purple-leaved Myrobalan plum but shorter. Plant 60cm (2ft) apart. To 1.5m (5ft) high. (*Boundary*)

Roses Various shrub and cluster-flowered (floribunda) roses make attractive flowering hedges but should not be trimmed formally. Some species can also be used and the sweetbriar, *Rosa rubiginosa*, can be clipped. Plant 45–60cm (18–24in) apart. To 1.5m (5ft) high. (*Flowering*)

Rosemary (*Rosmarinus officinalis*) Evergreen with small aromatic leaves and violet-blue flowers. It is not very hardy but makes an excellent small hedge in mild places. Plant 40cm (16in) apart. To 1.5m (5ft) high. (*Flowering*)

Thuja plicata An evergreen, much like Lawson cypress in appearance, available in dark green and yellow variegated ('Golden Wonder', 'Zebrina') varieties. Plant 60cm (2ft) apart. To 6m (20ft) high. (*Windbreak*)

Yew (*Taxus baccata*) Narrow-leaved evergreen in dark green- and yellow-leaved varieties. Grows in sun or shade; stands heavy clipping. Plant 50–60cm (20–24in) apart. To 3m (10ft) high. (*Formal*)

SHEAR FANTASY

Topiary is the name given to the very ancient art of clipping shrubs into ornamental shapes so that they can be used in gardens as focal points or eye-catchers. Topiary can vary from simple cones, pyramids or balls to fantastic figures of birds, animals or whatever takes the gardener's fancy. You can build it on the tops of hedges to give them a more interesting appearance or make free-standing specimens, used either singly or in rows or patterns.

Small-leaved, freely branched evergreen shrubs are the best for topiary work: yew and box in green-leaved and golden forms are the favourites, but many others can be used and for really large specimens Portugal laurel was at one time much in demand.

Simple shapes – cones, pyramids, columns, drums, globes, or even spirals – can be formed by the simple process of clipping the shrubs to the desired shapes. They may be small and a bit rudimentary at first but gradually each plant will gain in size and shapeliness and it should not take more than three or four years to produce an admirable topiary specimen.

'Seven Sisters' in pub garden, Oaksmere, Suffolk.

Dog (probably a poodle) graces a plot at Toller Porcorum, Dorset.

Commemorative topiary in Wells, Norfolk.

More elaborate forms, such as peacocks with widespread or flowing tails, doves, rabbits, running dogs, bears, or even chessmen, require more skill and time. Stems will need to be trained as well as clipped and for this you will need to tie them to some kind of framework. Lash canes together or fold wire netting to give you the basic skeleton. Fix this framework firmly to stakes driven well into the soil with the shrub at the centre. It will look fairly unsightly at first but, given good care in watering and feeding, the shrubs will soon make sufficient growth to screen the framework. Clip-ping and training go hand in hand, and within three or four years even the most elaborate fantasies should be recognizable. From then on it is simply a matter of improving the details, allowing specimens to increase in size until they reach the maximum desired, after which you simply clip and prune them to maintain them exactly as they are.

All you need for clipping topiary specimens are ordinary shears or hedge trimmers. The topiary 'season' runs from May to August.

A H

Lavandula spica 'Hidcote'.

VEGETABLES

Fresh vegetables from a well-stocked kitchen garden.

GETTING STARTED: A BUYER'S GUIDE TO SEED

In the vegetable garden almost everything starts with seed. There are a few notable exceptions – potatoes, Jerusalem and globe artichokes and some of the culinary herbs – but the great body of vegetables are raised from seed every year.

I never cease to be astonished at the storehouse of potential locked up in a seed: to think that that fragile, slightly furry tomato seed, sown in the chills of March, could grow into a plant 2–2.5m (7–8ft) high by September and produce between 2–4.5kg (4–10lb) of fruit; or that an admittedly far more robust-looking pumpkin seed will blanket 4m² of ground with its huge leaves and rampant stems, yielding pumpkins weighing as much as 27kg (60lb) before the onset of winter.

Most of us sow with optimism, shutting out of our minds the vicissitudes of weather, pests, diseases and even pure neglect which may beset the plant, thinking only of the future harvest. But while marvelling at what lies ahead, it is perhaps worth casting an eye back, for while the seed packet is the start of one cycle, it is the end-product of another. And knowing something about where today's seed comes from, and how it is produced, helps to explain both the high price, and the high quality, of modern seed.

Our seed is grown all over the world – in East Africa and California, Italy, Denmark and Holland, the Rhône and Loire valleys, Taiwan and Indonesia. Only a little – cress, kale and cabbage, perhaps – is home-grown, in East Anglia. The reasons for this are primarily climatic.

Growing seed is a highly skilled, labour-intensive business. Although the picture is changing, much seed is still grown under contract for the large seed companies by families who for generations have specialized in two or three seed crops. It's an international cottage industry.

The seed crops are raised from very carefully selected, top-quality 'mother seed', supplied by the parent seed company who inspect the growing crop regularly to check on quality. The grower needs to 'rogue' the crop several times to spot and remove any plants which are below-standard; he needs to judge the precise moment to harvest, which is still often done by hand. Certainly, one reason for the escalating costs of quality seed is the problem of matching these increasingly rare skills with suitable sites for seed growing.

Once harvested, the seed companies clean the seed with highly automated equipment which rejects poor and misshapen seed. Further refinements include removing the barbs from the coat of carrot seed, or the hard outer coat from beet – all steps to help in germination. The seed is then stored in air-conditioned warehouses, where temperature and humidity are carefully controlled. Finally, before it is sold, vegetable seed is tested for purity and germination (it has to comply with certain minimum standards), and in many cases for freedom from disease as well. By the time it reaches us, it *should* be good.

Gardeners generally buy their seed from garden centres and seed shops, or through the seed firms' mail-order catalogues. There are several advantages in the latter course. The seed companies usually hold a far wider range, especially of the less common varieites, than most shops can afford to stock; there is a lot of practical gardening information in the seed catalogues, which are almost always free; discounts are often offered, and the seed, one hopes, is stored under optimum conditions. (When it comes to seed potatoes, onion sets, shallots and so forth, which are heavy, bulky, costly to post and liable to be damaged in transit, there is an obvious advantage in buying from garden centres or shops.)

KEEPING SEED

There may be a gap of several months between buying and sowing seed. How to keep the seed in that intervening period, and between one sowing and the next, has a direct bearing on success.

If seed is to retain its viability, ie its ability to germinate *well*, it must be kept in dry, cool conditions. Seed keeps best at temperatures below zero, but for every 5°C (9°F) rise in temperature above freezing point, the storage life of seed is halved. So seed should be kept in the coolest, driest place available – never in a hot kitchen or damp garden shed. (A domestic refrigerator is an excellent place.)

If possible, keep seed in packets in an air-tight

Seeds: shaping up to quality

Any newcomer to vegetable growing is faced with a bewildering choice of varieties. (Which Savoy cabbage is it to be: 'January King' or 'Ice Queen'?) Finding varieties best suited to one's needs, tastes and locality is acquired with experience. But there are several pointers to good varieties, usually indicated on the packets or in the catalogues. Seed is nowadays also sold not only as 'naked seed', but in more practical forms.

Sweet corn (Kelvedon Glory)

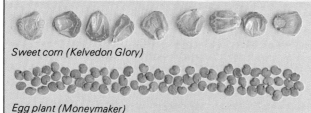

Egg plant (Moneymaker)

F1 Hybrids These are 'first generation' hybrids, in the plant breeder's jargon, made by crossing two pure parent lines which have been inbred for several generations. Plants raised from F1 seed are of exceptional quality and vigour, but because of the complex breeding process, this seed is more expensive than ordinary 'open pollinated' seed. Where vegetables are concerned it is almost always worth the extra outlay.

Calendula (Pot Marigold)

Onion (Brunswick)

Foil Packeted Seed packed in modern air-sealed foil packs keeps fresh and viable far longer than seed in conventional paper packets. Once foil packs are opened the seed starts to deteriorate in the usual way, but they are always worth buying initially.

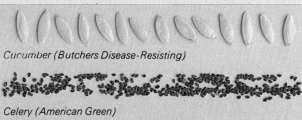

Runner bean (Enorma)

Beetroot (Boltardy)

Awards The Royal Horticultural Society in this country, and the All America Selections scheme in the United States, carry out trials of new varieties and make awards to those they find outstanding. The highest RHS recommendation is the First Class Certificate (FCC), followed by the Award of Merit (AM) and Highly Commended (HC). The All America Selections award Gold, Silver and Bronze medals.

Cucumber (Butchers Disease-Resisting)

Celery (American Green)

Free from Disease 1 Seed can be treated against certain seed-borne diseases which would become apparent after sowing. Celery and celeriac, for instance, can be treated against leaf spot. **2** Seed can be treated or dusted with chemicals which help combat those diseases in the soil which lead to germination failures. **3** Seed can be guaranteed free of certain seed-borne diseases, such as lettuce mosaic virus. **4** Varieties are often bred with resistance to certain diseases, for example, this cucumber seed is resistant to leaf spot.

Parsnip (Tender and True)

Carrot (Nantes Champion Scarlet Horn)

Pelleted Each seed is made into a tiny ball with a coating of protective substance which breaks down in the soil. Pellets were originally developed to meet the precision-drilling requirements of commercial growers, but their main asset for amateurs is that each seed is of a size which can be handled individually. This makes it very easy to sow seeds 2.5cm (1in) or even 1.5cm ($\frac{1}{2}$in) apart, as required, so eliminating – or simplifying – the need to thin germinated seed. The soil *must* be kept moist until the seed germinates.

Cucumber Simex F1 hybrid

Chitted or Pre-germinated This is a very recent development. The seed is germinated under laboratory conditions by the seed company, then despatched to customers for immediate planting. The point is that while high temperatures and good conditions are often essential to get seed to *germinate* (they need a heated propagator), once seed *has* germinated it can withstand lower temperatures and poorer conditions quite successfully.

All these varieties are available from most seed companies, except for the Cucumber Simex F1 hybrid, which is exclusively from Suttons

tin or jar, in which there is a bag or dish of silica gel to absorb moisture. It is worth getting cobalt-chloride-treated silica gel, which is blue when dry, pink when moist. Once it has become moist it can be dried out in a low oven and re-used.

Even when kept under perfect conditions, seed viability varies from species to species. Brassicas (members of the cabbage family), legumes (the pea and bean family) and tomatoes will all keep up to nine or ten years, but parsnips, salsify and scorzonera should be treated with suspicion after one year, and onions and leeks discarded after two. Most other vegetable seeds fall between these two extremes.

JL

'Mother' onion seed at the National Seed Development Organisation; later it goes to commercial distributors.

Mail-order catalogues of vegetable and flower seed

Alexander & Brown, South Methven Street, PO Box 13, Perth
Asmer Garden Shops Ltd, 29 North Street, Taunton TA1 1LP
J. W. Boyce, Soham, Ely, Cambridge CB7 5ED
Thomas Butcher Ltd, 60 Wickham Road, Shirley, Croydon, Surrey CR9 8AG
Chase Compost Seeds Ltd, Benhall, Saxmundham, Suffolk IP16 1HU
Samuel Dobie & Son Ltd, Upper Dee Mills, Llangollen, Clwyd LL20 8SD
S. E. Marshall & Co. Ltd, 21 Regal Road, Wisbech, Cambs. PE13 2RF
Suttons Seeds, Hele Road, Torquay, Devon TQ2 7QJ
Thompson & Morgan, London Road, Ipswich, Suffolk IP2 0BA
I. & S. Unwin Ltd, Oldfield Lane, Wisbech, Cambs. PE13 2HW
W. J. Unwin Ltd, Histon, Cambridge, CB4 4LE

SOWING FOR SUCCESS

Vegetables can be sown from seed in one of three ways:

Directly in the ground where they are to grow to maturity.

In a seedbed outdoors, being later transplanted into their permanent position.

'Indoors', ie under protection in a seed tray or pots, for planting outdoors as seedlings or small plants when conditions are favourable.

The choice of method depends on the circumstances. Direct sowing is used mainly for vegetables which are used as seedlings, eg cress, or are difficult or liable to be set back by being transplanted. Common examples are root vegetables such as carrots, parsnips, turnips and radishes; peas and beans (though they *can* be transplanted successfully); parsley, onions, and summer sowings of lettuce.

Seedbeds are essentially a means of saving space, and are mostly used for vegetables which either have a long growing season, or require a lot of space when mature. These are sown in close rows in the seedbed, where they remain until they are large enough for transplanting into a permanent position which, in the meantime, has been used for some other crop. Cabbages, Brussels sprouts, cauliflowers, leeks, perennial vegetables such as seakale and globe artichokes, as well as salad crops, are often raised in seedbeds.

Seeds are sown indoors to give them an earlier start, for one of several reasons. Celery, celeriac, leeks and onions will grow into larger specimens if given a longer growing season. Half-hardy vegetables such as tomatoes, sweetcorn, sweet peppers and French beans can't be planted out until the risk of frost is past and may fail to mature in poor seasons, so they also benefit from being started indoors. Earlier crops of lettuce, cabbages and cauliflowers, to name but three, can be obtained by sowing indoors a few weeks earlier than would be possible outdoors. (For indoor sowing methods *see* 'Colours of Summer: Growing Annuals and Biennials'.)

PREPARING A SEEDBED OUTDOORS

A seedbed needs to be carefully prepared. It should be reasonably firm and settled, but not so consolidated as to be impenetrable to roots. The surface should be free of large clods and stones, and raked into a good tilth, so that the soil crumbs on the surface are about the size of large breadcrumbs. For large seeds such as peas and beans a coarser tilth is adequate, even beneficial as it will discourage the germination of weed seeds.

If the ground has been dug over in the autumn, frost will have broken down the soil in winter and preparing the seedbed in spring will be relatively easy. The crucial factor is to choose a moment when the soil is neither too wet nor too dry. If the soil sticks to your feet when you walk on it, it is best to delay. Small areas of wet soil can be dried out with cloches, while if the soil has become too dry, it will have to be watered.

The first step is to break down clods with the back of the rake; then rake off any remaining clods or stones, finally raking backwards and forwards until the tilth is obtained. If it is inconvenient to sow immediately, cover the surface with a thin mulch of straw or similar material. This will preserve the tilth in good condition. (The mulch can be raked off just before sowing.) Otherwise the strong drying winds often encountered in spring dry out the surface very rapidly, making it difficult to sow.

Where the ground was not dug over in winter it is usually necessary, unless the soil is exceptionally light, to fork it over first to make it workable. Then tread it lightly to help the soil to settle before starting to rake down the surface.

It is often tempting to save space by making a seedbed in an out-of-the-way corner, perhaps behind a shed or alongside a hedge. Resist the temptation: the odds are that the seedlings will be drawn towards the light and turn pale and lanky. Make sure, too, that the ground is relatively free of both annual and perennial weeds, or the seedlings may be engulfed early in life. Weed seeds are more vigorous and inevitably germinate first.

If the soil is known to be full of weed seed (and this applies to any sowing outdoors) allow the first flush of weeds to germinate after you have prepared the seedbed. Then hoe off the weeds and sow your seeds. This is especially worthwhile when making the first sowings in gardens which have been neglected and have acquired a large legacy of weed seed.

Above: Plants grown in rows.

Right: Sugarloaf chicory sown broadcast – a useful method for salad crops.

SOWING METHODS

The commonest form of sowing outdoors is in straight drills, virtually slits made in the soil with the blade of a hoe or trowel. Seed is sown in the bottom of the drill and covered with soil. The depth of sowing depends on the size of the seed. Small seeds like lettuce and carrots should be about 1cm (½in) deep, sweetcorn and peas about 2.5cm (1in), beans about 4cm (1½in).

What matters most is the *condition* of the soil. Seeds germinate best in warm moist soil. In wet conditions they are liable to rot and be attacked by pests and diseases in the soil, though seed dressings can be used to counter these problems. In very dry soil they simply fail to germinate.

Steps can be taken to overcome hostile conditions. If the soil is very wet, the drill can either be lined with peat or sowing compost, or covered with cloches for a day or two to warm it up before sowing. If the soil is very dry, take out the drill, water only the bottom of the drill until it is almost muddy, sow the seed and cover it with dry soil. This acts as a mulch and prevents the moisture evaporating – an invaluable technique for summer sowings.

The golden rule is to sow thinly. If the seeds are large enough for individual handling, sow them at least 1–2.5cm (½–1in) apart, or 'station sow' in little groups of three or four at 'stations' a few inches apart; these will be much easier to thin than a continuous row. Nothing is ever gained by thick sowing; overcrowded seedlings are prone to attack by pests and diseases and never develop satisfactorily.

Large seeds like peas and beans are sometimes sown individually in holes made with a dibber or stick. Just make sure the seed touches the bottom of the hole and is not suspended in a pocket of air. Some large seeds such as marrow or sweetcorn can be sown direct and covered with a jam jar until they germinate. The jar acts as a miniature cloche.

An old-fashioned method of sowing which deserves a comeback is broadcasting. After preparing the seedbed, seed is simply scattered evenly and thinly on the surface. It is then raked over first in one direction and then at right angles to the first direction. This is a useful way of sowing early carrots and radishes, and for the cut-and-come-again seedling crops such as cress, Mediterranean rocket, lettuce and chicory which are grown for salads.

As with any sowing, germination is encouraged by covering the seedbed with sheets of newspaper or polythene film, which helps to maintain a moist atmosphere. Unless perforated plastic is used, the cover must be removed as soon as any seedlings appear, or they will become white and drawn.

VIRTUES OF THINNING

Thinning, the removal of surplus seedlings, is an important – if tedious – gardening operation. Ideally, one should sow so thinly that thinning is unnecessary: in practice this rarely happens. Thinning is best done in stages, starting as soon as the seedlings are large enough to handle, and thinning each time so that each seedling stands just clear of its neighbour. The final distance depends on the vegetable: radishes need be only 2.5cm (1in) apart, parsnips 12cm (5in), lettuces 22–25cm (9–10in). Instead of uprooting the unwanted seedlings, they can be nipped off at the base, which minimizes the disturbance to the remaining seedlings. All thinnings should be removed immediately, as their characteristic smell attracts the plant's pests. The carrot root fly is a classic example, homing in on carrots which have been thinned.

Where seedlings are being uprooted, do this when the ground is moist, or water the soil beforehand; afterwards, firm the soil around the base of the remaining seedlings. Similarly, before digging up plants for transplanting, water the seedbed if dry, to minimize disturbance to the roots.

A high proportion of failures with vegetables can be traced to that notoriously vulnerable stage between seed and seedling. We fail to get good results because we sow too early (those fatal itchy fingers that gardeners get in spring), too thickly, when it's too cold, too wet or too dry – mistakes all compounded by subsequently thinning or transplanting too late.

The Block Revolution

The relatively new technique of sowing individual seeds in small blocks of soil or peat compost overcomes many germination and early growth problems, and is ideal for anyone who wants relatively small numbers of vegetable plants. It is a simple alternative to the traditional system of raising prize vegetable specimens in small pots, guaranteeing plants the best conditions during their most vulnerable stages and in unfavourable conditions.

The blocks are compact cubes, measuring about 4cm (1½in) each way, with a small hole in the top in which the seed is sown. They are best made of peat blocking compost (a commercially prepared potting compost with an added adhesive agent), but peat-based compost or soil-based sowing compost or basic potting compost can be used. Blocks are pressed from moistened compost using a special tool. Professional growers use multiple blockers, but there is a type available to amateurs that makes one block at a time. Stand the blocks side by side in a standard seed tray.

Usually one seed is sown in each block, but several seeds can be sown to allow for low germination and later thinned to one per block. Large and pelleted seeds are easily sown by hand; smaller seeds can be pushed carefully off a piece of paper, or picked up on a paintbrush or label and dropped singly into the block. The seed is covered with soil from the edge of the hole.

Each seedling grows rapidly in its own block, unimpeded by competition, developing a vigorous

root system which permeates the whole block. No thinning is necessary. When the seedling shows signs of outgrowing its block, the whole is planted out as one unit; harden off first if necessary. There is no transplanting shock, nor the damage often done by tearing apart the intertwined root systems of plants raised in a seed tray. The protective nature of the block means that planting can be successfully carried out in conditions which would otherwise be considered too wet or too dry.

Blocking is the most flexible of systems. One seed tray holding forty blocks could, for example, be used to raise ten cabbage plants, five brussels sprout plants, twenty lettuces, five marrows and ten bedding plants or even French beans, which have a very high death rate when sown direct.

If you cannot get the proper equipment, improvise. Sow in a seed tray, space the seeds about 4cm (1½in) apart and with a knife divide the compost into squares.   JL

Left and right: Peat blocks are ideal for sowing vegetables.

Below left: Press out block, drop a seed into the hole. The entire block can be planted out without disturbing the roots.

UNDERCOVER OPERATIONS

'From first to last gardening in this country is a continuous conflict with difficulties.' So wrote the Victorian gardening writer Shirley Hibberd in 1877. Little has changed, because the main source of the conflict, now as then, is the short growing season allowed by our fickle climate.

Most of our vegetable crops start to grow when the average daytime temperature reaches 6°C (43°F) in spring and stop growing when it falls below this temperature in autumn. The number of 'growing days' any gardener has at his disposal depends entirely on where he lives. The main purpose of 'protection' – which embraces anything from cloches to frames to greenhouses and includes both the low and the newer 'walk-in' polythene tunnels – is to increase the number of these growing days. There is no doubt that a little protection of some kind, however makeshift, pays enormous dividends in the kitchen garden.

REASONS FOR PROTECTION

It raises the soil and air temperature extending both the growing season and the range of crops. Only with protection can borderline crops such as tomatoes, green peppers and melons be grown successfully, whatever the season.

It shields crops against the elements – rain, hail, salt spray in maritime areas and, most important of all, wind, thus improving both the yield and quality of vegetables. Protection is especially worthwhile against the lethal combination of cold winds and low temperatures.

It reduces bird damage in the garden. In some circumstances birds do more damage than any other outside agent, including pests, diseases and climatic extremes. Their repertoire ranges from sparrows eliminating all beetroot and spinach seedlings to pigeons plundering the winter greens.

It gives some defence against frost, although this is only complete when the protection is heated in some way. Frames, for example, can be electrically heated with soil cables.

It keeps crops clean, which means less wastage and, as a bonus, less vulnerability to the many pests and diseases which are encouraged by 'mucky' plants.

Apart from enabling us to grow more crops of a better quality over a longer period, protection is useful for all sorts of odd purposes, which include warming up the soil before sowing, hardening off seedlings and young plants, ripening tomatoes and drying off onions.

WHAT KIND OF PROTECTION

The sort of protection to choose depends on the size of your pocket as much as the size of your

Above: Mixing protection – modern plastic cloches surrounded by hoops covered with netting.

Left: Winter lettuce makes progress in an unheated greenhouse. Note the good ventilation – but glass is expensive and heavy to erect.

Scarecrow in a kitchen garden, an age-old remedy against birds. It must be moved frequently to be effective.

garden. Should you go for something permanent, like a traditional greenhouse? Or should it be semi-permanent, a 'walk-in' tunnel or greenhouse clad with polythene film? (These require no foundations as the edges are simply anchored with soil.) Or do you really want a temporary, mobile device such as a portable frame or set of cloches? (Check with the chart for the pros and cons of each system.)

The important point about any permanent structure is that if the same crop – tomatoes or cucumbers, for example – is grown for several years in the same soil, there is a buildup of pests and diseases which results in soil sickness, making it impossible to continue growing the crop. The only remedy is to change or sterilize the soil, or to grow future crops in some form of container such as growing bags, boxes or pots, or in a soilless system such as ring culture.

The other important consideration is the covering material. Glass transmits light best,

retains more heat at night and does not deteriorate with age; on the other hand, it is very expensive, heavy to erect and there is the risk of breakages. Some of the modern rigid and semi-rigid plastic materials are cheaper, transmit light reasonably enough (plants grow surprisingly well under the diffused light of some of the translucent materials such as Correx), but they lose heat more rapidly at night. Many plastics deteriorate within three to five years due to ultra-violet radiation, becoming discoloured and brittle. Polythene films are cheaper still, though the least durable. Thin films (150 gauge) are used over small hoops to make low tunnels (the cheapest form of protection for a vegetable garden) while heavier film (600 gauge) is used to cover the large galvanized steel hoops of walk-in tunnels, or structures made in the traditional greenhouse shape. All of these cheaper

Types of protection

Initial costs in relation to area protected	Durability	Advantages	Disadvantages	Main uses	
Cloches					
Moderate to expensive depending on type	Glass cloches permanent; plastic cloches average 3 years	Mobile and flexible to use: can be removed for watering, ventilation and other tasks. Can also be switched from crop to crop	Only really suitable for low-growing crops. Heat up rapidly so require fairly constant attention	Warming soil before sowing or planting in spring. Raising seedlings in boxes or pots in spring. Early sowing in spring, eg peas, broad beans, lettuce, carrots. (Later transferred to other crops.)	peppers, cucumbers, marrows. Extending the season in autumn by covering late crops, eg carrots, lettuce, radishes. Ripening off bush tomatoes and onions. Protecting salad crops, etc, in winter, eg lettuce, endives, corn salad, parsley, spinach.
Low polythene tunnels				Hardening off plants raised indoors, eg celery, sweet corn, tomatoes. Protection of half-hardy crops when first planted outdoors, eg. dwarf French beans, tomatoes,	Overwintering seedlings to be planted early in spring, eg cauliflowers, endives, lettuce
Cheap	Film lasts about 2 years; hoops indefinitely	Mobile and flexible as for cloches. Push the film back to one side for access	May be difficult to anchor in winds. Can be fiddly to erect and dismantle. Easily flattened by snow		
Frames					
Vary according to type	Many years	Better insulated than cloches. Mobility depends on whether portable, semi-portable, or permanent fixtures. Lids can be removed for watering and ventilation. Fairly tall crops can be grown	Not very flexible in use. If solid-sided, rather dark for some crops. Awkward to work in	Raising seedlings in seed boxes in spring. Early sowings, eg lettuce, carrots, radishes. Growing summer crops, eg tomatoes, melons, cucumbers. Overwintering	seedlings, eg cauliflowers, lettuce, endives. Growing winter crops, eg lettuce, endives. Blanching and forcing chicory, endives
Walk-in tunnels and greenhouse structures clad with film					
Cheap	Film lasts 2–3 years; steel or wood frame long-lasting	Can be moved to new site every 3 years so soil sickness avoided. Suitable for tall crops. Gardeners can work inside in poor weather	Watering has to be by hand. Heat is lost more rapidly than under glass at night, but temperatures build up rapidly during the day, encouraging pests and diseases unless well ventilated.	Starting plants early in spring in seed boxes or pots. Growing early crops of lettuce, radishes and seedlings. Growing half-hardy summer crops, eg tomatoes, peppers, melons, cucumbers.	Overwintering crops, eg winter salads, herbs, Chinese cabbage. Overwintering seedlings, eg cauliflowers, lettuce, endives
Greenhouses					
Expensive	Permanent	Substantial structures with good light transmission and good heat conservation easily ventilated. Kept frost-free by heating. Suitable for tall crops. Gardeners can work inside in poor weather	Watering has to be by hand; soil sickness builds up after about 3 years, so crops may have to be grown in containers.		

alternatives have much to offer the amateur vegetable grower.

To get most out of protective systems:

Put cloches, frames or polythene structures on the best available soil – fertile, rich in organic matter, well-drained and weed-free.

Anchor cloches, the lids of frames and low polythene tunnels as securely as possible, or they may blow away or be damaged in high winds. Where cloches have a small hoop on the top, run a string through the hoops and anchor it to stout stakes in the ground at either end.

Close the ends of cloches, for example with panes of glass; otherwise a chilling wind tunnel is created. This also helps to keep out the birds.

When using polythene film to make tunnels, frames or cloches:

Bind any rough edges on the framework, whether it is of wood or steel, with cloth or tape. This may give the film an extra year of life.

Mend any tears with plastic tape.

Put the film over the structure on a warm day, so that it can be pulled taut. Flapping film is subject to wear and tear. Plastic can be battened to a wooden frame to make it more rigid.

Make sure there is adequate ventilation. If possible put a door at either end of any structure more than about 6m (20ft) long, with screen netting in one half of the door; or cut holes the size of dinner plates about 45cm (18in) above ground level at either end. Tape a piece of polythene over the holes in winter.

Get longer-lasting ultra-violet treated film or plastics wherever possible.

FORCING THE PACE

Another way of beating the seasons is by forcing plants, that is, creating slightly warmer conditions so that they come into growth a little sooner. In the old days, it was done extensively with hot beds of fermenting stable manure – not a practical proposition for most modern gardens. Simple alternative methods are available, either by leaving the plants outdoors, or by lifting them and bringing them into slightly warmer conditions in greenhouses, sheds or in the house.

Forcing is often coupled with blanching, which means excluding light and so making plants white, tender and sweeter. Traditionally, many of the more bitter salad plants such as endives, dandelion and chicory were blanched.

Blanch endives and dandelions a few at a time as they may rot if not used soon after being blanched. Choose a dry day, or cover the plants

After fifteen days, off comes the covering to reveal a newly blanched endive: white, tender and sweeter.

beforehand with cloches to dry them off. Remove any dead or decayed leaves. Bunch up the leaves, and tie them towards the top with a piece of raffia, then cover the plants with a large flower pot with the holes blocked to exclude all light. The plants should be blanched within about fifteen days.

The 'chicons' of Witloof, the weather-resistant Belgian chicory, are easily produced at home, even if they look less elegant than shop-bought chicory. The chicory is sown in May or June and the plants thinned to about 15cm (6in) apart. They look like untidy dandelions.

In late October or November lift the roots. Reject any very thin or fanged roots, and trim the leaves off about 2.5cm (1in) above the root. If they are not required for immediate forcing (and it is best just to do a few at a time to keep a constant supply), store them horizontally in boxes of moist peat or sand in a dry shed.

Then, beginning in November, plant two or three roots close together, in ordinary soil, in a large 20–23cm (8–9in) flower pot or similar container. Cover the pot with an inverted pot of the same size, with the drainage hole blocked to exclude light. Bring the pot indoors. The temperature need be no higher than 10°C (50°F), though

Right: Rhubarb was traditionally forced under clay pots like these.

Below: Crowns overwintered and forced indoors in plastic sacks for an early crop.

growth will be faster at higher temperatures. Keep the soil moist. The chicons should form within about three weeks. Keep the cut chicons in the fridge when they are ready, as they will become green and bitter on exposure to light. A secondary crop of smaller leaves may be produced by the stump if it is left in the pot.

How to Force Rhubarb

Outdoors: Pack straw or dead leaves around the crowns in December or January, then cover them with upturned boxes, tea chests, ash buckets or traditional rhubarb pots. The stems will shoot up earlier and be exceptionally pink, sweet and tender.

Indoors: Dig up the plants in late autumn. If there has been no frost, leave them on the ground until after a period of cold weather to break their natural dormancy. Then plant the crowns under the staging in a greenhouse, or in large pots or boxes which can be brought indoors. Cover them with a similar container to exclude light if you want the stems blanched. The leaf stalks start to grow at temperatures of 7–16°C (45–61°F). Rhubarb can also be forced in black plastic sacks. The ideal temperature is 13°C (55°F): at higher temperatures the sticks are paler, and at lower temperatures development is slower.

How to Force Seakale

Outdoors: Force as for rhubarb, but cover with something that will allow the plants to grow up to 45cm (18in) high. Old seakale pots, of course, were designed for the purpose. The shoots will be ready between March and May, and have a wonderful texture and taste.

Indoors: Use plants at least two years old. Lift them in November, trim off side roots, and pot them up close together in boxes, pots, or a darkened area under the greenhouse staging. All light must be excluded to get the best flavoured shoots. The temperature for forcing should be 13–16°C (55–61°F). Forced plants have to be discarded after use.

JL

Left: Seakale can be forced outdoors under containers. By spring the stems will be crisp, tender and ready to eat.

PROTECTIVE LAYERS

Mulching is one of the most ancient horticultural techniques, utilized over the centuries by such highly skilled gardeners as the Arabs and Chinese. It was practised in England long ago: there are thirteenth-century records in Norwich of labourers paid for 'thatching' fields with straw.

While mulching has enabled crops to be grown in what would normally be considered impossibly hostile conditions, in places with exceptionally low rainfall, and on rocky, barren or salty soils, it also enables better crops to be grown under everyday conditions in ordinary gardens.

What exactly is mulching? It is simply covering the soil surface with a protective layer, a barrier between the soil and the air. Imitating nature, you might say, for in nature you rarely see bare ground. It is constantly being 'mulched', either by falling leaves and decaying plant debris, or by a living mulch of plant growth.

The main purpose of artificial mulching is to conserve moisture in the soil by preventing or reducing evaporation. Vegetables, especially leafy vegetables, are thirsty crops, and in most years most vegetables would give higher yields if they could have more water. Although we think of Britain as having a high rainfall, a tremendous proportion of it is lost through evaporation.

In the average summer the top few inches of the soil dry out through the effects of wind and sun. Not only does this deplete the reserves of moisture in the soil, but plant roots can only extract the nutrients they need – most of which are in the surface layers of the soil – from soil which is moist. When the soil becomes dry they are effectively deprived of both water and nutrients. Mulching prevents this happening, so growth can continue unchecked. It also, of course, prevents soil erosion, and is a very effective means of controlling weeds.

What to Use and When

The material used for mulching can be organic – seaweed, peat, or garden compost for example; an inert substance such as sand, gravel, stones or clinker; or manufactured material such as plastic

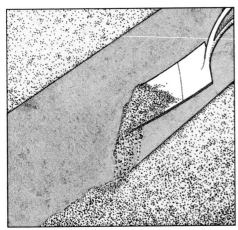

Use a black plastic mulch for potatoes: it saves earthing up and preserves moisture. When the leaves push up the plastic, cut slits in it and guide plants through.

film. In practice it is largely a question of what can be obtained without undue cost or effort.

On the whole, organic materials are best for mulching vegetables: when their mulching role is over, they can be dug into the soil to increase its humus content. Among suitable candidates are garden compost, spent mushroom compost (probably one of the very best mulching materials), seaweed (also excellent), very well rotted farmyard manure, debris from old haystacks, old reed straw and old hay, deep litter from poultry farms, spent hops, leafmould, bracken and lawn mowings. In short, you can use anything derived from living matter which will rot.

A cautionary note on lawn mowings. If fresh lawn mowings are put on in too thick a layer they tend to heat up when they start to rot, forming a thick unpleasant mass. Either let them dry out for a day or two, turning them to help the process, or put them on in layers of a couple of inches or so at a time.

Wood derivatives, such as sawdust, and pulverized or shredded bark, should also be used with caution in vegetable gardens. They break down slowly, robbing the soil of nitrogen in the process.

An important factor in choosing a mulch is texture. The ideal mulch should be slightly loose when settled, so that rain and air can penetrate through to the soil. Peat, though excellent for controlling weeds, is not very suitable for mulching vegetables since it absorbs rain on the surface and re-evaporates it, with the result that the soil remains dry beneath.

In Britain, sand, gravel and stones are rarely used for mulching, though there is scope for doing so on a small scale, for example in greenhouses. Moisture evaporates very rapidly from greenhouse soil during the day, and a mulch of sand or stone, 8cm (3in) deep around plants, can be invaluable for conserving moisture. Moreover, the heat absorbed by the mulch during the day is thrown out at night, so raising the greenhouse temperature a degree or so.

The important thing to remember about mulching is that it preserves the *status quo*. So never mulch when the soil is very dry, very wet or very cold. It will remain that way. The best time to mulch is in spring or early summer, when the soil has warmed up but is still moist.

It is easiest to mulch when planting out. Brassicas, courgettes, pumpkins, tomatoes, lettuces and beans, for example, can be given a good watering when planted, and then mulched. In many cases no further watering will be necessary.

For crops sown *in situ* it is best to delay mulching until the seedlings are through the soil and at least a couple of inches high. Otherwise they may be smothered by the mulch, especially if birds come and scratch about in it, as sometimes happens.

BLOT OUT WEEDS

Mulching is one of the best ways of controlling weeds in an established vetable garden, where weedkillers are often impracticable and hoeing leads to loss of moisture from the soil and may damage plant roots. Black plastic is excellent for this purpose. It completely excludes light so the seedlings of annual weeds cannot develop, while perennial weeds are, at the very least, held in abeyance.

Black plastic tends to have a cooling effect on the soil, so is best used for weed control on summer crops. There are two ways of planting through plastic. Either plant first, and then unroll the plastic over the plants, making cross-like slits in the plastic just above the plants and settling it over them. Alternatively, lay the plastic on the ground, cut small cross-slits in the film where the plants will be, and plant through the slits. In either case the sides and ends of the film can be buried in narrow slits made in the soil with a spade, or the edges held down with lumps of earth or stones. Where possible, dig up perennial weeds before planting. If the plastic gets torn, they will push through in an unsightly and damaging way.

The chief drawback to a black plastic mulch is that it prevents air and water reaching the soil, which in the long term would have adverse effects on the biological life in the soil. So remove it at the end of the growing season. Another way is to use the perforated plastic mulches which are now on the market. They allow air and water to pass into the soil, while still preventing weed growth. A secondary drawback is that on light soils mice, voles and moles sometimes wreak havoc under black plastic, but they are liable to do this with any mulch.

Black plastic is also used in growing potatoes to save earthing up. The potatoes are planted shallowly and covered with the film. When the leaves can be seen pushing it up, holes are cut and the stems pulled through. The plastic conserves moisture, controls weeds, and prevents the tubers from greening.

Transparent plastic film can also be used to help conserve moisture in the soil, but as it allows light through, it is useless for weed control.

Any of the organic mulching materials, provided they are used in a layer thick enough to exclude light, can be an effective means of weed control, particularly against annual weeds and to a lesser extent against perennials. However, any weeds which do penetrate an organic mulch are far easier to pull out by hand than if they were securely anchored in the ground.

You need to take care not to introduce weeds in organic mulches. Poorly made compost and stable manure are often full of weed seed. If a mulch is suspect, try it out first on a small scale. In most cases mulch is still worth using because, as already mentioned, weeds are easily pulled out of it. One of the great advantages of spent mushroom compost is that it is sterilized during the mushroom growing process, so is free of weed seed.

IMPROVING THE SOIL

It is widely recognized that mulching with organic materials improves soil fertility. 'Feed the soil, not the plants' is the motto of the 'organic' school, and one of the key methods of doing so is by mulching. It is perfectly feasible, and very effective, to cover the soil with a mulch 10–15cm (4–6in) deep using materials such as compost, well-rotted manure or seaweed. Any mulch which has not been worked into the soil by worms during the course of the season (and it is astonishing how it disappears), can be dug in at the end of the year. Where you use a thick mulch, planting is generally done through the mulch. If necessary, however, the mulch can be scraped to one side to enable seed to be sown in the soil.

Transparent plastic mulches are very useful for warming up the soil in spring, enabling sowings to be made earlier. Seeds of strong plants, such as marrows, pumpkins and beans, can be covered with a strip of plastic after sowing, and as soon as the seedlings are visible, a slit can be cut and the young plants eased through. The plastic mulch encourages germination by keeping the soil moist.

Perforated transparent films can be laid over the soil after the crop is sown or planted, and because of the numerous perforations in the film they stretch, virtually growing with the crop. After a certain period, which varies with the crop, they have to be removed; but by this time the crop has been given a very good start in life, and is well ahead of any sowings made completely in the open. Films are available by mail order from Transatlantic Plastics. Their address is: Garden Estate, Ventnor, Isle of Wight PO38 1YJ.

Protection against Frost

A thick blanket of organic material goes a long way towards preventing frost from penetrating the soil. It is particularly useful where root vegetables such as Jerusalem artichokes, carrots, swedes, celeriac and parsnips are being left in the soil during the winter. If the ground is frozen solid, lifting is normally impossible; but a mulch provides just enough protection to make it feasible.

In a garden without cloches a light mulch of bracken or straw can be used to protect over-wintering greens such as spinach, chard, winter lettuce, lamb's lettuce, endives and chicory from very heavy frost. If possible, the mulch should be laid over sticks or low wire hoops, trapping a layer of insulating air beneath it and preventing it from lying too heavily on the plant leaves. It should be removed if the weather turns mild or wet; otherwise it becomes soggy, encouraging slugs and making plants rot.

Sprouting your Own

One way of supplementing the limited supply of fresh vegetables in winter is to sprout seeds — perhaps the world's most productive form of vegetable growing! The time from sowing to harvest is often no more than four or five days; no soil and little space is required, and the end-product is highly nutritious, rich in vitamins and minerals.

All sorts of seed can be sprouted, but some of the most popular, and obtainable, are mung beans (the well-known Chinese bean sprouts), adzuki and soya beans, *whole* lentils, alfalfa, radish, fenugreek, rye, and brown unpolished rice. The seeds can be bought in wholefood shops or from seed firms: but make sure they are intended for sprouting, and have not been chemically treated. Once bought, store them like all seeds in cool, dry conditions.

Most can be used raw or cooked, though you should not eat large quantities of raw legume sprouts (beans, alfalfa, fenugreek, lentils). Sprouts are generally at their best when between $\frac{1}{2}$–2cm ($\frac{1}{4}$–$\frac{3}{4}$in) long. Seeds can be sprouted in the dark or the light; darkness makes the sprouts whiter and gives them a crisper texture.

All that is required to sprout seeds is to keep them moist and warm, but not in such close conditions that they become mouldy. This is the commonest cause of failure, and the reason for recommending twice-daily rinsing because this keeps them fresh.

Step-by-step guide to sprouting
1 Rinse the seeds in an ordinary culinary strainer, removing any which are chipped or off-colour.
2 Soak them overnight in cold water. This is optional, but speeds up the sprouting process.
3 Next morning tip them into a strainer, and run fresh cold water through them.
4 Put them, moist but drained, into a layer no more than 2cm ($\frac{3}{4}$in) deep in a jar, bowl or any kind of dish. This can be covered with a lid, plate or moisture-retaining material, partly to prevent them drying out, partly to keep them dark if whitened sprouts are preferred.
5 In winter put the container in a warm place (such as an airing cupboard); in summer it can be put anywhere. Most seeds sprout at a temperature between 13–21°C (55–70°F).
6 Each night and morning rinse the seeds by tipping them into a strainer, running cold water through, draining them, and returning them to the container. It need take no more than two minutes. Continue doing this until the sprouts are at least $\frac{1}{2}$cm ($\frac{1}{4}$in) long.

The sprouts are best eaten as soon as they are ready, when they are at their most nutritious and tasty. If delay is unavoidable, keep them in a bowl of cold water in a fridge, rinsing from time to time. Seeds can also be sprouted in commercial sprouters, most of which have perforations or holes in the lid to facilitate rinsing and draining.   JL

Seed mixtures sprouted in an airing cupboard can be ready in under a week. Keep warm, moist, well-rinsed.

WELL-FED AND WATERED

Plants are like babies – liquid continually going in at one end and coming out at the other, and a lot of work involved in the process. Only with plants the intake is at the bottom end, through the roots, and the moisture is lost at the top, through transpiration from the leaves.

Very little of this water is actually absorbed into the plant, but the constant 'throughput' is essential to keep the plant cells operating efficiently. Only then can the roots exert enough pressure to absorb nutrients from the soil, can the stomata (openings) on the leaves function so that respiration and photosynthesis (the conversion of energy from sunlight) take place, and nutrients move around the plant. As soon as there is a water shortage the plant becomes less efficient, until it eventually wilts and dies.

Watering is an energy- and time-consuming chore, and since water is frequently in short supply in summer it makes sense both to conserve what water there is in the soil, and to take measures to lessen the need for watering. Here, very briefly, are some suggestions:

Improve the soil structure by working in as much organic matter as possible (see also 'Soil Fertility').

Keep the soil mulched in summer to cut down evaporation, the principal means by which water is lost from the soil (see also 'Mulching').

Work the soil deeply every few years. This encourages roots to grow deeper, so drawing water from deeper reserves.

On steeply sloping land, cultivate across the slope; this minimizes loss of water through 'run off' down the slope.

In hot weather carry out as little surface cultivation as possible, pulling up weeds by hand, or hoeing only very shallowly. Once the top few inches of soil have dried out evaporation is slowed down, but it will increase if fresh moist soil is brought up to the surface.

Remove weeds, which not only compete with vegetables for water, but increase the loss of water through transpiration.

Where space is unlimited adopt wider spacing, so that plant roots can draw water from a larger volume of soil.

In exposed gardens in particular, erect artificial windbreaks around vegetables to cut down the force of the wind, which increases evaporation from the soil and transpiration from the leaves.

A postscript to these 'conservation measures' could be: 'Don't water when it isn't necessary.' Excessive watering may wash nitrogenous fertilizers below the root zone; it can discourage root growth, so making plants more susceptible to drought; it may increase the growth of the plant as a whole without necessarily increasing the edible part; worst of all, it may reduce the flavour.

However, there comes a time in most summers when vegetables need watering. The most important point to remember is that if watering is to be any good and reach the root zone of the plant, it must be thorough. Light sprinkling on the surface is useless. Soil becomes wet layer by layer, and until the top layer of the soil is saturated, the soil beneath remains completely dry.

Thorough wetting takes more water than you may realize. Poke a finger into the soil after what seemed like a good watering. More often than not only the top inch or so is wet! In hot weather it is not worth giving less than 9 litres/m² (2 galls/sq yd) at any one time – unless, of course, you are watering seedbeds, seedlings or young transplants.

Watering should, however, be as gentle as possible. Large droplets damage the soil surface, splash mud up onto plants, and can even destroy very young seedlings by knocking them over. These should always be watered with a fine rose on the can, turned upwards if necessary to soften the impact even more. If watering is automated, use a fine gentle sprinkler, or the perforated 'lay flat' polythene tubing which is laid on the ground between rows, and is very gentle in action.

The most economical way of watering large individual plants like marrows and pumpkins is to bury a clay pot in the ground near the roots, and confine watering to the pot. Water will slowly seep through to the plant. The best time to water is in the evening. This prevents water being lost through evaporation.

Much work has been done on how and when to water vegetables. Occasional good waterings can in many instances accomplish very nearly as much as frequent light waterings. This is most true of leafy vegetables such as spinach and cabbage, and has been demonstrated experimentally with summer cabbage. Yields were increased 100 per cent by watering eleven times between planting and harvesting; but by watering only twice, yields

Vegetables which give maximum response when watered at their moisture-sensitive stages

Crop	When to apply	How much	Comments
Peas and beans	At the start of flowering and throughout the pod-forming and picking period	18 litres/m² (4 galls/sq yd) per week depending on rainfall and weather	Improves pod set and quality (syringing runner beans doesn't in fact help setting)
Potatoes – early	For earliest crops water when potatoes size of marbles' (ie when plants flowering)	18 litres/m² (4 galls/sq yd)	Response depends on variety
– maincrop	For most varieties water at 'marble' stage and thereafter to increase yields	18 litres/m² (4 galls/sq yd)	Response depends on variety
Sweetcorn	At tasselling and cob-forming stages	18 litres/m² (4 galls/sq yd) on each occasion	Improves size and quality
Tomatoes	After transplanting to get plants established and at flowering and fruiting stages	9 litres/m² (2 galls/sq yd) twice a week or more	Very frequent watering increases yield, but reduces flavour. (Tomatoes restricted in growing bags and pots require more frequent watering)

were still increased by 80 per cent, and even a single watering, two weeks before harvest, gave increased yields of as much as 65 per cent.

This illustrates the point that many plants have critical periods in their development when shortage of water is particularly damaging, and the application of water particularly beneficial. Watering at these so-called 'moisture-sensitive' periods gives the highest returns.

The level of response depends on the type of vegetable. For example, most leafy vegetables (lettuce, celery, spinach, cauliflower, kale, calabrese) respond like the summer cabbage in the experiments quoted. With these vegetables the highest yields are obtained by frequent watering, which encourages the growth of leaves and shoots. They would benefit from 9–14 litres/m² (2–3 galls/sq yd) each week. Failing this, the best method is a single heavy watering, say 18 litres/m² (4 galls/sq yd), given ten to twenty days before the vegetable is ready for cutting. That is their critical period.

With vegetables grown for their fruits – for example tomatoes, marrows, cucumbers, sweetcorn, peas and beans (all 'fruits' in the botanical sense) – the critical period is when the fruits are setting and swelling. Generous watering at this stage pays dividends. With peas and beans, watering when the plants start to flower, at the rate of 4.5–9 litres/m² (1–2 galls/sq yd), results in

much higher yields. The underlying reason is that once plants start to flower and fruit their energies are concentrated on flowering and fruiting, and root growth is restricted as a result. So unless there is water within reach of the roots, the plant will suffer. The roots will not grow out in search of water as they do when the plant is younger.

With root crops, watering tends to encourage the growth of lush foliage at the expense of the roots, so it should be aimed at maintaining steady growth by preventing the soil from drying out. Potatoes are an exception, virtually always responding to watering, which can be timed to promote earlier cropping or higher yields. It must be pointed out, however, that different varieties of potato respond differently.

Moisture-sensitive periods apart, all vegetables are particularly vulnerable to water shortage when being sown and transplanted. So make sure they are not neglected at this stage. If sowing in dry conditions, water the seedbed several days in advance, or water the drills before sowing. If conditions are dry when transplanting – always a traumatic time for a plant – you can save water by watering just a small area, about 15cm (6in) in diameter, around the plant. This is one case where small daily waterings, no more than 0.1 litre (¼pt) each time, is the best policy until the plant shows signs of recovery. The roots, inevitably damaged by transplanting, can't cope with more.

Finally, a tip on emergency watering for individual vegetables, or plants in pots or growing bags, when you are away on holiday. Make wicks about 1cm ($\frac{1}{2}$in) thick with wool, soft string, or glass-fibre lagging. Place one end near the plant's roots or on the pot or bag, and dangle the other in a bucket of water. Water will seep along the wick to the plant. The same technique, using a mug instead of a bucket, can be used to keep mustard and cress moist on a window-sill.

SHELTER AND PROSPER

While it is obvious that vegetables need water, the necessity for shelter is far less obvious. Yet research has shown that if vegetables such as brassicas, carrots, tomatoes, lettuces, runner beans and radishes, among others, are sheltered from even light summer breezes yields will be between 20 and 30 per cent higher. These are higher increases than are usually obtained with irrigation or extra fertilizers.

Winds are both directly and indirectly detrimental to plant growth. The adverse effects of strong winds are obvious, buffeting plants like Brussels sprouts and other brassicas so that their root systems are loosened, tearing the foliage of climbing and dwarf French beans, impairing the quality of salad plants. Salt-laden coastal winds, extremely cold winds, and occasionally very warm winds are also harmful.

Even gentle winds have a desiccating effect, both on plants, so increasing transpiration, and on the soil, increasing evaporation. With spring-sown seedbeds a combination of low temperatures and high winds drying out the surface can result in very poor germination. In some parts of the country, soil 'blow' is a problem which can be alleviated by shelter.

Where sheltered conditions are created soil warms up faster, and many vegetables mature appreciably earlier if sheltered. Shelter also gives some protection against hail and driving rain, both of which destroy seedlings and even vegetables in more mature stages. Perhaps most important of all, pollinating and other beneficial insects are encouraged.

The purpose of any windbreak is simply to reduce the speed of the wind. The choice lies between living and artificial materials – trees, hedges, and tall wind-resistant plants on the one hand, and fences and netting on the other. Whatever is chosen it should be about 50 per cent permeable, so that the wind is filtered through it: otherwise damaging turbulence is created. It should also be as extensive as possible, for wind has a knack of nipping around the end of short barriers and attacking with still greater intensity.

As living windbreaks compete for nutrients, water and light, artificial windbreaks are more practical in the average smallish vegetable garden. Lath-and-wattle fences, bamboo-cane screens, hessian and coir netting (hop lewing), and the many plastic-net windbreak materials can all be used. A windbreak 150–180cm (5–6ft) high around the perimeter of the garden is invaluable. Alternatively, strips of netting or even hessian sacking, anything from 30–90cm (1–3ft) high depending on

Above: watering can continue in your absence by conveying water from bucket to pots along improvised wicks.

Left: A clay flower pot buried near a tomato plant makes an economical watering system.

the crop, can be strung between rows, or beds, of vegetables. Windbreak netting is usually battened to posts, but make sure it is put up securely, reinforcing corner posts if necessary. They take tremendous strain when a strong wind is blowing, the nets billowing like sails.

Living windbreaks that *are* justified in a vegetable garden are vegetable themselves: Jerusalem artichokes and sweetcorn are the two most appropriate. Jerusalem artichokes are among the most rugged of vegetables, and planted 30cm (1ft) apart in a band three rows deep, they filter the wind very effectively. They can grow over 240cm (8ft) high, but it is advisable to trim them back to 150–180cm (5–6ft) in late summer. This makes them more stable and encourages the tubers to swell.

Although less hardy, a belt of sweetcorn can similarly give useful protection to some of the more tender summer vegetables and herbs – dwarf French beans, tomatoes, green peppers, cucumbers, basil and so on. And although not generally regarded as a vegetable in spite of its edible seeds, sunflowers make a magnificently picturesque and functional frame to any vegetable patch.

J L

Grow a living windbreak of the tough and tall Jerusalem artichoke to protect more tender vegetables from cold winds. Once established, tubers left in the ground will sprout each year to renew the screen.

THE NEW BREEDS

While some of the more extravagant claims made for new and novel varieties of vegetables should be treated with suspicion, gardeners should overcome their natural conservatism, and take advantage of any useful spin-off from modern plant breeding. The disadvantage is that flavour, sadly, is low on the plant breeder's list of priorities. However, amateurs and commercial growers alike do benefit from high yields, tolerance to extreme weather conditions, resistance to disease, vigour, and ability to stand in the ground without deterioration – qualities which many good modern varieties undoubtedly have to offer.

Here we pick out a few of the outstanding introductions in recent years. But first a cautionary note. Never expect too much from any one variety, however praised. There are many variables in vegetable growing – geographical location, the season, the soil and seed quality being some of the most important, and no variety ever performs the same everywhere, every season. Before pronouncing a final judgement on a new variety it is worth trying it out for several seasons under your own conditions, ideally in comparison with an old favourite. This will enable you to decide if it really justifies the sometimes considerable extra price. Many of the new varieties are, after all, F1 hybrids, which are expensive.

From the many new vegetable varieties available, those selected below for 'special mention' are chosen in each case because I feel they represent a significant breakthrough of real value to the amateur gardener.

CABBAGE

In the last five or six years a host of new cabbage varieties have been launched on the commercial horticultural market, several of which are excellent in the garden. One of the very best is the F1 hybrid 'Minicole', a round-headed summer cabbage which can also be stored for winter. 'Minicole' was bred in Holland, and basically is the 'Dutch white' type of cabbage, ideally suited for shredding as cole slaw, but equally good cooked.

A very compact cabbage, one of the great attributes of 'Minicole' is its ability to stand in the ground for several months without deteriorating. Heads that mature in August can still be of prime quality in November. Its second highly commendable quality is that if cut in half, the remaining head 'browns' far less than most cabbage varieties – especially if kept, wrapped, in a fridge.

The earliest sowings can be made indoors in March, transplanting in May for a July harvest. This can be followed by sowing outdoors in early May, transplanting in mid-June for an August to September harvest. Also worth a try is a September sowing in which the seedlings overwinter in a cold frame for planting out in April. This may not succeed in a bad winter, but any plants which do come through will be ready very early the following summer.

'Minicole' will not stand very severe frost, so if lifting for storage (*see* 'Harvesting and Storing'), lift it before it has been affected by frost.

The same breeders have produced an excellent spring and summer cabbage, 'Hispi F1', which has already won a well-deserved place in many English gardens. A solid but pointed cabbage with a crisp

Compact 'Minicole' cabbage, a sturdy F1 hybrid.

sweet flavour, it is one of the fastest growing varieties, crops heavily, and is very adaptable in its use.

The earliest crops are obtained by sowing in a frame or cold greenhouse in September or October, planting out early in spring. It can also be sown under glass in February for a slightly later crop, followed by outdoor sowings in spring and summer, to crop between June and September.

I have found that both 'Minicole' and 'Hispi' respond well to 'cut-and-come-again' treatment (*see* 'Space Saving'), giving substantial secondary heads in late summer.

Red cabbage is one of the most undervalued of vegetables. It seems almost criminal to pickle it, when it is superb cooked with apples, onions, vinegar and brown sugar, and wonderful in summer and winter salads. To maintain continuity I always sow twice: in spring, for the main summer crop, storing any which are surplus in autumn; and again in autumn, overwintering seedlings in a cold frame and planting out in spring to get the earliest crop of the year. Not all the seedlings survive winter, but it is always worth a try. The variety 'Ruby Ball', an F1 from the United States, has an enviable reputation. It was awarded the prized All America Gold Medal, matures early, is very compact with little wasted leaf, and is said to be very sweet-flavoured.

CALABRESE

Calabrese, the green-sprouting broccoli, is one of the fastest growing brassicas, with a superb flavour, and ideal for freezing. Like cauliflower, to which it is closely related, it is not the easiest vegetable to grow, disliking setbacks such as water shortage, sudden temperature changes, even transplanting. For this reason it is best sown *in situ*, or raised in small individual pots for planting out. Sow it between April and July, space it 15cm (6in) apart in rows 30cm (12in) apart to get the highest yields, cut the main head first, and wait a few weeks before a secondary crop of sideshoots is ready for picking.

'Green Comet F1' is one of the best of the 'mainstream' calabrese. Also recommended is 'Romanesco', a large-headed, superbly flavoured variety which has only recently appeared, and for which May sowings are advised.

CUCUMBERS

With cucumbers, plant breeders have solved three problems. Cucumbers bear male and female flowers separately, and it has always been necessary, when growing the traditional long, smooth, greenhouse or frame cucumbers, to remove all the male flowers. Otherwise they were pollinated, resulting in bitter misshapen fruits.

The plant breeders, however, have now produced a number of 'all female' varieties, with no, or very few, male flowers. Apart from this tremendous advantage – no more flowers to pick off by hand – these new cucumbers often have good resistance to common cucumber diseases, come into bearing earlier than the older varieties, and fruit on the main stems as well as on the laterals so that far less training is necessary.

One of the most highly rated, among many useful all-female varieties, is 'Pepinex 69 Fl'. It is suitable for both heated and unheated greenhouses.

The other longstanding drawback to cucumbers has been that the long smooth type could only be grown under cover in greenhouses or frames. Outdoors one had to be satisfied with the hardier, gherkin-like 'ridge' cucumber – short, prickly, and rather coarse. But the Japanese have developed some remarkable long-fruited ridge cucumbers, tolerant of low temperatures and poor conditions, with considerable disease resistance. Although by no means as smooth and elegant as frame cucumbers, they are certainly the best bet for outdoor cucumbers in this country. They should,

The thinking gardener's cucumber is one you can dispose of at one sitting – hence the recent introduction of 'mini-cucs' like these, the heavy-cropping F1 'Petita'.

incidentally, be grown up some kind of support to get the best results and clean fruit. 'Burpee' and 'Burpless Tasty Green' are two of the most popular Fl hybrid Japanese cucumbers; ordinary, that is open-pollinated, varieties include 'Kyoto', 'Ochai Long Day' and 'Chinese Long Green'.

Another problem is that for many people cucumbers were too long. The second half lost its freshness while you consumed the first. The solution is the recently introduced 'mini-cucs', which are fully mature when 15–20cm (6–8in) long. (They immediately fell foul of EEC legislation: if they were that short they couldn't be cucumbers!)

The two mini-cucs currently available are the F1 hybrids 'Petita' and 'Fembaby'. They should be grown under glass, are all female (though occasional male flowers appear in 'Petita'), have good disease resistance, and are heavy-cropping. 'Fembaby' is said to perform well in a 25cm (10in) flower pot on a sunny windowsill, but 'Petita' should be trained as high, or as far, as it will go. This is because its best fruits are borne on the main stem, rather than on the laterals.

Onions

Another crop in which the Japanese plant breeders have made a notable contribution is bulb onions, as opposed to green 'spring' onions. There has

Japanese 'Imai Yellow' – bulb onions that you can sow in August to harvest during the following June–July.

always been a gap, in June and July, in the supply of bulb onions from the garden. Onions and shallots stored over the winter rarely last beyond April or May, while the maincrop raised by sowing seed or planting sets in spring is normally not ready for use until August. Attempts are made to fill the gap by sowing fairly hardy, traditional English overwintering varieties in autumn – 'Ailsa Craig', 'Reliance' and 'Autumn Queen' for example – which mature a little earlier than spring-sown varieties. But it only works in fairly mild parts of the country and in reasonable winters. More often than not the onions bolt in spring, or are killed off by severe weather. These failings have been overcome in the new, hardy, Japanese overwintering onions, which after trials over a number of years have proved beyond question their reliability in this country. They mature in June and July.

The sowing time for the Japanese onions is fairly critical, as they should ideally be about 15–20cm (6–8in) high in October. If sown too early they become too large and may bolt in spring; sown too late they risk being too small at the onset of winter, and may not survive in very bad weather. The recommended sowing times are as follows: north of England – first week in August; Midlands and east of England – third week in August; south of England – fourth week in August.

Seed is best sown *in situ* (transplanting may lead to bolting), thinning to about 2.5cm (1in) apart in autumn, 5cm (2in) apart in spring. Give a top dressing of nitro chalk in spring (60–90g/2–3oz per m²). Harvest them like any other onions. But remember they are not 'keepers', and can only be stored for two to three months.

'Express Yellow F1', 'Imai Early Yellow', and 'Senshu Semi-Globe Yellow' are three good varieties.

Sugar Peas

Sugar peas are one of the best 're-introductions' of recent years. These are the edible podded peas, the 'peascoddes' of Chaucerian times, esteemed for their exquisite flavour in East and West. Many types were known in the past, and now the plant breeders have begun to work on them. Quite rightly. They are much easier to grow than garden peas, heavier yielding, quicker to prepare, and well flavoured. Most varieties must, however, be picked when the faint shape of the peas can be seen inside the pod – otherwise they 'go over' and the flavour is lost. The exception is the new American variety

Sugar peas, with edible pods, are a popular resurrection of the mediaeval 'peascoddes' that Chaucer knew.

'Sugar Snap', which can be eaten immature and also when the peas are fully swollen. I can recommend 'Tezieravenir', 'Sugar Snap', and the Chinese variety 'Snow Pea'.

SWEETCORN

Although one of the most rewarding vegetables to pick fresh from the garden, sweetcorn is pushed to its natural limits here, and cannot be grown in those parts of the British Isles with short, chilly summers. But this is a crop which the plant breeders are continually improving, producing hardier and more reliable varieties. The following fairly new F1 varieties are all good: 'Earliking', 'Hurst Honeydew', 'Kelvedon Glory', 'Kelvedon Sweetheart' and 'Royal Crest'.

The most exciting recent introductions, however, are a range of what are technically known as 'synergistic' types. These have more sugar in their cobs, and after picking last much longer than ordinary types of sweetcorn without losing their sweetness. Look out for 'Seneca Pathfinder' and 'Seneca Warrior', 'Early Extra Sweet' and 'Kelvedon Kandy Cob' – all F1 hybrids. Their sweetness is outstanding. Grow them some distance away from other varieties, as the sweet quality is lost if they are pollinated 'outside the family'. To assist their own pollination, grow them, like all sweetcorn, in a block formation, the plants spaced 30–38cm (12–15in) apart.   JL

ALL THINGS BRIGHT AND BEAUTIFUL

'It is most miserable taste, to seek to poke away the kitchen garden in order to get it out of sight. If well managed, nothing is more beautiful than the kitchen garden.' That was William Cobbett, writing in *The English Gardener* in 1845. His views are particularly relevant today, when the majority of gardens are so small that it is impossible to 'poke the kitchen garden out of sight'.

And indeed why should we? Many vegetables have an innate beauty of their own, and there is infinite scope both for integrating vegetables into flower gardens and for creating a vegetable garden which is both ornamental and utilitarian.

The classic example of a decorative kitchen garden is the reconstructed Renaissance garden at Château Villandry in the Loire valley, where an intricate and colourful tapestry is woven with vegetables. Villandry reflects the period in the sixteenth century when the kitchen gardens of the great still bore the stamp of monastic gardens, but were being adapted to embrace the exciting new introductions from the American continent – peppers, tomatoes, beans and gourds. These new vegetables were planted near the house to enable their owners to watch their progress, but, so as not to offend the eye, they were surrounded by flower beds, fountains, arbours and trellised fencework, and set in prettily and symmetrically designed beds, edged with low-clipped box hedging.

Villandry is a source of inspiration for any vegetable grower. But such dramatic effects are not easily transferred to ordinary gardens, where vegetables are grown primarily to eat rather than to look at. However, let's look at what can be done, especially by using some slightly less common vegetables and varieties.

A vegetable which deservedly commands the epithet 'handsome' is the cardoon. It is closely related to the globe artichoke and grown, albeit rarely, for the blanched young stems. Its greyish-blue leaves are striking early in the season, and the plant rapidly grows to an impressive height of one metre or more, before sending out its magnificent thistle heads, opening first into showy purple tufts,

Curiouser and curiouser ... the scarlet stems of the ruby chard and its purple foliage trap the passing eye.

Red-skinned onions with white flesh.

eventually turning to a mass of down. Single plants, grouped plants, even a boundary hedge of cardoons would be an impressive feature in any garden. The globe artichoke itself is less noble in dimensions, but nevertheless a plant of attractive colour and habit.

Several herbs in the umbelliferous family make magnificent single specimens. Angelica and the celery-flavoured lovage are exceptionally handsome, angelica reaching heights of 2.5m (8ft), with lovage not far behind. Sweet cicely gradually attains a height of about 1.5m (5ft), and with its slightly downy, fern-like leaves is another beautiful plant. So is the delicately coloured, delicately textured bronze form of ordinary fennel. Both make a lovely backdrop to a bed of flowers or vegetables, and all are useful for flavouring.

Red orach, on the borderline between herbs and vegetables, is another striking plant. It is little known here, but has brilliant red foliage and can grow up to 1.5m (5ft) high. The leaves – if not appropriated for floral decoration – are cooked like spinach. Although orach seeds itself readily, it is best to nip off any flowering shoots to encourage strong foliage.

Better known is asparagus, valuable both for its culinary qualities and the decorative nature of its fern and berries. Odd asparagus plants can be worked very effectively into flower borders, manuring the ground well before planting.

STRANGELY FAMILIAR

Now for the more decorative forms of ordinary vegetables. Runner beans were originally introduced into our gardens in the seventeenth century for their visual qualities (so, incidentally, were tomatoes). Because they climb so willingly, runners can become colourful screens and focal points in gardens, trained up strings, canes or poles, over fences, even up trees or the sides of houses. In these last two cases make sure there is plenty of moisture and rich soil at their roots. Most modern varieties are white-flowered, but for visual effect try the old-fashioned variety 'Painted Lady', which has red and white flowers, or the newer 'Sunset', with pale pink flowers, and 'Red Knight' with red flowers.

Marvellous value too are the purple-podded French beans, found in both climbing and dwarf forms. The pods are deep purple and the flowers and foliage often have a pretty purplish tinge, but quite apart from their looks they are well worth growing for their excellent flavour. Climbing forms are usually called simply 'Climbing Purple'. 'Royalty' and 'Royal Burgundy' are two named dwarf varieties. There's also a purple-podded pea, a tall-growing old variety, handsome in both bloom and pod.

A very recent development in the pea world is the leafless pea, bred for mechanical harvesting for the processing industry. The fragile-looking stems twine together to give an impression of green barbed wire, and with the dainty white flowers make a pretty patch in the garden. Their novelty value may be higher than their culinary worth, but try the variety 'Bikini' now available from Thompson & Morgan.

The asparagus pea is not, technically, a pea at all, but has curious triangular pods which are delicately flavoured if used young. It is a very pretty, neat plant, with attractive foliage and lovely scarlet-brown flowers. If used to line the front garden path, no one would suspect its promotion from the kitchen garden.

A lot of beauty lurks in the pumpkin and marrow family. Where you have a dismal piece of waste ground or an ugly corner, pumpkins and to a lesser extent marrows make splendid, if unorthodox, ground-cover plants. To make sure their roots are in a fertile piece of ground, prepare a special hole filled with well-mixed earth and manure, and then allow them to romp freely in any direction. The morning dew on the huge spreading leaves of a healthy pumpkin plant is an unforget-

Brilliant capsicums (peppers).

Bright yellow courgettes.

Ornamental cabbage.

Chinese chives and nasturtiums – two salad plants that also make decorative edging in the kitchen garden.

table sight, while the large yellow flowers (which can be made into fritters or soups) and ripening pumpkins can be spectacular.

The range of picturesque pumpkins and gourds available in Europe and in the USA is far greater than here, eg the huge ribbed and warted French pumpkins, and the beautiful double-decker Turk's Cap or Turban gourd, with its marvellous subtle combinations of white, yellow, pink and orange. They occasionally turn up in packets of mixed ornamental gourds, but they are not merely ornamental; they store well and make good pies. Several marrows, which are both decorative and useful, can be bought in Britain, for example the fluted yellow custard marrows, the white 'Patty Pan', the green scallopini squashes, and the golden courgettes. As these are all bush, rather than trailing in form, they can be adapted to smaller spaces.

There are several colourful types of tomatoes: the tiny yellow currant tomatoes, red cherry tomatoes, plum- and pear-shaped tomatoes, and yellow- and orange-fruited tomatoes. These last I have always found exceptionally well flavoured. Of the many types of sweet pepper, the pendulous yellow-fruited and the flat 'bonnet' or tomato-shaped are particularly decorative. Chances of success with peppers are enhanced if they are grown with some protection, but they are nothing like as difficult as people imagine. A novelty which looks promising is strawberry corn, an edible popcorn with strawberry-shaped cobs and mahogany-coloured seeds.

The ornamental cabbages and kales or bore-coles are among the finest of the decorative vegetables. Stunning effects can be created when they are used as bedding plants in flower borders, or in a kitchen garden. They are usually variegated in colour, mixtures of cream, green and pinks, the leaves often beautifully fringed and veined. The colours tend to deepen during the winter months. They *are* edible, but are not generally as tender as standard cabbages. Ordinary curly kale is also a pretty vegetable, especially the dwarfer varieties which are now available.

Japanese mustard, green 'Mizuna', is a vegetable I have taken to in a big way; it is very decorative, easily grown, hardy and useful both cooked (Chinese 'stir fried') or raw in salads. The leaves are deeply indented, and the plants can be kept neat using the cut-and-come-again technique, to which it responds magnificently, or allowed to grow to 30cm (1ft) in height. The small young leaves are particularly tender.

The leaf beets or chards include some wonder-fully decorative plants, for example Ruby chard, with its purple foliage and crimson stems, and ordinary seakale beet or Swiss chard, with its crisp white mid-ribs and brilliant glossy foliage. I hardly dare mention foreign varieties again (unless it serves to stir British seedsmen from a long period of dormancy), but travellers on the Continent should look out for the gorgeous pink-stemmed Italian chard ('Bieta a coste rosate') – a magnificent, robust vegetable.

Many of the salad vegetables described in 'Salad Bonanza' make very colourful patches in the garden, such as the red and green 'Salad Bowl' and oak-leaved lettuces. As only a few leaves are picked at a time, the overall 'pattern' is not spoilt when they are used. Other colourful salad plants are red chicories, curled endives, cress, claytonia, golden summer purslane and iceplant to name a few.

Then there are the red-skinned but white-fleshed onions – 'Mammoth Red', 'Brunswick Blood Red', 'Red Italian' and 'Get Set Red'. Most of these are suitable for both summer use and storage for winter.

When you grow vegetables in flower beds; remember that vegetables are more demanding than flowers, so work plenty of manure or compost into the ground, give them plenty of space and light, and keep them well-watered. It is easier to establish them if they are transplanted rather than sown direct, and it is best to grow them in clumps or patches, or where appropriate as single specimens, rather than in rows.   J L

Suppliers of decorative vegetables
Some of the plants and varieties mentioned appear in standard mail-order seed catalogues.
J. W. Boyce, Soham, Ely, Cambridge CB7 5ED
John Chambers, 15 Westleigh Road, Barton Seagrave, Kettering, Northants NN15 5AJ
Chiltern Seeds, Bortree Stile, Ulverston, Cumbria
Samuel Dobie & Sons, Upper Dee Mills, Llangollen, Clwyd LL20 8SD
M. Holtzhausen, 14 High Cross Street, St Austell, Cornwall
S. E. Marshall & Co. Ltd, 21 Regal Rd, Wisbech, Cambs PE13 2BR
W. Robinson & Sons, Sunnybank, Forton, near Preston, Lancs PR3 0BN
Suffolk Herbs, Sawyers Farm, Little Cornard, Sudbury, Suffolk
Suttons Seeds Ltd, Hele Road, Torquay TQ2 7QJ
Thompson & Morgan, London Road, Ipswich, Suffolk IP2 0BA
W. J. Unwin Ltd, Histon, Cambridge CB4 4LE

QUICK CROPS

Is it worth growing vegetables in a small or very small garden? For those vegetables which take up a lot of room for many months – Brussels sprouts and maincrop potatoes for example – the answer is probably no. But where you can grow something tastier, fresher and different from anything you can buy, the answer is probably yes. What is certain is that if only a small area is available for vegetable growing, it pays to adopt space-saving techniques.

In the typical English kitchen garden vegetables are grown in orderly, widely spaced rows. It has not always been so. In the old days vegetables were grown closely, evenly spaced, in compact beds the width of 'a man's stretch', about 150cm (5ft). Where necessary, weeding between the plants was done by hand, though when plants are grown close together they eventually form a canopy which stifles most weed growth.

With the advent of the horse-drawn hoe market gardeners adapted their planting systems to the new technology and changed to our modern, widely spaced rows. They were copied by kitchen gardeners, albeit using hand hoes instead of horses. But today the pendulum is swinging back. Now vegetables are being grown on a field scale on farms, where the tractor is the tool. So farmers are reverting to a bed system, this time with beds of a width that a tractor can straddle, and, once again, plants grown closely at equidistant spacing within the bed.

This highly productive, intensive form of cultivation deserves to be imitated by space-starved amateurs. For modern research has shown that with many vegetables – carrots, onions, runner beans for example – growing vegetables at equidistant spacing in narrow beds or patches produces higher returns from any unit area of ground.

One factor which determines the spacing is the size of vegetable required. Take onions as an example: they can be sown or thinned to 1cm ($\frac{1}{2}$in) apart to get pickling onions, 2.5cm (1in) apart for green salad onions, 4cm ($1\frac{1}{2}$in) apart for medium-sized cooking onions, 5–7cm (2–2$\frac{1}{2}$in) apart for large onions.

Many vegetables benefit from being grown fairly closely together in patches: closely spaced self-blanching celery, 20cm (8in) apart, becomes more blanched; sweetcorn, 30–35cm (12–15in)

apart, will be cross-pollinated better when planted in a block; tomatoes, 45cm (18in) apart, and onions will ripen earlier; while broad beans, dwarf French beans, both 22cm (9in) apart, and even peas, 10cm (4in) apart, provided they are not too tall a variety, will to some extent hold each other up, so requiring less supplementary support. In all these cases space is saved.

Cut and Come Again

Patches are also the ideal format for the various techniques bracketed under the general heading of 'cut and come again', which are so productive and useful for small gardens. Provided the soil is reasonably fertile and there is adequate moisture, many vegetables will re-sprout after being cut. At one extreme, seedlings can be cut off and will burst into growth again; at the other the hoary old stump of a cabbage which has been cut in spring or early summer will, if a shallow cross is made in the stump, produce in due course four or five more heads, crammed together on the old stump.

In the past, seedlings of cress, mustard, turnip, radish and lettuce, to name a few, were sown broadcast in the garden. The leaves were cut when only a few inches high (their most nutritious stage, incidentally) for use in salads. This is still done on

The cut-and-come-again technique is useful for brassicas and salad crops in small gardens. *Top*: Cut a shallow cross in the stump of a cabbage. From this will emerge (*inset and above*) a cluster of new heads.

the Continent with plants such as lettuce, chicory, Mediterranean rocket, even spinach, which is cut when 10 or 12cm (4 or 5in) high. Most of these re-sprout to give a second, sometimes even a third or fourth crop, from the original sowing. The sheer weight of leaf which can thus be obtained from a small area is astonishing.

Using this principle, a method of growing non-hearted 'leaf lettuce' has been developed recently by the National Vegetable Research Station (NVRS). They use certain varieties of lettuce ('Lobjoits Cos' and 'Paris White Cos' are two of the most suitable) and sow seed in drills about 12cm (5in) apart, aiming at twelve to fifteen seeds per 30cm (12in) run. This close spacing prevents the formation of a hearted lettuce; instead the plants form crisp, upright leaves. The leaf is cut about 2.5cm (1in) above ground level when 10–12cm (4–5in) high, the plant being left to re-sprout.

It normally takes about eighty days for a hearted lettuce to form, but a far heavier crop of leaf lettuce is ready for cutting within forty to sixty days (depending on the season), from a far smaller piece of ground. To keep a family supplied with leaf lettuce from May until October the NVRS blueprint recommends small sowings at weekly intervals during the first four weeks of April and May, and again in the first three weeks of August, cutting each crop twice.

Many plants, ranging from salad vegetables to some of the more unusual brassicas such as Chinese cabbage and Japanese mustard, and kale and turnips when grown for 'tops' in spring, respond well to the cut and come again treatment. Of the salads, broad-leaved endive, 'Sugar Loaf' chicory (which forms a tightly packed conical head of crisp leaf), the red Italian chicories, Florence fennel and some lettuce, especially the 'Salad Bowl' type, are the most suitable. The stumps left in the ground after the main head is cut will shortly throw up a second crop of smaller but useful leaf.

This is particularly valuable during the colder months of the year; indeed, a few plants trans-planted or sown in a cold greenhouse in late summer or autumn for cutting may continue growing in mild spells during the winter. These trimmed plants seem able to survive lower temperatures than they would if larger and leafier.

DOUBLE CROPPING

Where conventionally spaced rows are used, space can be saved by various forms of double cropping,

An original way of saving space by growing some Swiss chard between rows of strawberries.

Runner beans trained to climb above low-growing courgettes.

such as intersowing, intercropping, or undercropping. In most of these cases a quick-growing crop is combined with, or grown very close to, a slower-growing, space-consuming crop. The idea is that the former has matured and is harvested before the space is required by the latter.

One of the best candidates for intersowing is the slow-growing parsnip. Parsnip seed can be 'station sown' at stations about 15cm (6in) apart along the row, with pinches of radish seed, or dwarf lettuces such as 'Little Gem' or 'Tom Thumb', sown in between. Radish seed can be mixed with onion, parsley, parsnip or carrot seed and sown in the drill with them. Because it germinates so much faster, radish helps to mark the rows (making weeding easier early on), also providing a quick crop long before the main crop will be ready.

Brassicas such as cauliflowers and Brussels

No space wasted here: from bottom right, parsnip, Hamburg parsley, scorzonera, salsify, chicory, onion.

Space-starved gardeners can revert to the traditional method of growing vegetables in compact 'narrow beds'.

sprouts have plenty of empty space around them when first planted, and at this stage can be intersown, or interplanted, with, say, salad plants or, again, radishes. They are also good subjects for intercropping: for example, they can be planted out in early summer between established rows of peas, and although they will be overshadowed at first by the peas, these will be over and cleared within a few weeks, leaving plenty of space for the brassicas to develop. If they had had to remain in the seedbed until the peas were finished several growing weeks would have been lost.

Sweetcorn is the best crop for undercropping as the lower leaves dry off as the crop matures. This means that plenty of light can penetrate the ground beneath, so that trailing marrows and pumpkins, dwarf French beans, lettuce and many other plants can grow happily beneath.

With any form of double cropping, soil resources are being fully stretched; so the soil must be fertile. If rainfall is low, the crops may need extra watering so that both can develop fully.

Climbing Vegetables

Perhaps the most delightful way of saving space is to grow climbing vegetables. Runner beans, indeed, were orignally introduced into gardens for their decorative qualities, but equally striking are the purple- and yellow-podded forms of climbing French beans and purple-podded peas, all of which can be trained into 'vegetable hedges' or screens. Other climbers are the outdoor Japanese cucumbers, which will reach several feet, and trailing pumpkins and marrows which will clamber over fences, or cover unsightly corners. Only their roots need to be in good soil.

Although runner beans will climb up old tree trunks, artificial supports usually have to be erected for peas and beans, as they need to curl their tendrils around twigs, net, wire or string. When grown against solid walls or fences, supports can either be erected upright against the wall or, if necessary, at a 45-degree angle. Beans will also climb up the side of a house on strings attached to eyes set in rawlplugs. The only drawback with walls is that soil dries out at the base: so make sure that plants are kept well watered.

Where there are no convenient walls or boundary fences, freestanding wigwams for climbing vegetables can be made by tying together four or five 240cm (8ft) long bamboo canes. Tie them near the top, and anchor them firmly in the ground. They will soon be covered with vegetation, followed by flowers and beans or peas, making an eye-catching, functional and space-saving feature in the smallest garden.

J L

SALAD BONANZA

I suspect we have our Victorian forebears to blame for the dreadful British habit of cooking and cooking vegetables, so destroying both their flavour and nutritional value. But it does seem that we're at last beginning to throw off the Victorian yoke and to appreciate, once again, the subtle delights of using vegetables raw in salads. Not only does this mean that vitamins and flavour survive intact, but we save on cooking fuel, and also on garden space, for salad vegetables, above all others, lend themselves to intensive cultivation in small areas, especially when using cut-and-come-again and broadcasting techniques (*see* 'Space Saving').

Salads have waxed and waned in popularity in this country. They 'came in', literally, with the Romans, who, appreciating their health-giving and fuel-saving qualities, encouraged their use. Radish, beetroot, endive, chicory, lettuce and cucumber were all introduced by the Romans – but after the Romans withdrew we stopped cultivating them.

There is little evidence of the cultivation of any but the most basic vegetables until the fifteenth century, when monastic and domestic herb gardens, previously devoted to medicinal herbs, began to branch out and grow culinary herbs for flavouring soups and sauces. This gradually developed to include what were then known as 'salad herbs'. A list of 'herbes for a salad' in a fifteenth-century cookery book now in the British Museum shows us the sort of plants being grown for that purpose: cresses, dandelion, chickweed, parsley, rocket, chives, wild garlic, wild celery, primrose buds, violet, daisy and borage flowers ... and so on.

From these quiet beginnings developed what can only be called a salad bonanza. From the late sixteenth until the mid-nineteenth centuries, salads ruled. The host of superb gardening books written in those early years by famous men such as Parkinson, Worledge, the diarist Evelyn, Batty Langley and many others, all assumed that vegetables were mainly for salads.

An astonishing range of plants was used in salads, either cultivated in the garden or collected from the wild. And all parts of plants were used, not just the leaves, but buds, flowers, seedlings and roots – the latter admittedly cooked and allowed to cool. One list given by Parkinson, in his 1629 gardening classic *Paradisus in Sole Terrestis*, included the following: asparagus, lettuce, lamb's lettuce, purslane, colewort (cabbage, in this case using the boiled mid-ribs), endive, succory (the blue-flowered wild chicory), chervil, rampion roots, cresses, rocket (Mediterranean, not garden rocket), salad burnet, mustard, tansy, parsley, fennel, pot marigold flowers ('pickled against the winter'), pickled clove gilliflower (clove-scented pink) and wild goat's beard.

An equally impressive range of techniques was used to ensure an all-year supply of 'salading'. Crops were brought on by forcing on hotbeds of fermenting manure. Some were covered with calico-topped frames, later superseded by glass frames and bell jars, all skilfully used to extend the natural season of salad crops. Many vegetables were blanched to make them white and sweet. This was done in dark cellars, under pots, by burying them in sand, wrapping them in straw, or simply by tying the leaves together (*see* 'Forcing and Blanching').

In those pre-freezer days, everything imaginable was pickled for winter: cucumber, the fleshy leaves of purslane, onions, leeks, globe artichokes, turnips, beetroots, broom and elder buds, radish pods, flowers, and herbs such as tarragon and chervil – all to add spice to winter salads.

Sometimes 'simple salads' of one ingredient were made. More often, it seems, they were 'compound' – compounded of a variety of plants, the 'mild and inspid' carefully balanced with the 'sharp and biting'. Garnished with flowers, what a wonderful blend of flavour, texture and colour those old salads must have been. Strange that they died out.

They never completely died out on the European continent, where, even today, cultivated and wild plants, herbs, seedlings and flowers are used in salads. Some common continental salad plants, endives, chicories, coloured lettuce for example, are almost unknown here, although easily grown and in some cases exceptionally hardy. Also neglected is our own heritage of native and naturalized salad plants – corn salad, rocket, land cress, claytonia or winter purslane, to name a few. There's no reason why these, and other less common plants, should not be grown today to add new dimensions to modern salads – both in summer and winter.

Here are some ideas for salad plants:

Starting with summer, the 'Salad Bowl' type of lettuce, still widely grown in the USA, is well worth trying. These don't form true hearts, but their pretty, frilly leaves can be picked individually over a long period. One type is known as 'Oak-Leaved', the leaves having rounded, indented edges very similar to oak. Both the ordinary and the 'Oak-Leaved' Salad Bowl have green and red forms, the latter very striking.

Of the more familiar, hearted, summer lettuces, the crisphead and cos type are infinitely better value in a salad than the soft, rounded 'cabbage' lettuce. Queen of them all to my mind is the semi-cos 'Little Gem', a sweet, neat and crunchy variety. Recommended crisphead varieties are 'Great Lakes', 'Iceberg', 'Minetto', 'Webb's Wonderful' and 'Windermere'.

That ancient salad herb purslane (*Portulaca oleracea*) contributes taste and texture to salads. The succulent, rounded leaves are normally green, although there is a golden form. Purslane thrives in hot weather, preferring a well-drained, sunny position: it is miserable in cold conditions, so start it indoors in April or outdoors in May or June.

The strange-looking iceplant, with its succulent leaves, thrives in hot conditions. It tastes good in a salad.

The same treatment should be meted out to its cousin the iceplant (*Mesembryanthemum crystallinum*); this owes its name to the glands on its substantial, succulent leaves, which sparkle like dew drops in the sunshine. Previously grown as a spinach substitute (it flourishes in the hot conditions in which spinach tends to run to seed), it has a distinctive flavour and striking appearance in a salad.

Raw peas have always had their advocates, but equally good raw are the membrane-free pods of mangetout or sugar peas, which have an excellent sweet flavour and crunchy texture. Another overlooked salad ingredient is radish pods. Every summer brings its quota of radish sowings which run to seed. Don't uproot them: the pods, picked plump and green when they still snap clean in half, are delicious. Flavour ranges from mild to hot depending on variety. If supply exceeds demand, pickle the surplus for winter.

Alternative ingredients for your salads'

lettuce 'Ramcos'

Japanese mustard 'Miike Giant'

dandelion

angelica

Japanese mustard 'Hon Tsai Tsai' and 'Tendergreen'

red chicory 'Treviso' blanched

endive 'Cornet de Bordeaux'

pot marigold

sorrel

clayt

radish 'Robino'

chervil

rocket

Japanese mustard 'Mizuna'

radish 'Long Black Winter'

viola

ornamental cabbage

salad burnet

garden daisy

chicory 'Witloof'

American land cress

bronze fennel

lamb's lettuce

endive 'Golda'

Chinese cabbage 'Tip Top'

Italian wild chicory

red cabbage

cress seedlings

red chicory 'Treviso' (natural)

lettuce 'Marvel of Four Seasons'

k-leaved ttuce

rocket seedlings

chickweed

chicory 'Grumolo'

sprouting seeds: adzuki, mung, lentils

Chinese garlic chives

hairy bitter cress

This photograph was taken in April. All these plants had been over-wintered in the open or in an unheated greenhouse.

Borage flowers are sweet in spring – but to stay within the law you must use your own garden-grown plants.

Eating Flowers

As for flowers, there is a huge choice of edible flowers for salads. It is now illegal to dig up wild flowers, so if violets, cowslips or primroses are wanted they must be sown in the garden. Among my salad favourites are the sky blue flowers of anchusa and borage, the latter wonderfully sweet in spring; violas and pansies, brightly coloured but mild flavoured; elderflowers, in moderation, to add their own musty sweetness; and the double form of the humble garden daisy, *Bellis perennis*.

Of very ancient use is pot marigold or calendula (*not* French and African marigold). The bright orange petals, reputed to have medicinal qualities, can be dried in gentle heat for winter. Another old-timer is nasturtium, adding both fiery looks and a fiery taste, for the flowers can be pepper-hot. The leaves can also be used: particularly recommended are the pretty, variegated leaves of the variety 'Alaska', smaller and less coarse than other nasturtiums, and the purplish leaves of 'Empress of India'.

Flowers are best sprinkled over the salad at the last minute, after it has been dressed with oil and vinegar, pulling the individual petals off any daisy-like flowers.

Winter Greenery

Let's turn to winter, when lettuces, the acknowledged backbone of summer salads, tend to succumb to diseases, and, if they survive, are insipid, heartless and tasteless (apart from the hardy, red-leaved varieties such as 'Marvel of Four Seasons'). Yet a surprising number of salad plants flourish in the cold damp months of winter. Endives are one example. Looking like rugged lettuce, they can be sown in July and August for use in autumn and early winter. When fully mature they produce large heads of slightly bitter leaf, but if the leaves are shredded, much of the bitterness is lost. Alternatively, the heads can be tied towards the top for about ten days to blanch the inner leaves. After cutting, leave the stump in the ground: secondary growth of tender leaf is usually produced. There are broad-leaved and curled endives, the former bulkier, the latter decorative.

Sugar Loaf chicory looks not unlike broad-leaved endive, though the densely packed inner leaves in the conical heads are naturally blanched by the outer leaves. It is sown and grown in much the same way as endive, and like endive it will not stand very severe frost, but responds well to cut-and-come-again treatment. It is one of the most accommodating seedling crops, giving very quick returns from autumn or spring sowings. The seedling leaves can be cut from about 6cm (2in) high. In Italy, they are considered a spring delicacy, served simply with chopped hard-boiled egg. A spring-sown patch may produce salad leaf continually until the following winter, but for a well-hearted crop, July-August sowings give the best result. Another intriguing green Italian chicory is 'Grumolo'. Sown broadcast in mid to late summer, it produces dandelion-like leaves at first, but very early in spring a beautiful rosette of small, green, rounded leaves. And it tolerates the worst soil conditions imaginable. Leave a few to run to seed and use the blue flowers fresh or pickled in salad.

Also from Italy are the large and varied family of red chicories, almost unknown in this country. They are green and upright in summer, but assume a wonderful range of red and variegated colours at the onset of colder weather. At the same time, the leaves of most varieties start to curl inwards, perhaps a protective mechanism against frost, eventually forming dense compact heads of beautifully coloured, crisp leaf. Varieties differ in their tolerance of frost. 'Red Verona' and 'Treviso' (which doesn't form a heart) are among those suitable for English winters. They die back at that time, but both varieties can be lifted and forced like Witloof chicory (see 'Forcing and Blanching') to give a continuous supply. And then in spring they shoot into growth again naturally.

An invaluable quartet for winter salads are corn salad or lamb's lettuce (*Valerianella locusta*), American land cress (*Barbarea praecox*), Mediterranean rocket (*Eruca sativa*) and winter purslane (*Claytonia perfoliata*). Corn salad is mildflavoured; land cress almost indistinguishable in flavour from watercress; rocket has a gorgeous spiciness, and claytonia, another succulent plant, a cool blandness.

All of these can be sown in July, or at the latest August, a time when there is often spare ground. They will stand several degrees of frost, but the quality of the leaf is improved, growth more vigorous, and the chances of survival enhanced if they are protected – at least by bracken, but preferably with cloches, low plastic tunnels or by being grown in a cold greenhouse. They are useful in autumn, winter and spring, when they are among the first to start back into growth, before running to seed in early summer. If a few seedling plants are left they will produce ample seedlings for planting out in late summer.

Several root vegetables are useful in winter salads. Celeriac has a distinct celery flavour, and is lovely cooked or grated raw into a salad. It needs a long growing season, so should be started indoors in February or March. Wonderful value are the huge 'Chinese' winter radishes: 'China Rose' and 'Black Spanish'. Given optimum conditions some varieties may grow up to 60cm (2ft) long, weighing up to 18kg (40lb). But even at that size they remain tender, and can be sliced or grated into a salad. But they can be very hot. Leftovers can be boiled like turnips. Like so many winter salad plants, they can be sown in July or August, thinning to about 22cm (9in) apart. They can be left in the soil until required, protected with straw to make lifting easier.

And finally, there is Chinese cabbage, now firmly established in greengrocers and gardens. It is most useful for autumn and early winter salads, two excellent varieties being the Fl hybrids 'Tip Top' and 'Nagaoka', though there are many others. Sow them *in situ* in July and August, taking precautions against slugs, that are magnetized by them. This vegetable has the essential qualities of a good salad plant: crisp texture in the white mid-ribs and leaves, refreshing unique flavour, and, with lime-green, beautifully veined leaves, visual appeal. Unfortunately, mature heads will not stand heavy frost, but cut just above ground level and left to re-sprout, they seem to survive far lower temperatures, producing useful leaf in the winter months. It is certainly worth a try, especially in a cold greenhouse which would otherwise be idle in winter.

It's no cause for despair if your radish runs to seed. The young pods can be snapped off and eaten raw in spring and summer, or pickled for winter.

Recipe for pickling flowers
Lay down flowers in layers in a container, covering each layer with sugar. Pack down fairly firmly. Boil up enough cider or wine vinegar to cover. Allow to cool and then pour over the flowers. They are ready for use in four days.

Recipe for pickling radish pods
Make a brine by dissolving 60g (2oz) salt in 1 pint of water. Bring it to the boil. Drop the radish pods into the hot brine and leave them there to cool. Drain and pack into jars. Fill with plain or spiced white vinegar. Close the jars.

Seed sources for unusual salad plants
Italian salads, and many English 'salad herbs' from Suffolk Herbs, Sawyers Farm, Little Cornard, Sudbury, Suffolk. General salad plants, Chinese cabbage, iceplant from Chiltern Seeds, Bortree Stile, Ulverston, Cumbria LA12 7PB. Edible wild plants and edible weeds from John Chambers, 15 Westleigh Road, Barton Seagrave, Kettering, Northants.

THE TOMATO BOOM

Being natives of South America, tomatoes don't take too kindly to our short, cold and clouded summers. But ever since they were introduced into this country in the sixteenth century they have steadily risen in our esteem, and probably more British gardening man-hours have been devoted to overcoming the problems of growing tomatoes than to any other edible plant. It seems ironic now that they were originally grown for their decorative qualities and that the fruits were thought poisonous. The tomato does, after all, belong to the deadly nightshade family.

Most tomatoes are what are technically known as 'indeterminate' in growth. Given a suitable climate, they will go on growing almost *ad infinitum*, throwing out numerous vigorous side-shoots which in turn bear flowers and fruit and go on growing. However, a few varieties are naturally dwarf, ceasing to grow once they are 30–60cm (1–2ft) high and remaining a compact bush. On the whole these dwarf types crop earlier and are more suitable for outdoor cultivation. They are also convenient for growing under cloches.

The tall types make more economic use of valuable greenhouse space. They have to be supported, and this is easily done by tying them to or twisting them around wires or strings, fixed securely to run from the greenhouse roof to ground level. Alternatively, indoors or out, they can be tied to strong canes, or to horizontal wires stretched between posts.

The tomato plant's yearning to keep growing has to be curbed or its energies are expended on vegetative growth rather than fruit. So side-shoots have to be nipped out (side-shooting) and eventually the growing point has to be cut off a couple of leaves above a flowering truss (stopping). Outdoor plants are usually stopped at the end of July or early August, allowing about three trusses to fruit in northern districts, and four or five in the south. Under glass, plants can be stopped later to leave six, seven or more fruiting trusses. One advantage of bush tomatoes is that they require no, or very little, side-shooting, stopping or staking.

Growing Under Glass

Tomatoes are the most popular summer crop for unheated greenhouses. Heavier and earlier crops can be obtained where greenhouses are heated, but for most amateurs this is no longer an economic proposition.

There is one major drawback to growing tomatoes year after year in the same greenhouse: the soil becomes infected with tomato diseases and the crop deteriorates. After cropping for two or three years the soil usually has to be sterilized, changed or an alternative method of growing tomatoes adopted.

Nip out side-shoots to control leaf growth, and stop the growing-point when enough fruit trusses have formed.

For amateurs, sterilizing is not easy. Dasomet (Basomid) is one of the few effective chemicals available, but is not sold in small packs, though gardening societies can buy large commercial packs. Replacing the greenhouse soil with fresh garden soil is laborious and something of a gamble, as it too may be infected. In practice the answer is to grow indoor tomatoes in 22cm (9in) pots, boxes or growing bags, using sterilized soil-based John Innes Potting Compost No. 3, or a peat-based compost, such as Levingtons, buying fresh supplies annually. Cover the greenhouse soil with a sheet of black plastic to prevent pots being reinfected from the old greenhouse soil.

It is not difficult to raise your own plants from seed. Sow, in unheated greenhouses, from mid-March to early April, using John Innes Potting

The importance of staking: most forms need to be trained vertically; only a bush plant should sprawl.

Compost No. 1 or a seed compost, and prick out into small 7cm (2½in) pots, filled with JI No. 2 or a peat potting compost, when the seedlings have three leaves. For best results, sow in gentle heat, about 10–15°C (50–60°F). Move the plants to their growing positions in mid-late April.

Compared with outdoor tomatoes, the indoor types grow very rapidly, but they are 'softer' and more prone to disease. Ventilation, feeding, watering and side-shooting require constant attention.

In the Open

Outdoor tomatoes are always at the mercy of the weather. They can do very well in warm summers in the warmer parts of the country, but are always a poor risk in the North. Any protection they can be given with cloches, frames, or even with nylon windbreak netting, increases the chances of obtaining a useful crop.

If you are starting them from seed, sow indoors or under glass in early April; the method is the same as for unheated greenhouses.

Tomatoes can be planted directly in the ground, or grown in pots or growing bags which can, of course, be put anywhere. Give your plants the most sheltered and sunniest position available, the ideal spot being against a south-facing wall. Don't plant them in the same piece of ground year after year or soil diseases will build up as they do indoors: rotate them on a three-year cycle. Avoid growing them near potatoes as they are easily infected by potato blight.

The soil should be fertile, well-drained, and limed if acid. Prepare it beforehand by working in very well-rotted manure or compost. About ten days before planting, the soil should be watered if dry, and a general fertilizer can be worked in.

Tomato seedlings are not as fragile as you might imagine, and can stand fairly severe drops in the night temperature, provided the days are warm. It is best to grow them 'hard' with no coddling, ie giving them plenty of ventilation and space. They should be ready for planting out 6–8 weeks after sowing. Harden them off carefully, and where possible plant them under cloches or in frames initially. The best stage to plant outdoor tomatoes is when the first flower truss is just showing: the plant is then usually about 17–20cm (7–8in) high. Allow about 35cm (15in) between plants.

If you prefer to buy plants (the main snag is the limited choice of variety), select short stocky plants in individual pots rather than boxes.

Tall varieties need to be supported either with horizontal wires or cane stakes 120cm (4ft) high. In either case the main stem is tied (loosely enough to allow for expansion) to the support as it grows. Side-shoots must be removed as they appear, and eventually the plants 'stopped'.

Bush varieties need less attention, but as they tend to sprawl on the ground (although they can be supported with short canes), it is advisable to cover the surface with plastic sheeting. Straw can also be used, but it is apt to harbour slugs and disease in a wet year.

When planted in well-prepared soil, outdoor tomatoes require no further feeding. Once they are flowering properly, water at the rate of about 9 litres/m^2 (2 gallons/sq yard) per week. This increases the yield, though it may lead to some loss of flavour. Tomatoes in pots or bags require more frequent watering, and should be fed with a proprietary tomato fertilizer, according to the manufacturer's recommendations. In wet, humid summers it may be necessary to spray against potato blight in July or August, using a copper fungicide or Bordeaux Mixture.

The outdoor crop is normally ready in August. By the end of September further ripening in the open is unlikely unless the plants can be cloched. For this purpose tall plants can be cut down from their stakes (though not uprooted) and laid horizontally under the cloches. Alternatively pull up the plants by their roots and hang them indoors, or in a glasshouse, where the fruits will ripen slowly over the months.

The tomatoes listed below are rated as reliable croppers with a good flavour.

There is no hard and fast division between outdoor and indoor varieties: some varieties, however, tolerate outdoor conditions better, though most so-called 'outdoor' varieties can be grown successfully indoors.

For indoors or out: 'Ailsa Craig', 'Alicante', 'Gardeners' Delight' ('Sugar-plum'), 'Harbinger', 'Pixie Fl' (dwarf).

Outdoors only: 'Alfresco Fl' (dwarf), 'Sleaford Abundance Fl' (dwarf), 'Ronaclave Fl', 'Supermarmande' (semi-dwarf, with the tasty but ugly continental-type tomatoes).

Indoors only: If growing tomatoes indoors primarily for cooking, where flavour is less important, it is worth growing the modern Fl greenhouse varieties which crop heavily and have remarkable disease resistance though unremarkable flavour. 'Curabel', 'Shirley', 'Sonatine' and 'Ostona' are recommended. The variety 'Herald Fl' combines their cropping virtues with good flavour.   J L

GREEN ARISTOCRATS

Asparagus, artichokes, cardoons and melons have always had high status in the kitchen garden. This must stem from the delights they offer at table (in ancient Rome, artichokes were thought so delicious that they were forbidden to commoners), not from the skill needed to grow them. The first three crop well with but the slightest attention, and a few melon plants, given the right temperature and a bit of help can produce royally.

All four crops are most easily and cheaply produced from seed. Roots of named varieties of asparagus and artichokes can be bought saving (if all goes well) a year's wait for the first asparagus spears, and a year's fun selecting the best variants of the artichoke crop. In general, asparagus varieties are poorly defined anyway, and good cultivation is more important than varietal difference. There are a number of artichoke varieties (mostly grown on the Continent), but a packet of seed will cover much of the range. Chose those with fleshy scale bases, or tough scales but large 'fonds', or tender young buds, or fancy colours, as you feel inclined. Once you've some plants you like, it's an easy matter to increase them.

Melon varieties are legion. I can only suggest that you experiment. I grow four or five different types a year, and have found that some of the modern 'Ogen' melons are early and delicious, though each fruit is only just large enough for two people. Some of the old cantaloup types send one's taste buds reeling. One of the pleasantest ways of finding seed is to taste as many melons as possible when abroad. Generally, field-grown melons come true from seed, so save a few seeds of those you like most and try them under home conditions.

ARTICHOKES

Sow seeds in gentle warmth as early as you can. Plant out in May 120cm (4ft) apart (the intervening space can be cropped with anything ready by the end of July). The plants like a sunny position, and good rich soil. Take care that the young plants don't dry out. By the end of September (earlier in the south), they should be producing the first crop of flower buds. Remember to mark the plants that give the best eating.

Artichoke heads. Limit them to four-five per plant.

Other than an annual manuring, and regular hoeing (the arching leaves provide a perfect cover for weeds), the plants require little further attention. They're fairly pest-proof, though earwigs can badly damage leaves early in the season, and black aphids are a nuisance on flower heads in southern parts.

ASPARAGUS

A few plants, if only to provide asparagus sauce for a boiled chicken, deserve a place in every garden. Most of my plants are grown from seed, and seem entirely satisfactory. Seed germinates easily if fresh, and the seedlings are put into their final spacing (45cm/18in) in their second year. They can be lightly cropped in the third, and more seriously in the fourth. By that time, female plants are producing more seed, and so you can either expand the crop, or start digging up mature roots for forcing in the greenhouse. Otherwise, buy one-year-old roots, which are easier to establish than older roots, and plant carefully with the crowns 10cm (4in) below the surface.

Crops are almost pest-proof, apart from asparagus beetle. It's important to stop the seedlings being smothered by weeds, and to ensure that the mature plants are either carefully staked or strung, or planted in a very sheltered situation. Stems that blow over and snap won't do anything

The plants die down to the root in winter, and it's usually recommended that the dormant plants are given a protection of straw. In my garden, by the Firth of Forth, I never get round to doing this and have not yet had plants killed by cold. But if you prefer to play safe, pot up your plants and let them overwinter under frost-free glass.

The following spring, each root sends up a number of shoots. Four or five is the maximum number allowable to each plant. The rest should be removed when about 20cm (8in) high, cutting as close to the main root as possible (a trowel is a good implement for this). If the plant was an especially good one, the pieces removed – with a few roots attached – can be treated as cuttings, and will root easily. They are inclined to flop terribly at first, but you can forestall this by shortening the leaves by half when planting.

If you have an excess of spare shoots, they can be given away, cooked as a vegetable (good), or pickled (delicious). The second-year plants should be cropping by the end of June, the rooted side-shoots by August, and there should still be some for eating at the end of October.

Asparagus spear ready for picking. The feather-like leaves (some are visible behind) grow from the scales.

to build up the root for next year's crop. Give the plants an annual feed of manure.

Some of my plants are permanent inhabitants of the formal flower borders, and still yield some very good spears. It's often suggested that plants should be grown on raised beds. If your soil drains easily, don't bother to do that; if it doesn't drain, it might be worth trying. It's also usually recommended that the spears are cut off below soil level. However, don't worry if you miss the right moment; the tops can be cut from stems a yard high, and still taste fine.

CARDOONS

The same botanical species as the artichoke, the cardoon is valued for its fleshy mid-ribs to the leaves, not its fleshy flower buds. The plants are a good deal taller, leafier, and very elegant.

They are grown rather differently. Seedlings are planted out at 120cm (4ft) spacings. No flower shoots are produced in the first year, and in

Cardoon in flower (you eat the mid-ribs of the leaves).

September the bunches of leaves are tied into a sheaf (a tricky job this, needing plenty of spare hands and yards of tape or soft twine). The lower two-thirds of the sheaf is then earthed up, or loosely wrapped with black polythene. Blanching is complete in about six weeks, but the leaf bunches can be harvested throughout the winter or stored in a cellar or sand-box. A well-grown bunch provides plenty of eating (whether raw or cooked) and is good as a dinner-party plant. Incidentally, the mid-ribs can be eaten unblanched, but they are then stringier and less well flavoured.

Any plants not eaten can be left in the ground and allowed to flower, whether for decoration (spectacular), or seed (if the plant is in a warm place). Most plants then die, but a few produce side-shoots which can be treated as those of the artichoke – planted, cooked or pickled.

MELONS

Often a frustrating crop, needing heat, a rich diet, and plenty of attention. However, a perfectly ripened melon of one's own growing is quite a sensation, and makes the fuss entirely worthwhile. They need a minimum temperature of 18°C (65°F), and are happier in a few degrees more.

The seeds are best sown singly in small pots in gentle heat. Don't try cheating and put in several seeds. The young plants hate root disturbance, even if that only means pulling out adjacent surplus seedlings, and will refuse to grow. Try to keep the plants moving on until they are ready for placing out in frames, under cloches, or in the greenhouse. Two happy plants will easily fill a frame 2m × 2m (6ft × 6ft). In the greenhouse, they can be grown up strings. Mine are planted in open beds; I've never managed to get more than three fruit from a pot-grown plant. Growing bags might be better.

When flowering, the plants produce male flowers in abundance, but females more rarely, usually on short side branches. The females need identifying (the potential melon is clearly visible beneath the flower), and fertilizing by hand.

Best conditions for fertilization are dry sunny days. On damp days the anthers of the male flowers don't open. Pick a male flower, roll the base gently between the fingers to encourage more pollen out, then strip off the petals and sepals. Dab the anthers onto the central part of the female flower. The latter are only open for a day or two, so the plants need careful watching if a good crop is to ensue.

Ogen melons.

Grown up strings, or along the ground under cloches, the side-shoots are stopped (ie nipped off) after three leaves if they bear no fruit, or at three leaves beyond the fruit if they do. Grown on the flat in frames, the plants are stopped early on (after about four or five leaves) to encourage lots of new stems, then I let them do as they please. Weak stems and yellowing leaves are removed. As the frame plants follow on from forced strawberries, I get a single season of six to eight fruits from each plant. (That's not all that high: in the early nineteenth century, and using manure heating, it was common for a three-light frame to produce anything up to a hundred fruits a year.)

The fruit should be placed base-down on tiles, or preferably on straw, to discourage slugs and woodlice as well as to give a little extra warmth. They should also be turned every few days, so that they ripen evenly and don't bruise and rot. Red spider mites adore melon plants, as do white fly.

Regular inspection and spraying is essential. Disease resistance is claimed for a number of new varieties, but I've not yet found any that are absolutely proof against attack. In moist conditions downy mildew can be a problem; keep it at bay by ventilating the plants generously during any spells of sunshine.

When some good fruits have formed, don't press them to see if they're ripe. A melon approaching ripeness begins to give off the most glorious smell. It's strong and quite unmistakable. Once you've noticed the smell, leave the fruit for a day or two, either on the plant or in a sunny and secure place. Then call your nearest and dearest together for the treat. If, after a while, even perfect melons tire your palate, try stuffing them with alpine strawberries.

One note of caution: don't eat a melon you suspect might be 'over the top', for it can do dire things to your innards. ᴅꜱ

THE SPECIAL BUNCH

No kitchen garden is complete without herbs, and perhaps nothing reflects the culinary idiosyncracies of a household so closely as the herbs they cultivate. Besides the hard core of common herbs – parsley, mint, chives, thyme, sage and rosemary – every gardener has some special favourites. Here then, are brief notes on a few of my personal favourites among the slightly less common culinary herbs.

BASIL

This tender Mediterranean herb, with its unique clove-like flower, is rarely on sale fresh. Dried basil is a poor substitute for the real thing, so it is well worth growing your own. Common or sweet basil grows at least a foot high and has large leaves, while bush basil is dwarfed with narrow leaves, and is better grown in pots. There's also a pretty red-leaved form, 'Dark Opal'.

Basil loves warmth, and is best grown in a greenhouse or frame. Otherwise plant it in a sheltered sunny spot outdoors. Sow in March or April indoors, and plant outdoors after all risk of frost is past, about 12cm (5in) apart. Outdoor plants will be killed off in late summer by the first hint of frost. To extend the season, cut back a few plants (preferably of bush basil) in early September, pot them up and bring them indoors for fresh leaf until November or December.

Basil is marvellous in many summer dishes, especially with tomatoes. It is a vital ingredient of the famous French vegetable soup *pistou*.

CHERVIL

A pretty fern-like annual herb, chervil is normally about 20cm (8in) high, though it shoots up to 60cm (2ft) high when it runs to seed. It is relatively

hardy, remaining green all winter, so is especially useful in the winter months when many herbs have died down.

Sow from February to April *in situ* outdoors for summer use, and in August, outdoors or in a cold greenhouse or frame, for winter and spring use. It runs to seed rapidly in hot weather and in dry soil, so make several sowings for a continuous supply. Choose a slightly shaded position in summer, but a warm sheltered position for winter. Thin to about 10cm (4in) apart.

Chervil, with its delicate aniseed flavour, is good chopped in sauces, green mayonnaise, herb butter, salads, egg dishes, and generally as a parsley substitute. Chervil soup is excellent.

CORIANDER

Also known as Chinese parsley, coriander is a hardy annual resembling broad-leaved parsley in appearance, and growing up to about 45cm (18in)

Below and left: Herbs make an attractive garden in their own right but look equally well in pots or wherever a few plants can be fitted in – preferably close to the kitchen.

high. It is one of the commonest herbs in the world, but has been neglected in modern times in this country. The leaves have an unusual, musty, mild spiciness, and the seeds a flavour said to be reminiscent of oranges.

Sow in February (indoors) and March to June (outdoors) for the main summer crop. (The earlier sowing is necessary if it is being grown for seed.) Sow *in situ* outdoors, or in a frame, from August to September, to overwinter for early summer use. Thin to about 22cm (9in) apart. The fresh green leaf can be sprinkled on curries about ten minutes before serving. The seed is used as a pickling spice, and in many Arabic and Greek dishes.

DILL

This is a most attractive annual herb with feathery bluish foliage and bronzy yellow umbelliferous (parsley-like) seedheads, both of which are used in cooking. It is easily confused with fennel, but is smaller and daintier, growing up to 90cm (3ft) high.

Grow dill in well-drained, reasonably good soil in a sheltered position, keeping it watered in dry

Dill is smaller and daintier than fennel.

weather. Sow from April to June *in situ* outdoors, sprinkling the seed on the surface. Thin to about 10cm (4in) apart if growing it for the leaf, 22cm (9in) apart if seedheads are required. Keep it well weeded or it may be overrun. Plants left to seed in autumn tend to self-sow themselves, producing offspring the following year which seem to be more robust than the parents!

With its distinct aromatic flavour, dill is used with fish, or combined with yogurt or sour cream in soups and sauces, or used in open Scandinavian sandwiches. The sharper flavoured seedheads are essential for making dill pickles.

Lemon Balm (Melissa)

A spreading and tenacious perennial herb, lemon balm is not unlike dead nettle in appearance. It is ground-hugging early in the year (in fact is a useful ground-cover plant), growing to about 60cm (2ft) high when flowering, dying down completely in winter. Its leaves have a very pleasant lemon fragrance and flavour.

Extremely easy to grow, it is usually raised by dividing old plants and replanting pieces of root. It can also be raised from cuttings taken in spring or autumn, or by sowing seed in spring, for transplanting in autumn. Germination, however, can be very erratic, so be patient. Space the plants about 45cm (18in) apart.

The leaves are generally chopped and used alone or combined with other herbs in salads, soups, drinks, or for flavouring lemon ice cream. A single leaf makes a marvellously refreshing lemon-flavoured tea.

Lemon Verbena

A perennial shrubby plant growing up to 3m (10ft) high outdoors, lemon verbena is frequently grown successfully in tubs or large flower pots. It is slightly tender, but withstands low temperatures better if grown in well-drained soil.

Buy a plant, or raise it from soft- or hard-wood cuttings. Plant outside in well-drained, light soil in a sheltered south-facing position; it should be on poor soil or the growth will be too lush. Protect the roots in winter with a mulch of leafmould. The leaves die in winter, and there is often no sign of life until May. So don't write the plant off for dead after a severe winter: the odds are it will recover.

The dried and fresh leaf with its long-lasting lemon-lime scent and flavour makes a wonderful tea. It is also a valuable substitute for lemon and vanilla flavouring in desserts such as custards, infused in milk; it can be chopped into jellies and fruit salads, and is also used in savoury sauces.

Lovage

One of the most handsome of herbs, lovage has dark green, shiny, celery-like leaves borne on tall hollow stems and has a very strong celery flavour. A large plant growing up to 2½m (8ft), it has the flat seedheads characteristic of an umbellifer.

It is one of the first herbs to appear above ground in spring; the young shoots are a very beautiful bronze colour. In the past they were blanched for use as a spring vegetable. Although lovage prefers deep, moist, rich soil, it tolerates a very wide range of soil and conditions, doing well even in shade. It is usually propagated by dividing established plants in spring, making sure each piece of root has a shoot. It can also be raised from seed, preferably sowing fresh seed in August; otherwise sow in spring. A third method is to allow plants to seed naturally, transplanting self-sown seedlings. Planting is best done in spring, allowing 60–90cm (2–3ft) between plants. One plant would be sufficient for most households.

Pieces of stem can be candied like angelica. The seed can be used as a substitute for fennel and aniseed in cakes, bread, biscuits and desserts. Crushed leaves can be rubbed around a salad bowl to impart a celery flavour; chopped leaves can be added to a salad, but no more than half a teaspoonful. They can also be used in sauces and stews, but above all lovage is the herb to flavour soups, mellowing deliciously with cooking.

Marjoram

Natives of the Mediterranean, the many forms of marjoram have a long history of cultivation. Sweet or knotted marjoram is perennial in mild climates, but half-hardy here. It is a neat, bushy, soft-leaved little plant no more than a few inches high; the name comes from the knot-like clusters of buds which form on the stem in late summer. Wild marjoram or oregano is much hardier, truly perennial, with woodier stems. (Note: the name 'pot marjoram' is misleadingly used both for wild marjoram, and for the uncommon French marjoram, *Origanum onites*.) Wild marjoram is a spreading plant making pretty ground-hugging mounds from which tall flowering spikes are thrown up in summer. There are several very attractive forms – golden, variegated gold, and pink and white flowered. Some are compact, others sprawling.

Marjoram.

One of the hardiest of all the marjorams is winter marjoram, a tiny neat plant with bright green leaves, white flowers and a good flavour. It, too, is perennial and grown like wild marjoram.

The marjorams have a subtle pleasant flavour, not unlike that of thyme. Sweet marjoram is sweeter and very strong, but the flavour is destroyed by prolonged cooking; wild marjoram has a slightly bitter edge but is more durable in cooking. Both dry well for winter use; sweet marjoram freezes well.

Marjoram does best in light, well-drained soil in a sunny position. Sweet marjoram is raised from seed sown in spring. The seeds are tiny and not too robust, so are best sown indoors, keeping them in warm moist conditions until well established. Plant about 18cm (7in) apart. For winter use, pot up a few plants in late summer and bring them indoors, though established plants may retain plenty of leaf throughout the winter in favourable areas.

Wild marjoram can also be raised from seed, but is usually propagated by cuttings in spring and summer, or by dividing established plants in spring or autumn. Plant them about 30cm (1ft) apart. Trim back the straggly growths in autumn.

Marjoram is often used as a substitute for thyme or mixed with thyme. It can be chopped into salads, omelettes or stuffing, or used to flavour meat dishes, sausages, poultry, game and tomato dishes. Altogether a lovely and versatile herb.

Tarragon

Like basil, tarragon is a superb culinary herb. It's worth cultivating as it is difficult to buy and scarcely recognizable when dried. A bushy perennial plant 75–90cm (2½–3ft) high, tarragon dies down completely in winter. It is much hardier than it is reputed to be. There are two forms: French and Russian. Gourmets say the French is infinitely superior with a strong, unusual, and very individual flavour.

Tarragon needs a sunny position in well-drained but not particularly rich soil. (Like many herbs, the flavour is diminished by growing it in lush conditions.) Because French tarragon is nearly always sterile, seed is virtually unobtainable at present; so either buy plants, or divide old plants, planting shoots with pieces of root attached. Plant in spring, about 60cm (2ft) apart. Autumn plantings are very likely to fail. Traditional advice is to lift, divide and move the plants every three or four years to prevent the flavour deteriorating. Not everyone agrees. If your tarragon bushes are performing well they should probably be left undisturbed.

It is an essential element in French cooking and is used in salads, with vegetables, meat, fish, game, cheese, in soups, in many sauces, to make tarragon vinegar and even to make a liqueur.

Sages: purple is culinary; golden is decorative.

Preserving Herbs for Winter

There is nothing to touch fresh herbs, but as only a handful remain green in winter, it is worth preserving one's favourites, either by drying, or in the case of succulent herbs like parsley, chives and basil, by freezing. For drying, herbs should be picked in their prime, usually just before flowering. Pick them in the morning just after the dew has dried. Dry them slowly and gently out of the sunlight. This can be done in a *very* low oven, stirring them from time to time, or by hanging them in a kitchen, protected with a muslin cloth to keep them clean. When the leaves are brittle rub them off the stems, and store them in airtight jars.

Sprigs of herbs can be frozen fresh, or chopped into water in ice cube trays so that they freeze in the ice cube blocks. When required, the blocks are simply melted in a strainer, leaving the herbs ready for use.

A FEAST IN STORE

Summer surpluses and winter shortages – gluts and gaps. It's the tale of many a kitchen garden. One of the challenges of growing vegetables has always been to store enough of the summer produce to keep one going during the winter, though the advent of deep freezers has to some extent lessened the need for conventional storing.

Root vegetables have always been considered the mainstay of the winter kitchen, some being left in the ground until required, others lifted and stored in boxes or clamps.

Only the very hardiest can be left in the soil without deteriorating or being damaged by frost. Jerusalem artichokes, parsnips, Hamburg parsley, Chinese winter radishes, salsify, scorzonera and celeriac are prime examples. Parsnips, indeed, are said to improve in the soil, becoming sweeter. Where these roots are left in the ground, mark the ends of the rows with sticks so that they can be found even if it snows. It is also worth covering the rows with straw, bracken or dead leaves, to try and prevent the ground from being frozen solid. Otherwise it may prove impossible to lift the roots in severe weather.

Swedes, turnips and carrots tolerate a fair amount of frost, but tend to lay down cellulose in winter, becoming progressively woodier and less palatable. There is also the risk of damage by slugs, mice and even rabbits if they are left in the soil. So they are normally lifted and stored in boxes or clamps. In very light soil they are sometimes left in the ground, though the carrots would normally be covered with straw as protection against frost. But in most circumstances it is easier and pleasanter, in the depths of winter, to retrieve vegetables from boxes or clamps than to dig them out of muddy ground.

With potatoes there is no option: they are easily damaged by frost so must be lifted by late autumn, dried in the sun for a couple of hours, then stored in clamps outdoors, or under cover in hessian sacks or double-thickness paper sacks, tied at the neck. If kept in sheds or cellars they are best stood up against an inside wall. Give them extra protection with sacking or straw if severe frost threatens. The ideal temperature for storing potatoes is between 4–10°C (39–50°F); at lower temperatures they may become unpleasantly sweetened. They should always be kept in the dark, or the tubers become green with the formation of poisonous alkaloids. (Any green parts should be cut out before cooking.)

There are a few 'golden rules' of storage:

Discard any diseased or damaged vegetables, as they will rot quickly in store. If necessary store them separately and use them first.

Handle vegetables for storage *very* gently. Even invisible bruises and tiny surface scratches provide a foothold for storage rots and diseases. This is especially true of onions and garlic. They should be handled like peaches!

Carefully rub off surplus mud and remove rotting leaves. The foliage of root crops should be cut off an inch or so above the root. With beet it should be twisted off to minimize bleeding.

Store under cool conditions. With root crops (other than potatoes), onions, and cabbage the temperature should be as near zero as possible. In most cases the atmosphere should not be too dry or the vegetables will shrivel.

Inspect stored vegetables regularly and remove any which are rotting.

The simplest method of storing lifted roots is in some kind of a box, tub or bin, laying them down in layers separated by slightly moist sand, peat, coke or coal ashes, or even soil. The largest roots are put at the bottom, the smallest, because they dry out first, at the top. Cover the top layer when the box is full. If mice are likely to be a problem, set traps or put down poison: it is astonishing how they nose out stored roots in winter.

Cross-section of a Root Clamp

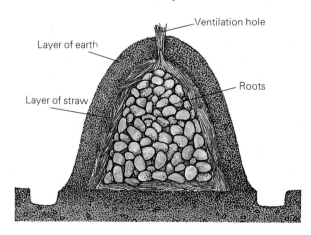

Ventilation hole

Layer of earth

Roots

Layer of straw

Above: Trimmed Witloof chicory is stored in peat until required for forcing.

Below: Store carrots in boxes of soil.

Storing vegetables in clamps may be rather old-fashioned, but it is an excellent way of conserving their flavour and quality. Choose a well-drained piece of ground, and start with a layer of straw about 20cm (8in) thick. Pile up the roots in a neat heap, covering the top layer with another 20cm (8in) of straw. Then leave them to sweat for a few days, before covering the whole heap with a 15cm (6in) layer of earth. This can be taken from the perimeter of the clamp, so making a dip around it which will serve for drainage. You can omit the soil layer for swedes, which are the hardiest of the vegetables normally lifted.

Stored onions, shallots and garlic need both low temperatures and plenty of ventilation. They are best hung in nets or old nylon stockings, or if there is enough leaf attached to the bulb, plaited into ropes. Otherwise, spread them out in trays, rejecting any thick-necked onions which never store well.

The key to successful storing lies in good

Garlic, roots and all, after harvesting. Store the bulbs in nets or bunches in a cool and well-ventilated place.

Chili peppers keep for several years on a plant hung
in a warm place.

harvesting. Onions, shallots and garlic should be
left in the soil until the foliage has died down
naturally (the practice of bending over the tops
does nothing to help the process; if anything it is
harmful). Then ease them gently out of the
ground, and leave them to dry in the sun for a week
or so, preferably raised off the ground on sacks or
upturned boxes. Try to dry them as fast and
thoroughly as possible, so that the skins are tanned
and crisp. However, if the weather is damp, bring
them inside after a few days, and complete the
drying under cover – in an airy kitchen, for
example.

Pumpkins are one of the most under-utilized of
winter vegetables, the basis for superb sweet and
savoury pies, soups, marmalade and pickles. But,
like onions, they will only store well if harvested
well. Leave them on the plants as long as possible,
that is, until the skins feel hard, or frost seems
likely (although pumpkins will stand light frost).
Then cut them off the plant with a piece of stem to
serve as a handle, and put them in a warm sunny

spot, a wall is ideal, for several days. This allows
them to colour up and harden further.

They can be stored on shelves or suspended in
nets in a cool, airy, frost-free shed, but cover them
up if very frosty conditions are expected. All the
winter gourds – Hubbard, acorn and butternut
squash, for example, can be harvested and stored
in the same way.

We don't usually think of peppers in terms of
storage, but although green peppers freeze well,
one of the simplest methods of storage is to uproot
the plants at the end of the season before they are
affected by frost, and to hang the whole plant in a
cool airy place, peppers attached. The peppers
keep in a reasonable condition for several months.

Hot cayenne peppers can be treated similarly,
but they can be hung in a kitchen. Even when
shrivelled by the warm atmosphere their hot
flavour is unimpaired; in fact they will keep up to
two years 'on the branch'.

Again, where peas and beans are grown for
drying, the plants can be left in the ground until
the end of the season so that the pods can, as far as
possible, mature and dry on the plant. When the
pods seem reasonably dry, or when damp au-
tumnal weather makes further drying seem
unlikely, uproot the plants and hang them
somewhere airy and dry until the pods are crisp
enough to snap open. Shell them, and store the
peas or beans in screw-top jars for winter.

Strangely enough, there is no tradition of
storing cabbage in this country. Instead, we rely
on our hardy Savoy cabbages, which can let us
down in very hard winters. Yet the less hardy red
cabbages, and the Dutch winter white cabbages
can be stored, and are a wonderful winter standby.

Cabbages destined for storage should be cut
before the outer leaves are affected by frost. Cut
the heads with several inches of stalk, which is
useful for handling, and also tends to rot first, so
prolonging the useful life of the head. They can be
stored in a cold frame, the cabbages just raised off
the ground on wooden slats. Cover the frame lights
with sacking or mats in cold weather, but open
them up for ventilation on warm days. Alternatively, they can be stored in cellars or sheds, on
racks, suspended in nets, or simply built up in
heaps. In all cases cover them with straw or
sacking in exceptionally cold weather. Inspect the
cabbages from time to time, and with the palm of
the hand, gently rub off any shrivelled outer
leaves.

J L

FRUIT

The ripe fruits of late summer – apples, pears, plums, peaches, grapes and blackberries.

FRUIT GLORIOUS FRUIT

Growing your own fruit brings its own rewards apart from the basic satisfaction of eating from your very own crop. One good reason is that there is such a limited range of varieties to buy in the shops: you certainly won't be able to purchase such delights as Ribston Pippin and Ashmead's Kernel apples or Royal Sovereign strawberries. Again, you may prefer fruit that has not been sprayed.

Don't be put off fruit growing because it seems complicated or because you have to wait such a long time for results. Neither assumption is necessarily true, so take up the challenge and have a go. Shop-bought fruit will never taste the same again.

Britain's fickle climate affects where and what fruit you can grow best. South-facing walls are a bonus for peaches.

WHAT TO GROW AND WHEN

As most fruit plants have a long life, it is important to spend some time planning what you are going to grow and where. Far better to discover your mistakes in the planning stage than ten years later when the tree that you planted to provide cocktail cherries for your parties is in fact a dessert variety that has never cropped.

What you choose to grow will be limited by your local climate, the space available and your type of soil, as well as your family's preferences.

Local climate is an important factor for commercial production but less so for the gardener whose livelihood does not depend on regular heavy crops. Nevertheless you will want your crops to be fairly reliable, so it is worth considering in what parts of the country most of the commercial crops are grown. Apples, plums and cherries do best south of a line from the Wash through to Shropshire, while pears are fairly reliable in the south-east, parts of East Anglia and the West Midlands. Cane fruit, such as raspberries and blackberries, grow well further north with raspberries especially famous in south-east Scotland. Currants, gooseberries and strawberries are quite happy in most areas of the country.

John Righall

Too little rain can result in poor plant growth, reduced fruit size and an increase in pests and diseases, but you can overcome this to a large extent by regular watering. On the other hand, too much rain can encourage soft growth, which increases the risk of diseases like apple scab and bacterial canker in stone fruits. These can be difficult to control.

Temperature affects the length of the growing season: overall lower temperatures in the north mean that the growing season is about fifty days shorter than in the south, so that the choice for northerners may be limited to soft fruit and the early ripening varieties of tree fruits. Altitude also affects the growing season: a garden 150m (500ft) above sea level, for example, will have a shorter growing season (by about forty-five days) than one at sea level.

Winter frosts, when the plants are dormant, are not usually damaging. But spring frosts are, so if these occur frequently in your garden settle for late-flowering crops such as raspberries and blackberries and later flowering varieties of tree fruits. Even so, you may still need to take precautions to avoid frost damage such as covering the plants at night (*see* 'Crop Regulation').

You *must* grow your fruit in a sunny part of the garden if you want large, well-coloured and tasty fruit. In the dull summer of 1980, for example, only strawberries from the sunniest sites tasted as good as they should.

Many fruits can be grown against walls, fences and trellises which not only saves space (*see* 'Space Saving'), but can improve the environment sufficiently to permit the growth of sensitive species such as peaches and nectarines; and also apples, pears and plums if you live in a cool and wet climate. South-facing walls in Britain are the warmest, and are best for peaches, nectarines, apricots, grapes, figs and pears. Soil at the base of south-facing walls, however, tends to dry out quickly so be prepared to water frequently. Similar crops can be grown against west-facing walls, which receive less sun, but are wetter. Cane and bush fruit also grow well in this position. Eastern aspects should only be used for the hardier species, while shaded northern walls are best avoided.

Apples in Kent – where they do best.

THE GROUND BENEATH

Gardeners can't choose their soil but have to make the best of what they've got, whether it's a rich dark loam in an established garden or a mixture of rubble, subsoil and builders' rubbish around a new house. If, on the face of it, your soil seems unsuitable, don't be disheartened; most fruit will grow on a wide range of soil types as long as they are suitably modified.

Once the site of the fruit garden has been cleared of rubble and rubbish, soil preparation can be started in earnest. Destroy weeds such as docks, nettles, couch and bindweed with an appropriate herbicide (*see* 'Pests and Diseases') or dig them out making sure no roots remain. Time and effort spent at this stage will make life much easier later.

Soil for fruit needs to be well drained as waterlogging causes root death and plant losses. Heavy clay soils that hold water most readily can be improved by incorporating bulky organic matter like manure, compost or peat. At the other extreme, very light sandy soils dry out readily and their water- and nutrient-holding capacity will also be improved by adding organic matter. Soil drainage can be hampered if an impervious barrier or 'pan' forms beneath the top layer of soil. These pans are caused if heavy construction machinery has compacted the soil or if a rotavator has been used when the soil is too wet. (If you are going to use a rotavator, only use it when the soil is dry enough.) The only way to break up a pan is by double digging, which is hard work – even harder if you are correcting somebody else's mistake.

Almost the final step before planting in a garden new to you is to test the pH of your soil. You can easily do this with a soil pH testing kit available from most garden shops. pH is a measure of the acidity/alkalinity of the soil: pH 0–7 is acid and 7–14 is alkaline. Most fruit crops grow best in a soil of pH 6.5, that is, just on the acid side of neutral. Those crops in the heather family, however, such as blueberries, require a pH of 4.0–5.5.

If your soil is too acid you can raise the pH by incorporating lime, usually in the form of ground limestone. As lime and fertilizers react against each other, lime is usually added in the autumn and fertilizers in the spring. Avoid over liming though, as it is much more difficult to reduce soil pH and very alkaline soils are unsuitable for most fruit crops. If you are on a chalky soil you can add sulphur to lower the pH but you will have to do this regularly because as soon as you stop, the soil will revert to being too alkaline.   P D

HOW TO BE CHOOSY

All gardeners want regular, reasonably heavy crops of fruit from varieties that are not too difficult to grow, but more than that you will want flavour, a quality that may well be disappearing with modern varieties and cultural techniques.

The chart of varieties includes some to suit most tastes, whether you prefer the aniseed flavour of the apple 'Ellison's Orange', the nuttiness of 'Egremont Russet' or the weak raspberry flavour of 'Worcester Pearmain'. Those varieties marked with three asterisks for flavour are the best, but each has its own individual qualities.

So how do you choose? You can be guided, of course, with a list such as this and by referring to fruit descriptions by experts. Ultimately though, it's best to taste the varieties yourself; seek out the expert at your local gardening society who may have some or, at least, know somebody who has.

In the list I have also attempted to indicate how easy a variety is to grow. A variety may be difficult for a number of reasons. It may be very susceptible to diseases, such as 'Cox's Orange Pippin' or the strawberry 'Royal Sovereign'. Or it

Apple 'Discovery'.

Apples

(T) triploid   (B) sometimes biennial

VARIETY	Ease of growing * difficult ** average *** easy	Growth * weak ** average *** vigorous	Crop * light ** average *** heavy	Season	Flavour * weak ** average *** rich
(dessert)					
Ashmead's Kernel	***	**	*	Dec–Mar	***
Cox's Orange Pippin	*	**	**	Oct–Dec	***
Discovery	**	**	**	Sept	**
Egremont Russet	***	**	***	Oct–Dec	***
Ellison's Orange	**	**	*** (B)	Sept–Oct	**–***
Greensleeves	***	*	***	Sept–Nov	*
Jonagold	***	**	**	Oct–Feb	***
Katja	**	**	***	Sept–Oct	*–**
Kidd's Orange Red	***	**	***	Nov–Feb	***
Laxton's Superb	**	***	*** (B)	Nov–Feb	**
Orleans Reinette	***	***	**	Dec–Feb	***
Ribston Pippin	** (T)	**	***	Nov–Jan	***
St Edmund's Pippin	***	*–**	***	Sept–Oct	***
Sunset	***	*	***	Nov–Dec	***
Worcester Pearmain	**	**	* initially then **	Sept–Oct	*–***
(culinary)					
Annie Elizabeth	***	***	***	Dec–June	***
Blenheim Orange	** (T)	***	** (B)	Nov–Jan	***
Bramley's Seedling	** (T)	***	** (B)	Nov–Mar	***
Golden Noble	**	**–***	***	Sept–Jan	***
Lane's Prince Albert	***	*	***	Jan–Mar	***

Pears

VARIETY	Ease of growing	Growth	Crop	Season	Flavour
(dessert)					
Beurre Superfin	***	**	**	Oct	***
Conference	***	**–***	***	Oct–Nov	**
Doyenné du Comice	*–**	***	*–**	Oct–Nov	***
Joséphine de Malines	***	*–**	***	Dec–Jan	***
Onward	**	***	**	Sept	**–***
Packham's Triumph	***	*	***	Nov–Dec	**–***
Williams' Bon Chrétien	**	**	***	Sept	**–***
(culinary)					
Catillac (stewing)	** (T)	***	*** (B)	Dec–Apr	***
Pitmaston Duchess (bottling)	**	***	**	Oct–Nov	***

Plums and gages

VARIETY	Ease of growing	Growth	Crop	Season	Flavour
(dessert)					
Cambridge Gage	**	***	*–**	Aug–Sept	***
Coe's Golden Drop	**	**	*	Sept	***
Early Transparent Gage	***	**	**	Aug	***
Jefferson	**	***	*–**	Aug–Sept	***
Kirke's	***	*–**	**	Aug–Sept	***
Victoria	***	**	***	Aug–Sept	**
(culinary)					
Czar	***	**	***	Aug	**
Early Rivers	**	**	***	July–Aug	**
Marjorie's Seedling	***	***	***	Sept–Oct	**
Shropshire Damson	***	*–**	**	Sept–Oct	***
Victoria	***	**	***	Aug–Sept	**

Cherries

VARIETY	Ease of growing * difficult ** average *** easy	Growth * weak ** average *** vigorous	Crop * light ** average *** heavy	Season	Flavour * weak ** average *** rich
(sweet)					
Bradbourne Black	**	***	**—***	July	**
Early Rivers	**	***	***	June	***
Merton Bigarreau	**	***	**—***	July	***
Merton Favourite	**	***	**	July	***
Merton Glory	**	***	***	July	**
Roundel	**	***	**	July	***
Stella	***	***	**—***	July	**
Van	**	***	***	July	**
(acid)					
Morello	***	**	***	Aug–Sept	**

Strawberries

Aromel	***	**	**	July–Oct	***
Cambridge Favourite	***	**	***	June–July	*—**
Cambridge Vigour	***	*	***	May–June	***
Domanil	***	***	***	July	**
Pantagruella	***	*	**	May–June	**
Redgauntlet	***	**	***	June–July	*—**
Royal Sovereign	*	**	**	June	***

Raspberries

Delight	*—**	***	***	July	**
Fallgold	***	***	**	Sept–Oct	**
Glen Cova	**	***	***	July	**
Heritage	***	**—*	***	Sept–Oct	*—**
Leo	**	*—**	***	July–Aug	**—***
Malling Admiral	**	***	***	July–Aug	**—***
Malling Jewel	***	*—**	***	July	**—***
Malling Orion	**	***	***	July	**—***

Blackberries

Bedford Giant	**	***	**	July–Aug	*—**
Himalaya Giant	**	***	***	Aug–Sept	**
Smoothstem	***	**	**—***	Aug–Sept	**

Blackcurrants

Baldwin	***	**	**	July	**
Ben Lomond	***	**	***	July–Aug	**
Jet	***	***	***	Aug	*—**

Redcurrants

Jonkheer van Tets	**	**—***	***	July	**
Laxton's No. 1	***	***	**	July	**
Red Lake	***	**—***	**	July–Aug	**

Gooseberries

Careless	**	**	***	June–July	**
Keepsake	**	**	**	June–July	***
Leveller	**	**	***	July	***
May Duke	**	**	**	May–June	**
Whitesmith	**	**	***	July	***

may be difficult from the pollination point of view, such as the triploid apples and pears marked on the list which cannot be used as pollinators for other varieties. Some varieties are also prone to attacks from birds, such as the cherries and early red apples, so although easy to grow need some extra effort to guarantee a crop.

The growth rating is obviously more important for tree fruits than soft fruits, and is a consideration if your space is limited. By using the ratings given here for each variety in conjunction with the table of calculating planting distances (*see* 'Planting'), you should be able to work out which varieties will fit in where in your garden.

Generally, all these varieties crop well and regularly. The only exceptions (those marked with one asterisk) are included because they have a notably fine flavour. Such varieties include the apple 'Ashmead's Kernel', a true connoisseur's variety; 'Doyenne du Comice' pear, nearly everyone's favourite but a fickle cropper; and 'Coe's Golden Drop' plum with its rich flavour rather like that of an apricot. Some varieties, like the apple 'Laxton's Superb', tend to crop heavily one year and very lightly the next. This biennial habit is indicated with a '(B)' in the lists.

Finally, the season when the variety is ready for eating is indicated. For soft fruits, plums and cherries this also coincides with the picking period but this is not so with mid-season and late varieties of apples and pears, which usually need a period of storage to mature to their best.

Above: Dessert pear 'Onward'.

Left: Culinary and dessert plum 'Victoria'.

Below: Strawberry 'Redgauntlet'.

Above: Redcurrant 'Red Lake'.

Above right: Gooseberry 'Careless'.

Right: Raspberry 'Malling Delight'.

NURSERY TACTICS

When buying fruit plants it is best to go to a specialist fruit nursery or a good garden centre. These will have a better range of varieties which most likely will be of good quality. Stock that is certified virus-free is available for most common varieties and you would do well to insist on it. When you check the quality of the tree, look particularly for a good number of wide-angled branches; with bush and cane fruit, look for healthy strong growth. Avoid plants with broken shoots, only a few roots, labels that have damaged the bark or those with pests or diseases.

Finally, check the variety (and rootstock for a tree) on the label and make sure it's exactly what you want *before* you buy. Because few fruit trees grow true from seed, they are cultivated in the nursery from two components. A compatible rootstock, which has been standardized and classified, forms the base, and onto it is grafted a cutting or scion of the fruit variety. Thus it is doubly important to buy the plant that is right for your garden. So if you have decided that 'Bramley Seedling' on M27 dwarfing rootstock is right for you don't be fobbed off with a tree labelled just 'Bramley Seedling', or 'Bramley Seedling on dwarfing rootstock'. There is a range of so-called dwarfing rootstocks, some a lot more vigorous than others.

Having bought your top-quality plant, don't just tie it to the roof rack with its roots bare to the drying wind. Make sure the roots are kept moist by putting the root system or the whole plant into a polythene bag for the journey. Containerized plants still in leaf need similar protection. (I once saw a couple pay well into double figures for a trained peach tree at a garden centre. They had difficulty getting it into the boot of the car and so broke off most of the branches and main stem. I sat among the gnomes nearby and wept.)

Whether you collect from a nursery or garden centre or order by mail, when the plants arrive at home remove the packaging and heel them in straight away. To do this, dig a hole in a sheltered part of the garden and place the root system in it, then cover it with soil to keep it moist. You can move the plant to its final position at your leisure when conditions are fully suitable.

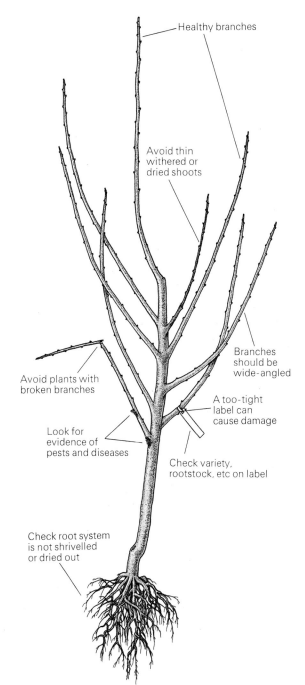

Healthy branches

Avoid thin withered or dried shoots

Branches should be wide-angled

Avoid plants with broken branches

A too-tight label can cause damage

Look for evidence of pests and diseases

Check variety, rootstock, etc on label

Check root system is not shrivelled or dried out

A Healthy Plant? Points to Check.

Distance apart of commonly grown fruit trees

Distances between plants depend on the vigour of the variety: plants of a non-vigorous variety should be spaced according to the smaller of the recommended figures

	APPLES		PEARS		PLUMS		CHERRIES	
	between plants	between rows	between plants	between rows	between plants	between rows	between plants	between rows
CENTRE LEADER BUSH	semi-dwarfing rootstock 4–6m / dwarfing rootstock 2–5m	4–6m / 3–6m	2–6m	4–6m	3–6m	4–6m	*Sweet* 5–8m *Sour* 4–6m	*Sweet* 5–8m *Sour* 4–6m
ESPALIER	4–6m	2m	3–6m	2m				
OBLIQUE CORDON	1m	2m	1m	2m				
FAN	4–6m		4–6m		4–6m		*Sweet* 5–8m *Sour* 4–6m	*Sour* 4–6m
STANDARD	6–10m	6–10m	6–10m	6–10m	6–8m	6–8m	*Sweet* 7–12m	

Spacing for soft fruit

	in the rows	between the rows
Strawberries	30–45cm	1m
Raspberries	45cm	2m
Blackberries and loganberries	3–5m	2m
Blackcurrants (bush)	1–2m	2m
Red and white currants	1–2m (bush) / 30–45cm (cordon)	2m (bush) / 1.5m (cordon)
Gooseberries	1–2m (bush) / 30–45cm (cordon)	1.5m (bush) / 1.5m (cordon)

SPACING AND SUPPORT

When it comes to choosing the right planting distance, particularly for fruit trees, many gardeners come sadly adrift. If you plant too far apart, you're wasting land; if you plant too close, which is more common, you are letting yourself in for a never-ending struggle to keep the plant within bounds.

To get your spacing right, you should take into account the vigour of the variety, the rootstock (if a tree), your soil type and the training system you propose to use.

Centre leader bush trees can be grown without support on the more vigorous rootstocks, particularly if the garden is sheltered from strong winds. Trees on the more dwarfing rootstocks, however, which tend to have poor root systems with brittle roots, need permanent support and should be tied to stakes. Stakes 2.5m (8ft) long are the most suitable for centre leader trees where the central stem can be tied to the post at several points. Open-centre bush trees are tied to 1.5m (5ft) stakes, usually at only one point. When planting, always use new stakes; treat them with a preservative or dip the base in creosote.

Raspberry 'Delight'.

PLANTING METHODS

Containerized material can be planted out at any time, but bare-rooted plants must be put in when dormant between late October and March. Strawberries, however, should be planted in August or September for cropping the following year, or spring planted and then deflowered to aid establishment. You will need to water any spring-planted material as the ground often dries out quickly and the north-easterly winds experienced at that time of year can desiccate plants very rapidly.

Having given a great deal of attention to planting correctly, it is most important to follow this up to give the plant a really good chance to establish itself. Any immediate pruning that is required should be done and the cut surfaces coated with a pruning paint. In the spring, apply a mulch around the plant, but away from the stem, to help conserve soil moisture as the ground dries out.

Mulching with manure or compost also adds nutrients. The plants should also be checked frequently for pests and diseases and to make sure they are adequately supported.

Finally, a thought should be given to the cropping history of your plot. Many fruit plants do not establish well if they are planted in ground previously occupied by similar crops. This rejection is caused by 'replant diseases' which particularly affect apples on dwarfing rootstocks. If you cannot avoid planting your trees in the same spot as old ones of a similar species, dig a hole 2m (6½ft) in diameter and refill it with either fresh soil from another part of the garden or a mixture of fresh soil and compost or peat (avoid using too much peat as it easily dries out, and you may lose your tree). In this way, the trees are given a good start and, once established and growing away well, will not be seriously affected when the roots eventually penetrate the surrounding 'infected' soil.

Strawberries also suffer from replant diseases and are best grown on fresh sites wherever possible.   P D

Some suppliers of good-quality fruit plants

Scott's Nurseries (Merriott) Ltd, Merriott, Somerset TA16 5PL

W. Seabrook & Sons Ltd, Boreham, Chelmsford, Essex CM3 3AE

Thomas Rivers & Sons Ltd, The Nurseries, Sawbridgeworth, Herts CM21 0HJ

Soft fruit specialist
Ken Muir, Honeypot Fruit Farm, Clacton-on-Sea, Essex CO16 9BJ

YOU AND THE BEES

Irregular cropping is one of the commonest problems with fruit trees. There are two main causes. Firstly, a lack of pollinators among species that require them, such as cherry, apple and pear; secondly, frosts damage the flowers so that fruit-set and development is impossible.

Fruit species that flower early in the year are going to be more prone to frost damage and therefore erratic in their cropping than later-flowering ones. So if you garden in an area troubled with regular spring frosts, you would be advised to concentrate on the later-flowering species, only growing the earlier-flowering ones if you can protect them.

Not only do different species flower at different times but varieties within a species vary too. For example, an apple variety like 'Ashmead's Kernel' flowers in most years about ten days later than 'Cox's' and is therefore more likely to miss spring frosts.

Having reduced the risk of frost damage by choosing your crops and varieties carefully, it is then important that you don't plant them in a frosty corner of the garden. As cold air sinks it tends to accumulate in the lowest part of the garden – a natural frostpocket – or in an area where its flow down a slope is impeded, say by a wall, solid fence or hedge. As far as possible, therefore, do not allow solid barriers to run *across* slopes.

A more direct form of protection is to cover the plants when frost is suspected. Unless you have a large spread of a sensitive crop, this technique is quite easy and fairly reliable. Many different materials are suitable, but I find several layers of plastic bird netting draped over the plants an easy and effective way of combating all but the severest

Encourage bees: without their help your crop will be poor. Don't use insecticides when bees are around.

of frosts. Remove the net during the day to allow insects to visit the flowers and pollinate them. Depending on your faith in local weather forecasts, you can either phone up each evening during the sensitive period to see what is in store that night or you can cover your plants every evening just in case.

Most fruits cannot develop from flowers without adequate pollination. All soft fruits are self-fertile, that is they will set fruit with their own pollen so that pollinator varieties are unnecessary. Tree fruits are different. Without pollinators, many won't set a crop at all, while others will only set a light one. Apples, pears and sweet cherries (except 'Stella') need pollinators; so do some plums, damsons and gages. Figs, peaches, nectarines, apricots, mulberries, quinces, medlars, cobnuts and filberts do not need pollinators.

Many species, however, even the self-fertile ones, will set heavier crops if additional pollinator varieties are provided, so if room allows, it's well worth it. When choosing pollinators, make sure that they flower at the same time as the main variety and produce pollen that is compatible to induce fruit setting. Some varieties are quite unsuitable as pollinators so it is essential to check your combinations of varieties before planting.

One of the pleasures of spring and early summer is to hear bees busily working the fruit flowers, especially when you know that without them you will get much lighter or poorer-quality crops. You don't need a hive of bees, but it is important to encourage the wild ones as much as possible and *not* spray with insecticides when they are around.

Crops that flower early in the year, or are grown under protection, will not be visited adequately by bees and other insects so you will have to transfer the pollen yourself. Wait for dry and warm conditions, and then transfer the pollen from the anthers to the stigmas with a small camel-hair brush. Although this process is rather time-consuming and tedious it is well worth it, as it certainly will increase your chances of getting a good crop.

With frost protection and good pollination, crops should be much more reliable and heavier, but with some species it is possible to set too heavy a crop. When this happens only a few flowers are produced the following year. Apple, pear, plum and peach varieties as well as gooseberries and grapes should have some fruitlets removed so that the plant is not 'overworked' and too many small fruits – as opposed to big ones – are produced.

With apples and pears, thin the fruitlets in mid-June to one or two per cluster, plums to a single fruit, and peaches and nectarines to a single fruit when they are not more than 3cm (1¼in) in diameter. Gooseberries can be thinned in late May or early June to every other fruit: use the thinnings for cooking while leaving the rest to swell up and ripen.

You can easily thin these crops with your fingers, but for dessert grapes you will need a pair of scissors with long thin blades as you have to remove fruitlets from within the bunch. This should be done when the fruits are swelling rapidly and while the fruit stalks are still accessible. Cut out those that are inside the bunch or are split or damaged.

P D

Blackcurrants, continually sprayed with water during frost, form a coating of ice to protect flowers from frost.

CUT BACK WITH CONFIDENCE

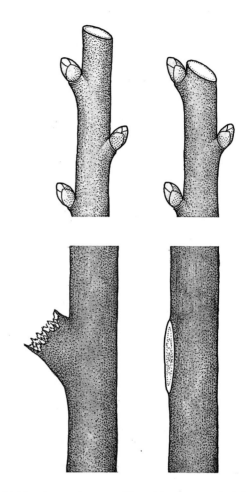

Pruning is one of the most important jobs for the fruit gardener, yet unless it is done correctly it can lead to all sorts of problems. I am often told that it seems quite straightforward when reading about it, but as soon as you are standing in front of a tree or bush, secateurs in hand, your confidence vanishes. As valuable as books are, with their rule of thumb guides to pruning, I am convinced that the subject becomes much more straightforward if you appreciate the principles first and understand how different plants respond, and only then put theory into practice.

So why prune fruit trees? Consider what happens if we don't. The tree will initially continue to grow happily, but as time goes on, it will set more and more fruit – very small and of poor quality – and produce less and less growth. In fact, it will lose the balance that must be maintained to produce quality fruit and healthy plants. On the other hand, if you overprune – easily done once you have started and got up steam – the balance swings the other way, and the tree produces too much vegetative growth and too little fruit. In practice it pays to prune lightly in the early years to encourage the plant to set fruit, pruning more heavily after it has carried several good crops.

Maintaining the balance is the main reason for pruning, but there are also other reasons: to allow light to get into the plant because shade results in poorer fruit the following year, and to provide good air circulation within the plant which helps prevent diseases. You will, even so, get some pest and disease problems so the more 'open' the plant, the easier the penetration of pesticide and fungicide sprays. As the plant develops, some branches may nevertheless become severely diseased; these should be removed along with those growing awkwardly in the wrong place.

But what actually happens when a branch is pruned? Obviously its length is reduced, but the harder it is pruned, that is, the further it is cut back, the more you will increase vegetative growth and the stiffness of the remaining branch. This applies particularly to winter pruning (when the buds are dormant). On the other hand, summer

Making the pruning cuts. *Above:* The shoot on the left is cut too far away from the bud. The other shoot, cut close is correct. *Below:* Avoid rough-cut stubs when pruning large branches – cut smooth with a knife.

Espalier apple tree in blossom.

Espalier Pruning and Training
Top left: After planting, cut back leader to just above bottom wire. Train laterals and new leader up canes as shown. *Top right*: In late autumn, lower laterals to the horizontal. Cut back weak laterals to three buds, the leader to just above the next wire, and tip the laterals to stimulate growth. *Above*: train next tier of laterals as before, and as growth stops prune back all new shoots to three leaves.

pruning, usually carried out when growth has almost stopped, does not encourage growth and is therefore used on intensive training systems such as espaliers and cordons.

These systems are very popular with gardeners, although they need attention, especially initially, and they can also be a little slow coming into cropping. Most trees are easier to manage if you encourage their natural growth habit, and for tree fruits this means a tree with a central stem rather like a Christmas tree. With most varieties of fruit, this tree habit is easy to maintain, especially if you bear in mind the fact that the more vertically a branch grows the more vigorously its grows, whereas a branch growing more or less horizontally will not be vigorous and will readily produce fruit buds.

As this sort of tree grows, fruit will be borne on the lower branches where it is easily reached while much of the shoot growth will be nearer the top of the tree. To maintain a balance of fruiting and shoot growth at the lower branches, the top of the tree should be used as the controlling mechanism, allowing it to grow away. This then reduces the vigour of the tree lower down. Alternatively, you can prune the central leader to a fruiting branch to induce vigour and maintain fruit size lower down.

If you find that you are short of space or prefer decorative shapes, apples and pears in particular can be grown as cordons or espaliers. Cordons can be grown against fences or walls, as well as in the open along wires, whereas espaliers are particularly effective against walls or along wires.

Plums and cherries can be grown as centre leader trees, as described for apples and pears, but with these and other stone fruits, such as peaches and nectarines, the most important point to remember is never to prune during winter as this will increase the risk of infection from bacterial canker and silver leaf diseases. Similarly, it is important that whatever training system is adopted, ties and so on must not damage the shoots leaving wounds through which disease can enter.

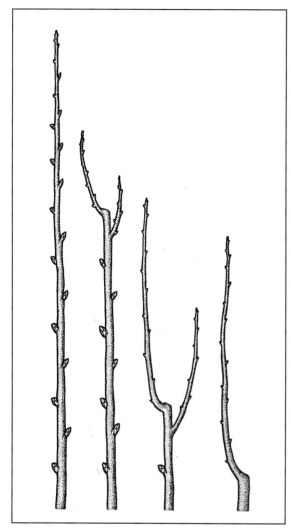

Where you cut affects the future growth of the shoot – and ultimately it affects what sort of fruit crop is produced.

Cordon-trained 'Discovery'.

Plums and cherries respond well to fan training, a system that is especially suitable for peaches and nectarines grown against the south face of a wall. You may prefer to buy trees trained as fans by the nurseryman or start from scratch yourself.

If you move house and find yourself saddled with sadly neglected trees, there are remedies. If the tree is producing lots of fruit bud and little shoot growth, the fruiting spurs should be thinned by pruning each to a few buds only and spacing the retained spurs 10cm (4in) or so apart. This, coupled with the removal of branches, should stimulate shoot growth and regain the balance between fruiting and growth.

On the other hand, you may have trees that are growing very vigorously and producing no fruit. This may be due to over-enthusiastic pruning, too vigorous a root stock, a tree planted too deep so that the variety has rooted, or, as so often happens, insufficient pollination is provided to set fruit. To redress the balance, cut out overcrowded shoots and branches, in late summer; do not feed the tree; allow grass to grow around it; and make sure that adequate pollination is provided.

Pruning soft fruit is much more straightforward. With summer-fruiting raspberries, for instance, all that is required is to cut to ground level cane that has carried a crop. The remaining cane, which will fruit the following year, should be thinned leaving eight to ten of the strongest and healthiest canes per plant. These canes should then be tied to the wirework, preferably before winter is too advanced. Autumn-fruiting varieties of raspberry produce fruit on the current season's growth and are therefore pruned differently. When fruiting has ceased they should be cut down to ground level and new cane will shoot up in spring.

Blackberries and loganberries crop on the previous year's growth and so are pruned in the same way as summer-fruiting raspberries. Although blackcurrants produce fruit on all wood except the current year's growth, the best quality fruit is borne on the previous year's growth. It is important therefore to cut out shoots comprising mainly older wood and stimulate a cycle of new growth.

Redcurrents and gooseberries fruit on older wood at the bases of the previous season's growth.

Cordon Pruning and Training

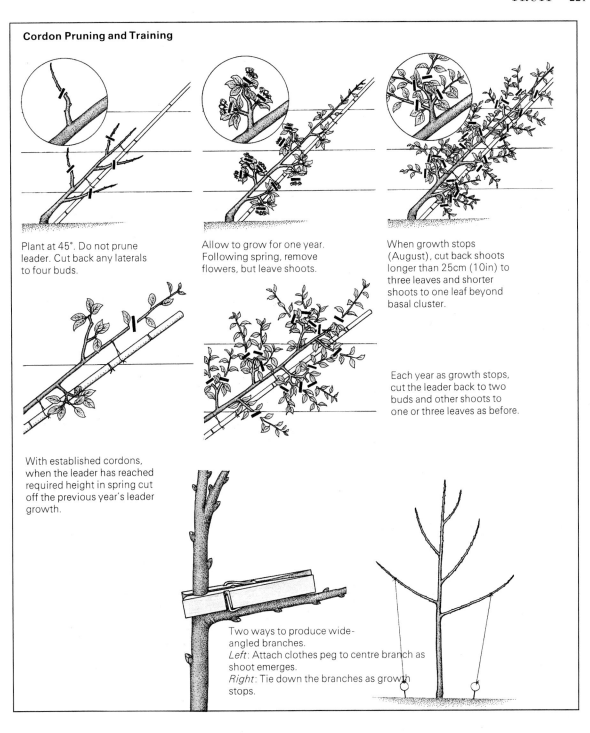

Plant at 45°. Do not prune leader. Cut back any laterals to four buds.

Allow to grow for one year. Following spring, remove flowers, but leave shoots.

When growth stops (August), cut back shoots longer than 25cm (10in) to three leaves and shorter shoots to one leaf beyond basal cluster.

Each year as growth stops, cut the leader back to two buds and other shoots to one or three leaves as before.

With established cordons, when the leader has reached required height in spring cut off the previous year's leader growth.

Two ways to produce wide-angled branches.
Left: Attach clothes peg to centre branch as shoot emerges.
Right: Tie down the branches as growth stops.

If grown as bushes, a permanent framework of branches is required, but once established, all new growth should be pruned back to a couple of buds. As these two fruits respond so well to this method, known as 'spur pruning', they also do well when grown as cordons.

There is no mystique in pruning. Study the fruiting habit of each type of fruit and adjust your pruning to produce the balanced growth so necessary for top-quality fruit.

P D

IN PRAISE OF A SHELTERED UPBRINGING

'Watering fruit trees in a climate like ours?' said the disbelieving gardener sitting squarely in the front row of a village gardening society I was addressing. What a good start, I thought, I've only announced the title of the talk and someone disagrees already.

Even in our notorious climate most fruit plants suffer from a shortage of water at some stage during the summer. The only exceptions are very large trees in good deep soils whose roots go down so far that they barely notice a drought. The shallower the rooting of the plant, the more prone it is to a shortage of water.

With all fruit crops, watering will give you bigger fruits in greater profusion. In addition, your plants will grow that much better and so are likely to give you heavier crops in subsequent years. Experiments during the hot dry summers of 1975 and 1976 showed that the yield and fruit size of blackcurrants, for instance, could sometimes be doubled with irrigation.

Garden sprinklers are quite suitable for water-ing strawberries and cane fruit since these need only one application. With bush and tree fruits, however, where the plants benefit from water being applied over a longer period, a drip system should be installed. The cheapest and simplest available is perforated polythene tubing which is especially suitable for bush fruits and trees on dwarfing rootstocks planted close together. Trees on semi-vigorous rootstocks such as MM106 for apples and Quince A for pears should be irrigated with a drip system with two nozzles for each tree, one on either side of the trunk at a quarter of the distance between the trees.

Mulches can help fruit as well as vegetables. The important thing to remember is to put the mulch on in the spring *before* the soil has dried out too much. Sadly, I have seen many trees in gardens that have been 'popped in' at the last minute in spring into already dry soil, and mulched heavily with straw which then prevents rainwater from reaching the roots.

Polythene mulches are particularly suitable for strawberries and bush fruits, but not for cane fruits. These will lift the polythene which will then be blown around the garden.

SAFE FROM THE WINDS

Within the temperate growing regions of the world we live in one of the windiest. All crops – whether fruit, vegetable or ornamental – benefit to a certain extent from shelter so we should do all we can to create an amenable environment for them to grow in and, ultimately, for us to enjoy them.

Few crops benefit more from shelter than fruit crops. Some of the advantages are obvious, for

Watering guide		* Roughly equivalent to 20 litres/m² (4½ galls/sq. yd)
Crop	**When to apply**	**How much**
Strawberries –planting –fruiting	one day before planting as fruits swell	single application of 2.5–5cm (1–2in)*
Cane fruits Raspberries Blackberries, Loganberries	as fruits swell and turn pink	single application of 5cm (2in)*
Bush fruits Blackcurrants Red and white currants Gooseberries	May–August June–July May–July	drip irrigation with perforated tubing drip irrigation with perforated tubing drip irrigation with perforated tubing
Tree fruits Apples and pears	May–August/September	drip irrigation 2 nozzles per tree; 1–5 litres (2–9pt) per hour per nozzle
Cherries and plums	May–July	drip irrigation 2 nozzles per tree; 1–5 litres (2–9pt) per hour per nozzle

example warmth, others less so, for example the calmer conditions will encourage bees and other pollinating insects to visit and increase fruit set.

If your garden is sheltered you will get better growth from most plants and, of course, much less damage. The most obvious wind damage tends to occur in late summer and autumn when strong gusty south-westerlies blow fruit off our trees, damage raspberry canes that we haven't tied in, and blow over our broccoli and sprouts so that they take on an unnatural creeping habit. Some damage, though, will be less obvious, and is often caused by spring north-easterlies. Leaves may emerge smaller, bruised and tattered, and fruits may have rougher skins.

The final major advantage of shelter is that it increases the number of opportunities you have to spray for pests, disease or weeds. With all chemicals you must avoid spray drift. In an exposed garden you might have to wait for days for the wind to drop sufficiently, which can make your particular problem more difficult to control.

Ideally, shelters or windbreaks should be semi-permeable and not solid, otherwise you will get turbulence on the sheltered side which is just as bad as being fully exposed. Obviously you can't remove every other brick from your neighbour's wall or knock holes in his fence, but in exposed areas of the garden you can put up windbreaks. These should be at least as high as the tallest plant you wish to protect. When siting your windbreak, avoid funnelling air through a gap or shading the crop.

Trees such as poplars, alders and Leyland cypresses are often used to shelter commercial orchards. The important thing with fruit crops is that they must be in leaf by the time the fruit blossom comes out. Poplars can probably be ruled out for all but the biggest gardens, and even then I wouldn't recommend them as they are so vigorous, greedy and far from attractive. A Leyland hedge, too, is not to be recommended as it is much too solid; but a hedge consisting of alternate Leylands and alders or silver birch is far more suitable.

In smaller gardens, you won't have room for a living windbreak and so your choice is limited to artificial ones. These can be made by erecting plastic windbreak materials (about 50 per cent porous) on poles and wires. They are ideal for protecting all fruit plants, except for the biggest trees, as well as vegetables, ornamentals and the glasshouse. Sheltering the glasshouse will also help to prevent breakages. There are several plastic windbreaks on the market but, as for bird netting, avoid unnatural green ones; black is best. **P D**

DWARFS IN THEIR ELEMENT

Fruit growing tends to be sacrificed if space is at a premium, but this doesn't have to be so. It's now possible to obtain more and more fruit from smaller and smaller plants grown closer together. No longer do growers have to wait fifteen years or so for sweet cherries to start cropping, and then pick them from the top of a fifty-rung ladder. Cropping in three or four years is now possible, and picking can be done from, at most, a pair of steps.

Various growing techniques are now available to amateurs: there are compact trees on dwarfing rootstocks, restricted growing systems trained against walls or fences, plants in pots, tubs, window boxes, hanging baskets or specimen fruit plants grown in the lawn or flower border.

With tree fruits, restrict your choice to the 'non-vigorous' varieties (*see* 'Fruit Varieties') grafted on to the more dwarfing rootstocks. Good dwarfing rootstocks for apples are M26 and M9, the latter inducing smaller trees. If you want more vigorous varieties, such as 'Bramley's Seedling', the rootstock to choose is the very dwarfing M27, which you can now buy from certain nurseries. The choice of rootstocks for pears is much more limited – only Quince A and Quince C are available. Quince A is more common, but Quince C is more dwarfing, so get it if you can.

The only plum rootstock suitable for the smaller garden is St Julien A. However, a new dwarfing rootstock for plums, called Pixy, may come on the market in the next few years, although it does tend to induce smaller fruits, particularly on light soils.

The standard rootstock for both sweet and acid cherries is Mazzard F12/1. All sweet cherry varieties, however, produce prohibitively large trees on it. Acid cherries on this rootstock are less vigorous, and are suitable in small spaces, especially if fan-trained up a wall or fence. There is, however, a new cherry rootstock called Colt, which, with many 'sweet' cherry varieties, can be kept to a height of about 5m (16ft) in an area 5–7m (16–23ft) wide. But a really dwarfing rootstock for cherries is, sadly, still a way off.

Space-saving gooseberries and currants.

Another advantage of trees on dwarf root-stocks is that as well as being smaller they start cropping at a much younger age than the same varieties on more vigorous rootstocks: you can hope to see fruit of most varieties by the second or third year.

Summer pruning is another way of keeping fruit-tree size under control. It restricts growth, as opposed to winter pruning, which encourages it. Summer pruning is useful, particularly on training systems such as cordons and espaliers (*see* 'Pruning and Training'). As shoot growth begins to slow up towards the middle of August, the current season's shoots coming from the main branches are cut back to three buds. This induces fruit bud formation on the remaining shoot spurs. Cut back shoots from existing spurs and laterals to just one bud. Then once the trees have grown to the height you require, cut back the previous season's leader growth to one bud in May. Repeat this process every year.

If you're growing tree fruits in a limited space avoid high levels of nitrogen in your soil because these encourage growth; ensure adequate pollination and frost protection because heavy crops tend to limit shoot growth.

When space is short, traditional boundaries have to be disregarded. So when you have filled the fruit garden, try and put a specimen tree or two in other parts of the garden; a naked expanse of lawn could be brightened up by a tree or two and a fruiting – and decorative – one is as good a choice as any.

It's obviously much easier to fit soft fruit into a small garden. You can grow blackberries and loganberries up fences or trellises; they do need room, but they are very productive so you only need one or two plants. Choose regular and heavy cropping varieties for a small garden. With bush fruits, like blackcurrants, choose the more compact varieties and plant them closer together at about one metre apart to form a cropping 'hedge'.

Some fruits like gooseberries and redcurrants can be grown as cordons planted 30cm (12in) apart, bordering a path perhaps or as a screen; or put blueberries among heathers and azaleas in the flower bed to show off their autumn colour.

Most fruit can be grown in pots, barrels, growing bags, window boxes, even hanging baskets. Indeed, growing fruit in containers has many advantages: they can be given their ideal soil and are more easily protected from frost, wind and birds.

Strawberries are the most popular fruit for container growing, doing well in anything from pots, troughs, window boxes and growing bags, to old sinks, polythene tubes of compost as well as in nutrient film in gutters. Alpine strawberries, too, do very well in hanging baskets.

Raspberries are not suitable for container growing, neither are the vigorous blackberries. Heavy-cropping loganberries, however, can be pot grown as long as adequate supplies of water and nutrients are available. This, of course, applies to all crops grown in this way and, certainly, container-grown plants need more attention than those in the soil. With figs the restricted root growth in pots checks the vigour and so increases cropping. You can grow all bush fruits in pots, and if you garden on chalky soil this is the only way you can grow acid-lovers like blueberries.   P D

LOVELY TO LOOK AT

The massed blossom of an orchard is one of the delights of spring but the effect, alas, is shortlived; and once the petals start to fall the trees become quite dull until the fruits begin to colour. Sadly, many of the flowering apples, plums and cherries provide a very short, sharp burst of colour for a week or so in spring and nothing at all for the rest of the year. I will never understand why those ornamental varieties, often with sterile multi-petalled flowers of unnaturally vivid hues, are so popular. The showy, blowsy *Prunus* 'Danzan', for example, hasn't much to offer the rest of the year. You would do better to settle down with a much more natural-fruiting variety whose subtle beauty and productivity will be far more satisfying.

Many fruiting varieties have attractive flowers, like the apples 'Arthur Turner' or 'Brownlees Russet', as well as the more familiar 'Bramley's Seedling'. Individual flowers of some varieties of pear, plum and cherry may not be too exciting, but *en masse*, against a bright blue sky, they are fine.

Fruits particularly noted for their decorative flowers include the less common quinces and blueberries. Quince flowers are most attractive – they are larger than apple or pear and often have a subtle hint of pink. They show up particularly well against the bright green backdrop of the foliage and are followed by interestingly shaped fruits.

Blueberry flowers are similar in shape to those of heather, to which they are related, but instead of whites, pinks and reds, the flowers are a soft creamy colour often hanging down on arched stems. For ornamental value the blueberry must take some beating, for not only are the flowers attractive but the fruits and red autumn foliage are, too.

Leaves of many of the popular fruit varieties are not particularly interesting but those of some of the more exotic crops are. Figs, for example, have very ornamental leaves being quite large with three or five lobes. A fig growing against a light sandstone wall really shows off the foliage, as well as providing an abundance of delicious juicy fruits. You don't have to have a wall for a fig though, you can easily grow them in pots. Surely an ideal plant for your patio to bring back

The variegated leaf-patterns and forms of the Brandt vine make an extraordinary jigsaw.

memories of days lazing in the Mediterranean sun in the shade of the large lobed leaves. In some countries, the leaves of some fig species are smoked, along with opium, but that's another story.

Apricots, too, have attractive leaves, albeit much smaller than those of fig. They are mid-green, almost leathery in appearance and again look particularly fine against a light-coloured wall. Apricot flowers are quite large and white, and some have a pink flush. They are produced in clusters, before the leaves come out, sometimes as early as February, when they are especially welcome.

Among the soft fruits, the parsley-leaved or cut-leaved blackberry must be one of the favourites for decorative foliage. It is worthwhile planting it in ornamental beds on the strength of its distinctive leaves alone, and people who try this often decide to add to its numbers in the fruit garden as it produces quite heavy crops of sharp but excellently flavoured large berries.

The foliage of many trees and shrubs is spectacular in autumn but unfortunately only a few fruit plants can be included in this category. As

well as those of blueberries, leaves of many grape vines turn in autumn to shades of red and purple – some consolation if the year's crop is not up to expectation.

Most people's idea of ornamental fruits is confined to crab apples, many of which produce prolific numbers of brightly coloured fruits. Two crabs that can be eaten – and look good – are 'John Downie' and 'Veitch's Scarlet', both of which have conical, bright orange and red fruits that glow in the low autumn sun and then drop, ready for gathering to make the most delicious clear-pink, crab-apple jelly.

Dessert apples that are particularly attractive to look at include 'Gala' with its bright orange fruits, 'Greensleeves' – a pleasantly shaped green apple with a clean skin, and 'St Edmund's Pippin' – a partly russet apple with a bright orange flush. If you like red apples the early variety 'Discovery' is an attractive one, but if you prefer dark, almost blue-red fruits, try 'Spartan'. Several culinary

An aristocrat among ornamental fruits – the crab-apple, whose leaves and fruits glow ever deeper before the autumn ripening.

apples are fairly attractive, and one of the best is 'Golden Noble' with its round, yellow-gold fruits.

For most people, an attractive pear is a plump 'Comice' with a pink flush. There are a few though that have red skins such as 'Glow Red Williams', which is available from a few nurseries and is worth considering if you want something a bit different.

People naturally have different ideas on what is attractive, and nowhere is this more true than with plums. If you like pale yellow fruits, 'Early Transparent' is a good one; whereas if you prefer dark blue plums, 'Kirke's' is one of the best. Most people, however, like large red plums, so try the most attractive, 'Pond's Seedling'. But it is deceptive, for there is little else to commend it: its flavour is particularly weak. The opposite, of course, is true of greengages, being small and green and not visually attractive at all. The flavour though is outstanding.

Sweet cherries tend to be classified as either black or white. Depending on variety, 'blacks' can be anything from a very dark red through mahogany to jet black, and 'whites' can be pale yellow or cream to bright red. Three attractive 'black' varieties are 'Van', 'Merton Bigarreau' and 'Stella', while one of the very best 'whites' is 'Merton Glory' – a very large-fruited red variety.

I am sometimes asked if I can suggest a weeping fruit tree that can be grown, in the lawn perhaps, instead of the more usual purely ornamental *Pyrus salicifolia pendula* or *Prunus avium pendula*. There are several varieties of fruit tree that do tend to weep, such as 'Merton Gem' plum and 'Catillac' pear, but nowhere to the same extent as the ornamental weepers. Both of these varieties produce reasonable fruit. 'Merton Gem' is a self-fertile late plum with yellow and red fruits, which turn purple when fully ripe. In some years this variety produces a second flush of flowers which, if the weather is favourable, can give fruit well into October. 'Catillac' is a very old pear variety dating back to the fifteenth century. It produces large dull green, almost round fruits, which, when ripe, are excellent for stewing. These varieties have a natural tendency to weep but you can, depending on your idea of beauty, train many fruits to grow in different ways.

I have already briefly mentioned cordons, espaliers, fans, bush and standard trees which is the usual range of training systems from which gardeners in this country choose. There are many others, however, some of which you may have noticed on the Continent, particularly if you have visited châteaux gardens in France. You may have seen vase- or goblet-shaped pear trees and palmettes in a range of guises: with three, four or five vertical branches, or perhaps 'Y' shapes looking like giant catapults. The French also grow trees as espaliers and cordons but often modified to create some interesting forms, some pleasing, some a little curious. Recently I saw *horizontal* cordons of 'Golden Delicious' with the main stems just 40cm (16in) above the edge of a path in du Roy's *potager* at Versailles; it was being used, like the more usual box, as an edging plant.

P D

WARM IS BOUNTIFUL

To pick and eat fresh fruits when they are in short supply and expensive in the shops is one of the pinnacles of the home gardener's year. You can reach these heights by two main routes. The easier is to include early and late varieties among those you plant in the open. Alternatively, you can grow the crop under protection and extend the season even further.

How successful you are in extending the season will depend to a certain extent on where you live. If, for instance, you have a south-facing garden near the south coast and choose to grow early varieties of strawberries, they will be as early as any grown in the country and they will still be scarce and expensive in the shops. If, however, you grow the same early variety in the north it may crop at the same time as the bulk of the main crop in the south and these will already be available in your shops at relatively low prices.

The length of your growing season will also influence which early and late varieties you can grow as you need to accommodate the period from flowering to harvest in your frost-free growing

Early and late varieties for outdoor cropping

Crop	Early varieties	Ripening time	Late varieties	Ripening time	
Strawberries	Cambridge Vigour Cambridge Prizewinner Gorella Pantagruella	Early June	Ostara* Rabunda* Aromel*	Until first frosts	
Raspberries	Malling Promise Glen Clova	Early July	September** Zeva** Heritage**	Until first frosts	
Blackcurrants	Baldwin Ben Lomond	End July	Jet	End August	
Gooseberries	May Duke Keepsake	End May	Lancashire Lad	End June	
Plums (culinary) (dessert)	Early Rivers Czar Early Laxton	End July Early August	Marjorie's Seedling Jefferson Golden Transparent	Early October Mid September	
Cherries (sweet) Cherries (sour)	Early Rivers Roundel	Mid June	Bradbourne Black Stella Morello	End July End August	
				Pick	**Store**
Apples (culinary)	Early Victoria Grenadier	End July Early August	Bramley's Seedling Annie Elizabeth	Mid Oct. Mid Oct.	March June
Apples (dessert)	Discovery Katja Worcester Pearmain	End August Early Sept. Mid Sept.	Crispin Gala Ashmead's Kernel	Mid Oct. Mid Oct. Mid Oct.	Early March Early March Early March
Pears (dessert)	Williams' Ben Chrétien Onward	September September	Doyenné du Comice Thompson's Winter Nelis	November November November	November November January

*Perpetual varieties, new plants of which need to be planted every year to produce large fruit.
**Autumn-fruiting varieties which crop on the current season's cane and are cut down to ground level after cropping.

season. A variety that ripens early may also flower early right in the middle of your regular spring frosts.

Raising the temperature of the growing environment is, of course, the time-honoured way of extending the growing season. With fruit you can cover the plants with cloches or low polythene tunnels or plant your crops in frames, walk-in tunnels or greenhouses. For an even longer season the last three structures can be heated but this is phenomenally expensive.

Only strawberries can be grown under glass cloches, the other crops are too big. For the best results use them only on the earliest varieties, when you should start picking up to three weeks before the unprotected crop. Glass cloches are relatively expensive and difficult to handle, and low polythene tunnels tend to be used instead, although they are not quite so effective in advancing the season, most varieties cropping a week or so later than under cloches.

For protected growing, new strawberry plants should be planted in August or early September. Put in the plants 20–30cm (8–12in) apart in single or double rows depending on the width of your cloches or tunnels. The plants should be covered from late January and ventilation started on warm sunny days as flowering commences. You can do this by opening one roof pane on each cloche or by lifting the side of your polythene tunnel. This not only prevents high temperatures building up but also allows pollinating insects to visit the flowers – essential for good cropping and preventing misshapen fruits.

Both walk-in tunnels and polythene greenhouses produce slightly earlier crops than low tunnels and it is easier to get to the plants. This, plus the fact that you too will be protected, means the plants are likely to be inspected more frequently.

Ripening can be brought forward even more by growing your crop on ridges or raised beds. This is particularly effective if you also cover the ridge or bed around the plants with polythene to raise the soil temperature. Clear polythene gives the highest soil temperatures but black is best because, by denying light, it also prevents weeds growing. Lay a perforated polythene irrigation tube along the row or bed under the polythene sheet so that water can be applied to the soil as the fruits begin to swell.

You can also use tunnels and cloches to lengthen the season in the autumn where perpetual or autumn-fruiting varieties of strawberries are grown. Polythene, unfortunately, will not protect your precious fruit from frosts. Cover the plants with a couple of layers of newspaper when frosts are forecast and this will keep the fruit coming for a little longer.

If you have a glasshouse or conservatory you can grow dessert grapes, figs, peaches and nectarines. They can all be trained against a wall leaving plenty of room for other crops and your bench. You can also grow grapes, peaches and nectarines

A fine old fig tree trained against a greenhouse wall. It will leave room for other plants if correctly pruned.

Blackcurrant 'Baldwin' (fairly early)

Plum 'Golden transparent' (late)

Raspberry 'Malling Promise' (late)

Gooseberry 'Lancashire Lad' (late)

Apple 'Bramley's Seeding' (late)

Apple 'Worcester Pearmain' (late)

Pear 'Williams' Bon Chrétien' (early)   Pear 'Doyenné du Comice' (late)

in pots, with the added advantage that you can move them out for the summer so that the space can be used for something else.

Varieties suitable for growing in an unheated glasshouse include:

Grapes 'Buckland Sweetwater', 'Foster's Seedling', 'Lady Hutt'.

Figs 'Brown Turkey', 'White Marseilles', 'Bourjasotte Grise'.

Peaches 'Duke of York', 'Hales' Early', 'Peregrine', 'Red Haven', 'Rochester', 'Royal George'.

Nectarines 'Early Rivers', 'Lord Napier', 'Humboldt', 'Pine Apple'.

These varieties should crop well in an unheated glasshouse but it is wise to have a heater on standby so that if a heavy frost is forecast during flowering time, damage can be avoided.

A fig grown against a wall should have its root-run restricted to prevent it from growing too vigorously and to encourage it to fruit. It can be grown quite easily as a fan and will only need its lateral shoots pinched back to about four leaves and its non-fruiting shoots thinned out to prevent congested growth.

Peaches and nectarines are treated in the same way as they are grown outdoors, except that as pollinating insects don't venture into glasshouses in adequate numbers, hand-pollination of flowers is necessary to set a crop. If you have room, dessert grapes must be one of the most rewarding crops to grow in the greenhouse. Once established, the vine is trained on the rod-and-spur system (*see* 'Pruning and Training') and will give you regular crops of juicy grapes.

STRAWBERRIES FOR CHRISTMAS

If you want to do something different in the depth of winter, try producing fresh strawberries for Christmas. A dozen or so plants of 'Redgauntlet' in a tower pot on a sunny window sill in a warm room kept at about 20°C (68°F) will give you enough fruit to add that little extra to the Christmas table. To do this successfully you need to pot them up in early July and let them get established, then in August allow them to be exposed to light for only eight hours a day.

This is easily done by covering the pots for the rest of the time with black polythene. The plants should start flowering towards the end of October when you should dust each one over with a small paintbrush to make sure each is pollinated and will produce a fruit. Keep the plants watered and fed and you should be rewarded with ripe strawberries through Christmas and into the New Year.　P D

BEYOND THE FRUIT BOWL

Once you have mastered growing the more common fruit crops you can turn your attention to the less usual ones such as apricots, peaches, nectarines and grapes, which need a favourable site and a little encouragement to be reliably productive, or those like mulberries and medlars which you can't buy in the shops since they have 'an acquired taste'.

Apricots, apart from their decorative value, are well worth growing for fruit and taste quite different from the familiar tinned or dried products. Like peaches and their smooth-skinned variants – nectarines – they are best fan-trained against a south-facing wall where they can be protected from spring frosts – the main problem with any early-flowering crop.

If you haven't a south-facing wall, try growing these fruits in pots on the patio where the frost risk is less and where they could be covered if necessary. Whichever method you adopt, choose St Julien A rootstock which will prevent the tree from becoming too vigorous and induce it to crop early. Apricots, peaches and nectarines are all self-fertile so you don't need to plant separate pollinator varieties. Two of the best and most reliable apricot varieties are 'Farmingdale' and 'Moorpark', both of which will produce heavy crops of delicious golden fruit in August. There are

Nectarine 'Early Rivers'.

Quince 'Champion'.

several varieties of peach to tempt us but I find 'Peregrine' one of the best flavoured and 'Rochester' one of the hardiest and most reliable. There are not so many nectarine varieties to choose from but one that is well worth looking out for is 'Early Rivers' which ripens towards the end of July and has a particularly rich juicy flavour. For heavy cropping, 'Lord Napier' and 'Humboldt' are two of the best varieties with quite a rich flavour but not quite up to 'Early Rivers'. All of these peach and nectarine varieties can also be grown in the glasshouse where they are easier to protect from frost and peach leaf curl.

Figs, apart from their decorative qualities, are one of the most delicious fruits when picked straight from the tree. In the tropics figs can crop three times a year but in temperate regions we have to be satisfied with only one crop. In Britain we don't depend on insects pollinating the flowers as the fruits develop without pollination and fertilization, so single trees can be planted. Figs like plenty of space if they are to flourish as bushes and fruit well. If you can't afford to give them much room, they should still fruit well enough in a large pot, given regular feeds and plenty of water.

'Brown Turkey' is a popular heavy-cropping variety that produces delicious red-fleshed rich fruits whilst 'White Marseilles' is a transparent-fleshed variety with a pale skin which is quite reliable in our climate. Both are also suitable for glasshouse cultivation, but if you have a glasshouse try 'Bourjasotte Grise', one of the sweetest and most richly flavoured of all figs.

Quinces and medlars, as well as being ornamental, produce very interesting fruits. Quinces grown for their fruit belong to the genus *Cydonia* (not to be confused with the ornamental Japanese quinces belonging to the genus *Chaenomeles*). When grown in this country they do not ripen as

they do around the Mediterranean and so are not generally eaten as fresh fruit. They do, however, make delicious jelly, preserves and marmalade.

Medlars also make a fine jelly but their reputation as a connoisseur's fruit is based on the flavour of the over-ripe or 'bletted' fruits when they are eaten after the flesh has become very soft and brown. Neither quinces nor medlars require pollinator varieties so you can easily start off with just one tree of each. The most popular and reliable quince variety is 'Vranja' which produces large pear-shaped fruits, even from young trees. Two medlar varieties that are often grown are 'Dutch', which makes a weeping tree and has pleasantly flavoured fruits, and 'Royal' which is more upright and produces heavy crops of smaller but better-flavoured fruits.

NUTS AND BERRIES

Nuts are not commonly grown in gardens nowadays but are worth considering if you have room. Cobnuts and filberts don't require much space but walnuts and sweet chestnuts certainly do, and with these you'll have to wait five or ten years before you get much of a crop. For really good flavour try the 'Franquette' or 'Mayette' walnuts and the 'Doré du Lyons' chestnut.

Cobnuts and filberts make pleasant specimen trees or bushes and are also useful as windbreaks. 'Kentish Cob' is the best-known variety in this country and produces heavy crops of long large

Ripe medlars.

nuts. Two better-flavoured varieties are 'Purple Filbert' and 'Red Filbert'; the former is very attractive with long dark red catkins and nuts with purple husks.

There are several soft fruits that are not commonly grown, such as 'hybrid berries' – which are relatives of the blackberry – blueberries and mulberries. Most hybrid berries are less vigorous than blackberries and some don't have thorns. Loganberries are included in this group, two clones of which are popular with gardeners: LY59 which has thorns and L 654 which hasn't. Both crop heavily and the fruits can be eaten fresh, frozen, or made into jam. A new hybrid berry, recently bred at the Scottish Crop Research Institute, is the 'Tayberry' which crops very heavily having fruits similar to those of the loganberry but with a mildly sweet flavour. All hybrid berries are grown like blackberries – along horizontal wires or up a fence.

Blueberries are easy to grow as long as the soil is sufficiently acid (pH 4.0–5.5). Varieties that do well in my garden include 'Early Blue', 'Bluecrop' and 'Jersey'. All produce heavy crops of large blue fruits which are excellent for pies although the flavour is weaker than that of the wild bilberry.

A fruit that is similar in appearance to loganberries is the mulberry. Mulberries are usually grown as large specimen trees in lawns where they make a fine sight, even if propped up in old age. For fruit production though, it's better to grow them against a wall or fence with horizontal branches every 50cm (20in); here they are much easier to protect from birds which otherwise devastate the crop.

Walnut

Suppliers of less common fruit plants
Deacons Nursery, Godshill, Isle of Wight PO38 3HW
Michael Pirie, 82 Kingston Road, Oxford OX2 6RJ
Thomas Rivers & Son Ltd, The Nurseries, Sawbridgeworth, Herts CM21 0HJ
R. V. Roger Ltd, The Nurseries, Pickering, North Yorks YO18 7HG
Scott's Nurseries (Merriott) Ltd, Merriott, Somerset TA16 5PL
Chris Bowers, Westerly Farm, Outwell, nr Wisbech, Cambs PE14 8QR

Tayberries – a new form of hybrid berry.

RIPE PICKINGS

Even the best-flavoured varieties of fruit will taste very ordinary if not harvested at the correct time. During ripening, acids in fruits become weaker, sugars accumulate and the aromatic compounds develop, to give their characteristic flavours. If you then pick too early, out of impatience or because you fear the birds will get the crop before you do, you finish up with fruit that is perhaps rather sour and almost certainly lacking in flavour. On the other hand, fruit picked too late lacks acidity, is oversweet and may have developed 'off' flavours.

Strawberries should be picked when the fruit has developed its full red colour but before it turns dull and soft. Raspberries, too, are ready for picking only when they have developed their full colour, are still firm and come away from the plug

easily. Similarly their close relatives, blackberries and loganberries, should be picked at this stage but here the plug comes away with the fruit. Most blackberry and loganberry varieties have rather vicious thorns, but don't wear gloves because picking fruits at the right stage is a delicate operation. Fruits hard won, taste even better.

These soft fruits do not all ripen together but over a period, perhaps of several weeks. Make sure you pick them over regularly, every other day is not too often.

From the point of view of picking, gooseberries are peculiar in that, for culinary purposes, they are often picked while still very under-ripe. Early varieties such as 'May Duke' are picked as soon as they have reached a respectable size usually during May and early June. Gooseberries for dessert use, however, are best picked when almost ripe but before they become too soft. They also have a tendency to split if a shower occurs as harvest time approaches, so deciding when to pick can become quite a nerve-racking affair. Currants, whether black, red or white, are not so problematic since they should be picked when most of the fruits on each string are ripe. Wait too long though, and

Some of the many fruits which ripen in the autumn, ready to be be preserved for the winter ahead: apples, pears, raspberries, blackberries and plums, and autumn jelly made with sloes, elderberries, blackberries and apples.

some varieties, especially of blackcurrants will start to drop.

Of the tree fruits, cherries and plums are quite straightforward. They are ready when the skin has turned the characteristic colour of the variety and the flesh starts to soften and is sweet. Again, many varieties of cherries, particularly when ripe, will split in the slightest shower of rain so do not leave them on too long. If wasps are troublesome, plums can be picked a few days early – not before since flavour will be lost – and finished off under cover.

It is the picking of apples and pears that is the most difficult. Early and mid-season dessert apples, for more or less immediate consumption, are ready when they have attained their full colour and the flesh is softening and tasting sweet (a good excuse for regular sampling). Late-season apples and pears to be stored will not however reach this stage on the tree and will continue to ripen in store. Different criteria are used with these to determine picking date ; the most useful is the ease with which the fruits can be detached from the tree. Each fruit should come away freely, if lifted slightly and gently twisted.

All fruits should be picked and handled carefully especially if they are to be stored. Soft fruits, cherries, plums and early apples will only keep for very short periods, but late apples and pears with care and given the right conditions can be kept for several months. Frost-free parts of sheds or garages are ideal for storage, where they should be placed in loosely folded polythene bags – these prevent shrivelling but allow the fruits to 'breathe'. Inspect them regularly and discard any rotting ones.

P D

Preservation: the art of keeping your fruit for winter feasts

Method of preservation	Deep freezing	Bottling	Jams, jellies cheeses, butters	Pickles	Sauces and chutneys
General comment	May need sugar added; can freeze made-up dish eg pie	In sugar syrup or as puree with added sugar	Proportion of sugar varies according to fruit. Butters have added spices	Vinegar (malt or distilled), spices and sugar (brown or white)	Vinegar, salt, sugar, spices with onion, dates, raisins, ginger, etc.
Apples	Puree or slices	Slices or rings	Jelly good with ginger or pineapple for flavour	Spiced crab-apples	Apples make a good chutney; often used in others too
Pears		Dessert – halved or quartered	Not recommended, except for quinces, which are good for cheese and jelly	●	●
Plums	In sugar syrup	Whole or halved	Damsons good for cheese	Damson pickle – improves in storage	Plum sauce very good
Cherries	In sugar syrup	Whole or stoned	Acid cherries best here		Morellos good here
Blackcurrants, Redcurrants	●	●	Redcurrant for jelly, and juice for added pectin		
Gooseberries	●	●	Juice used for added pectin		
Raspberries, Blackberries, Loganberries	●	●	Blackberries often used, with apple to give necessary pectin		Blackberry good
Strawberries	Not recommended unless as puree, ice cream, sorbets, etc.	Not recommended – they shrink and lose colour	May need added pectin for jams		
Rhubarb	●	●	May need added pectin and flavourings, eg ginger and orange	Sweet spiced rhubarb	●

...ying	Candying	Chemical (sulphur dioxide)	Syrups	Juices	Vinegars
...ds correct ...perature and ...tilation	Long process but worthwhile	Before eating boil well to remove preservative	High proportion sugar: dilute juice to taste	Less sugar than used for syrups. No need to dilute	Use ½kg (1lb) fruit to ½l (1pt) best malt vinegar
...windfalls in ...s – popular ...n children	Small crab-apples suitable	Peel, core and slice		No sugar needed. Use mixture of dessert and cooking varieties	
	●				
	●	●			
	●				
			Add water to extract juice	●	●
			●	●	Raspberry vinegar eases sore throats and colds
			●	●	

Fruit for bottling or freezing should be firm, fresh and ripe but not over-ripe. Riper fruit is better used in chutneys, sauces, syrups or juices; whereas a proportion of under-ripe fruit aids setting in jams, jellies, cheeses and butters, particularly if the ripe fruit used is low in pectin, for example, strawberries.

● indicates suitability of fruit for particular process.
All these fruits can usefully be made into wine.

GARDEN EQUIPMENT

Cloches

Cloches are used for warming up the soil prior to planting and for protecting early plants. Traditionally, they were made of glass but plastic ones are cheaper and lighter. Tunnel cloches are made from corrugated PVC held in position by wire hoops or from lightweight polythene which is laid over a series of hoops and held in place by a second set of hoops. Cloches made of corrugated PVC are probably the most practical as they last longer than glass, which breaks easily, or lightweight polythene, which deteriorates in sunlight.

If there is any danger of frost the cloche can be covered with several thicknesses of newspapers held in place with stones.

Fertilizers (Inorganic)

Fertilizers supply nutrients which may not be present in sufficient quantities in the soil and which are essential to the plant's growth. A general fertilizer, one containing a balanced blend of phosphorus, nitrogen and potassium, is the easiest type to use. Applying specialized fertilizers such as sulphate of ammonia or superphosphate of lime needs careful measurement and can lead to an imbalance of nutrients in the soil.

Foliar feeds should be used on the plant's leaves, but other fertilizers must not come into contact with either stem or leaves. They are most effective sprinkled around the plant in a circle as wide as the growth above. A general fertilizer should not be dug into the soil. Use it before seeds are sown or before planting out and then at intervals as the plant is growing. Do not use fertilizers in the winter as plants are dormant at this time, or when the ground is very dry as they will not be absorbed by the plants.

Liquid fertilizers are more expensive than others but are more easily taken in by the plants and so give quicker results. However, they can be washed out of the soil very quickly if it rains.

Frame

A frame, usually referred to as a cold frame, is a topless, bottomless box with a cover made of glass or plastic. It can be built from wood, brick, concrete blocks or even, in an emergency, turves or bales of straw. It is generally used to harden off plants.

Greenhouses

There are many different types available with either cedarwood or low-maintenance aluminium frames. Among the most popular are the following :

Traditional vertical-sided greenhouses which are free-standing and are often timber-clad up to the level of the staging.

Dutch light greenhouses which have sloping sides and large glass panels reaching the ground on all sides.

Lean-to greenhouses which are three-sided, the fourth side being a house or garden wall. A lean-to greenhouse built against a house wall will be warmer than any other type.

Circular greenhouses which are becoming increasingly popular as the gardener can work on all parts of the greenhouse simply by turning around. This wastes less space than other houses.

An east-west alignment is usually considered to be ideal for the greenhouse as it then gets light throughout the day. Obviously the greenhouse should not be sited under trees or where it will be overshadowed by any other building, nor should it be sited too near a fence or hedge as this may make maintenance difficult.

A greenhouse must have a good ventilation system with two or more roof ventilators and at least one at a lower level. Automatic ventilators are available and are very useful for gardeners who are out all day. They must, however, be connected to the main electricity supply. The other essential is a regular and plentiful supply of water. Again, automatic systems are available. Capillary irrigation is a system by which water flows from a tank into a trough from which it is drawn into a sand tray by means of a wick. A second capillary system involves standing the plant pots on an absorbent mat which takes water from a tank. This type of watering is really only suitable for very small plants or for seedlings. Trickle irrigation is suitable for larger plants. A pipe is laid near the plants and nozzles from it are placed in each pot releasing into them a steady stream of water.

The greenhouse will probably need some form of shading to protect the plants from direct sunlight during very hot weather. Slatted blinds are the most efficient way of supplying shade, but there is also a liquid screen which you can spray onto the glass. It becomes opaque in bright sunlight but transparent on dull days.

Unless you intend to use the greenhouse as a cold house it will need some form of heating during the winter. Gas, paraffin and electric heaters are all available. Electric heating is the most expensive, but it is automatic and more versatile than the other systems. The conventional form of heating greenhouses is by hot-water pipes from a boiler, which may be fired by gas, oil or solid fuel. This is not suitable for small structures, but where a lean-to greenhouse is built against a house-wall it may be possible to extend the central heating system to warm the lean-to as well.

Greenhouse staging, or slatted benches, can be made using 2½-inch (5cm) timber for the legs and 2 × 1 inch (5 × 2.5cm) timber for the framework of the bench area. Battens made from 2½ × ½ inch (5 × 1cm) timber are nailed to the top to form slats. The bench is strengthened by the addition of crossbracing, made from 2 × 1 inch (5 × 2.5cm) timber, between the legs and top. The staging should be placed on a firm surface, such as stone slabs, to ensure that it remains steady.

The greenhouse must be kept clean and should be fumigated with pesticidal and fungicidal smoke 'bombs' at the end of each growing season. The smoke reaches all parts of the greenhouse but is harmless to food crops. The bombs must be used in calm weather, but not in bright sunshine. The ventilators should be shut and any gaps blocked before the bombs are lit. Light the first bomb at the end of the greenhouse furthest from the door and work backwards towards the door. Close and lock the door. The following day you can open the door, but wait for a few minutes before going in to open the ventilators.

You can use disinfectant to clean the inside of the greenhouse. Both sides of the glass panes should be cleaned so that as much light as possible reaches the plants. This is best done before spring sowing begins.

Pots

Plants will grow in almost any container provided it has adequate drainage, although those in general use are either clay, peat or plastic. Clay and plastic pots must be thoroughly clean before they are used.

CLAY

This is the traditional material for plant pots and they are available in many sizes from a width of 2 inches (5cm) upwards. Always soak a new clay pot in water for several days before using it. As these pots are porous they absorb moisture and consequently the soil in them dries out more quickly than in other types of pot.

PEAT

These pots, made from Irish moss peat, are becoming increasingly popular. They are available in several sizes and are ideal for raising seedlings or cuttings as the whole pot can be planted out complete with its contents. The roots grow through the walls of the pot into the earth and the pot itself eventually decomposes adding humus to the soil.

PLASTIC

These pots are very popular as they are light and easy to clean. They are also less likely to break than clay pots. As they retain moisture, there is a danger of overwatering the plants contained in them.

Sprays

Chemical sprays are of three kinds; insecticides, fungicides and herbicides. All should be treated with great caution for as well as killing insects, fungus diseases and weeds, they can injure human beings and domestic animals, sometimes with fatal consequences. Always use a sprayer with a nozzle which will produce a fine spray pattern with good coverage of the plants. Always read the instructions on the packet or bottle and follow them. Never mix chemicals together unless the manufacturer's instructions on the packet or bottle suggest that you should. There are an enormous number of chemical sprays available which are divided into different types according to the way in which they work. Systemic sprays are carried in the sap to all parts of the plant and will therefore affect pests or diseases in any part of the plant. A non-systemic spray is not carried around the plant and kills pests by poisoning the surfaces on which they feed.

Weedkillers are available in three types: selective weedkillers, mostly used for weeds in lawns; contact weedkillers, which kill all parts of the plant with which they come into contact; and residual weedkillers which remain near the surface to kill weed seedlings as they emerge. Weedkillers should not be used near fruit and vegetable plants nor should they be used where plants are growing close together. Remove weeds from such areas by hand. Unlike insecticides and fungicides, herbicides can be applied with a watering-can, but make sure that it is washed well after use. If possible keep a watering-can solely for this purpose.

RULES FOR SPRAYING

1 Always read and follow the manufacturer's instructions.
2 Always wash off accidental splashes immediately and always wash your hands after using a spray.
3 Always keep containers well stoppered, ensure they are correctly labelled, and lock them up.
4 Always put empty containers in the refuse bin.
5 Always wash the spray equipment immediately after use, and never use spray equipment for any other purpose.
6 Never inhale the vapour.
7 Never spray open flowers during the day. This will prevent helpful insects such as bees being killed.
8 Never harvest crops until the period of time given in the instructions has elapsed.
9 Never spray when there is a breeze.
10 Never mix up more solution than you need – it cannot be kept.
11 Never spray the whole garden – spray only those plants that are being attacked by pests or disease.

Tools

Any job is more easily carried out using the correct tools. The tools that a gardener needs are a spade, fork, hoe, rake, trowel, dibber, garden line, secateurs, hose, watering-can and wheelbarrow. Buy the best tools you can afford. Stainless steel tools are expensive but they are unlikely to rust and will give good service for longer than any other types.

As far as caring for garden tools is concerned, they should always be cleaned after use and stored in a dry place where they can be hung up out of the way – to prevent damage to both the tools and yourself.

Spades and forks are available with either a 'T' or 'D' shaped top to their handles. Choice is a matter of personal preference. What matters most is that they should be comfortable.

DIBBER, DIBBLE

Any blunt pointed stick can be used as a dibber but it is more comfortable if it has a handle. It is used for making holes in the soil when transplanting seedlings.

FORK

Like the spade, (see below) the fork is available in two sizes (standard and border). It has four tines and is invaluable for breaking up lumpy soil, for lifting garden crops, and for shifting compost.

GARDEN LINE, HOEING LINE

Two sticks with a length of cord tied between them are adequate for marking a straight line for hoeing or making a seed drill, but a ready-made line is easier to use. The line must be long enough to span the width of the plot. First one stick is pushed firmly into the earth, the line is unravelled until it reaches the other side of the plot, it is then pulled taut and the second stick is pushed firmly into the earth.

HOE

The Dutch hoe is used to break up the surface of the soil to dispose of small weeds. It has a 'D' shaped or flat-bladed head and is used while the gardener walks backwards so that he does not tread on the ground he has just hoed.

The draw hoe has a rectangular-shaped blade which is fixed at right angles to the handle. It is used to dispose of larger weeds and is used while walking forwards.

The onion hoe has a short handle and must therefore be used while kneeling if the gardener is not to damage his back. It is very useful for working close to plants.

HOSE AND WATERING-CAN

Both are essential. The watering-can is used for selective watering and for applying liquid fertilizers and weedkillers. It should have a capacity of about 2 gallons (9l) and both a coarse and fine rose are essential. If you intend to use a watering-can for weedkiller, it is safer to have a can solely for that purpose. The hose is used for giving plants a thorough soaking. A hose reel will prevent the hose becoming impossibly tangled during storage.

RAKE

This is used for levelling the soil, working in fertilizers and pulling out weeds. It usually has 12 teeth, but rakes with wide heads and more teeth are available. A fan-shaped wire rake is useful for removing cut grass and leaves but is not an essential tool unless you have a very large expanse of grass or are surrounded by trees.

SECATEURS

A good quality pair of secateurs is essential. They are used for pruning and should be light and easy to use. The blades must be sharp and hard-wearing. When using them ensure that the cutting blade is on top.

Two types of secateurs are available – the anvil

type, which has a single cutting blade which cuts against a broad 'anvil' blade, and the parrot-bill type, which has a scissors action.

SPADE

Two types are available, the standard size, which has a blade measuring 7 × 11 inches (18 × 28cm), and the border size, which has a blade measuring 6 × 9 inches (15 × 23cm). The smaller size is easier to handle and is usually perfectly adequate for the small garden. A modern development which has made digging easier for people with weak backs is the semi-automatic spade, such as the Wolf-Terrex.

TROWEL

This tool is used for planting out and weeding. If you can remember its overall length and the lengths of the blade and the handle it can be used as a rough guide to spacing plants when planting out. Forks are available in the same sizes as trowels and these tools are also available in miniature form for use with houseplants.

WHEELBARROW

The barrow must be sturdy as it will be used for moving all types of material about the garden.

GLOSSARY

Acid soil

Such soils have a pH of less than 6.6. Acidity can check the growth of some plants and few of them will grow in a very acid soil. It can be corrected by the addition of lime, but the overuse of lime can be disastrous, taking up to 15 years to correct. Peat soils are acidic. (*See also* soil testing.)

Alkaline soil

Such soils have a pH of 7 or over. They are chalky soils, that is, they contain carbonate of lime in the form of chalk. It is difficult to correct this type of soil as rain washes more lime into the soil from the underlying chalk. Adding peat, leafmould or grass cuttings will gradually make the soil more acidic, but the process takes a long time. Alkaline soils tend to suffer from a lack of nitrogen and potassium, both of which are essential to healthy plant growth. (*See also* soil testing.)

Annual

A plant which germinates, flowers, produces seeds and dies within a year. Examples are *Alyssum maritimum*, *Centaurea cyanus* (cornflower) and *Malcolmia maritima* (Virginian stock).

Bedding out

A term used for setting out bedding plants, hardy or half-hardy annuals, biennials or perennials which are used for display during the summer. They can usually be bought ready for bedding out from a nursery. Bang the sides of the container to loosen the soil and ease the plants gently out. Separate them carefully so that each plant has a good root with soil attached. Use a trowel to dig a hole which is big enough for the plant's root ball, put in the plant and replace the soil slightly above the level of the original soil. Firm down well and water.

Biennial

A plant which has a life cycle spread over two years. During the first year the plant produces leafy growth; during the second year, it produces flowers and seeds, then dies. Examples are *Dianthus barbatus* (sweet william), *Lunaria annua* (honesty) and *Oenothera trichocalyx* (evening primrose). Some perennials (*qv*) are treated as biennials, for example *Cheiranthus cheiri* (wallflower).

Blanching

This process keeps light away from plants such as celery and chicory, so that the leaves or stems do not form chlorophyll and are less bitter to eat. The plant to be blanched can be earthed up, wrapped in newspaper or covered over with a flower pot.

Bolting

Plants are said to have 'bolted' when they run prematurely to seed. Spinach, lettuce and beetroot are especially prone to this during periods of drought. Plants may also bolt as a result of being grown on soil that is in poor condition.

Broadcast

A way of scattering seeds widely over an irregular patch, rather than sowing them in straight lines or drills. Lawn seed is usually broadcast.

Calyx

The outer green part of a flower, where sepals have joined together to form a bowl, or funnel, out of which the petals grow.

Capsule

A dry fruit which usually contains loose seeds.

Catch crop

A catch crop is a quick-growing vegetable such as lettuce or radish, that is grown between rows of slower growing crops, or is grown in the space from which one main crop has been harvested before a second main crop is planted.

Chlorosis

The loss of green colouring (chlorophyll) in a leaf, which makes it look bleached or yellowish. In extreme cases, the plant may die. It is sometimes caused by a virus, but is usually due to a lack of essential minerals in the soil.

Clamp

A clamp can be used to store root crops such as potatoes or turnips outdoors. Remove any soil adhering to the roots and heap them up in a ridge shape on a bed of straw about 6in (150mm) thick. Cover the heap with a 6in (150mm) layer of straw. Cover the layer of straw with some soil to keep it in place and leave the heap for 24 hours. After 24 hours dig a drainage trench around the heap. Use the soil removed from this trench to cover the straw with a 6in (150mm) layer of soil. Ensure that the soil covering the clamp is smooth by beating it flat with a spade, which will enable the clamp to shed rain. Ventilation holes should be left at 36in (915mm) intervals along the top of the clamp. Pull up tufts of straw through the soil layer to keep the ventilation holes open. Inspect the stored roots that you can see each time you open the clamp and remove any rotten ones. If you discover many rotten ones you must remake the clamp.

Clone

The descendants of a plant that has been propagated solely by vegetative means. Many clones are sterile, but even if the plants set seed, the offspring would not be regarded as part of the clone.

Compost

Either a manure substitute produced from rotting vegetable waste, or a specialized soil mixture used for raising seedlings and potting on houseplants.

Cordon

Usually applied to a specially trained and pruned apple or pear tree which bears fruit on a single main stem. Diagonal cordons can be trained on wires to form a decorative and productive hedge.

Corm

The swollen underground stem of flowers such as crocus or gladiolus. After flowering the old corm withers while a new one grows on top of it.

Corolla

The ring of petals in the flower as a whole.

Corona

The trumpet- or cup-shaped part of the flower which lies between the petals and the stamens.

Cotyledon

The first seedling leaf or leaves to appear at germination. These leaves are frequently different in shape from the plants' adult leaves. (See also Dicotyledon; Monocotyledon.)

Crocks

These are broken pieces of a clay pot which are placed over the drainage hole of a container.

Crop Rotation

In agriculture crop rotation is used to minimize the problem of soil-borne diseases. These are usually specific to one plant or at least to one family of plants and if this plant is not grown on the same ground for some four years there is a good chance that the disease will die out. Unfortunately with rather small areas such as the normal vegetable plot the distances between the various crops are so small, that the disease can more easily travel from one part of the plot to another. What this means is that if you get a really pestilential infection, such as club root in brassicas, growing your brassicas in a different part of the garden will probably not be effective and the only sure method of eliminating this disease will be to avoid growing brassicas for several years. Even so it is usually inadvisable to grow the same sort of vegetable in the same place two years in succession. Many people seem to grow runner beans on the same ground year after year without any deterioration in the crop and many growers once they have made a well-established onion bed, continue to grow onions on it until there are signs of deterioration. Root vegetables may well get split roots if grown on freshly-manured ground, which brassicas will enjoy, so it is advantageous to use your manure where you hope to grow brassicas and grow root crops on this ground the following year. Pulse crops, ie peas and beans, put nitrogen into the soil, so that they can usefully follow the root crops, which can be followed by salad crops or by onions if no separate onion bed has been made.

Crown

The base of an herbaceous perennial, for example rhubarb, from which both shoots and roots grow.

Cultivar

A variant of a plant, either species or hybrid, which has arisen in cultivation and is not known in the wild. Wild variants are known either as varietas, abbreviated var. or forma, abreviated f. The latter are given Latin names, while cultivars (abbreviated cv.) are given names in the language of the country in which they were raised.

Deciduous

A tree or shrub that loses its leaves at the end of each growing season.

Dicotyledon

Plants in this group have two seed leaves (see Cotyledon).

Digging

Digging is essential to the creation of a fertile soil. It should be carried out in autumn so that the soil can be broken down by frost and rain during the winter. The process aerates the soil and manure or compost can be incorporated at the same time.

There are two types of digging; single digging which consists of turning over the top spit of soil and double digging which consists of turning over the soil to a depth of two spits. Double digging should be used on soil that has been neglected for a long time, or which is badly aerated.

Disbud

To remove a certain number of secondary flower buds below the main one, so that this will develop into a bigger flower. Carnations, chrysanthemums, roses and dahlias can all be disbudded.

Disk (Disc) Floret see Floret

Double Flowers

Abnormal flowers in which the stamens and/or pistils have been transformed into petals. Fully double flowers are, therefore, completely sterile, but some double flowers still have a few stamens and often undamaged pistils, from which seed can be raised. In semi-double flowers only a few of the sexual organs have become petaloid. Plants of the daisy family with all ray florets are often termed double, but this is inaccurate; there is no such thing as a single dandelion, for example.

Drawn

A plant which is growing in a group that is too closely packed or in a poorly lighted position is inclined to become long and thin and is often pallid in colour. Such a plant is said to be 'drawn'.

Drill

A straight, shallow U- or V-shaped furrow in which seeds are sown. The easiest way to make a drill is with a rake or hoe.

Espalier

A type of specially trained fruit tree that is grown flat against wires or a wall, with horizontal branches leading out in pairs from the main stem.

Etiolate

A plant is said to be 'etiolated' when lack of light draws it up into lanky, pallid growth. Young seedlings are especially prone to this if they are not given maximum light as they are growing.

Evergreen

A tree or shrub which bears foliage throughout the year.

F_1

A hybrid plant which is the first generation of a controlled crossing of parent plants. Seeds from F_1 hybrids do not come true and so the crossing has to be repeated to reproduce the original hybrid.

F_2

A hybrid plant which is the second generation of a controlled crossing of parent plants.

Fastigiate

This refers to a tall, thin habit of growth, especially in trees, such as the Lombardy poplar or the Irish yew.

Fertility

Some plants and trees will set seed when fertilized with their own pollen. Such plants are called 'self-fertile'. Others, referred to as 'self-sterile', need cross-pollinating with different varieties in order to produce fruit and seed.

Floret

An individual flower which forms part of a large flowerhead or inflorescence. Disk florets are tubular, petalless florets found in many plants of the daisy family. Sometimes they are surrounded by the more conspicuous ray florets, as in the common daisy. Groundsel is composed entirely of disk florets, while some chrysanthemums are composed entirely of ray florets.

Forcing

Applied to plants which are encouraged to come into growth before their natural time. Hyacinths and some narcissus are forced by keeping in darkness the pots in which they are planted. Tall bell-shaped earthenware pots are used to force rhubarb into early growth.

Friable

A soil which is crumbly and therefore can be easily worked.

Fungicide

A chemical used for killing fungal diseases.

Genus

A division of a plant family which is based on the plant's botanical characteristics. A plant's genus is indicated by its first botanical name. For example, cornflower belongs to the genus Centaurea. The plural form of genus is genera.

Germination

The first stage in the development of a plant from a seed.

Ground Cover

Plants referred to as 'ground cover plants' are used to cover the soil, usually under trees or between shrubs. Besides bringing colour to the planting scheme they provide a dense weedproof cover. *Hypericum calycinum* (St John's wort) is an excellent ground cover plant.

Growing medium see Compost

Half-hardy

This refers to plants from tropical and sub-tropical regions which require protection during the winter when grown in temperate climates. It may also refer to certain shrubs and herbaceous perennials which will survive average – but not severe – winters out of doors if grown in sheltered positions or in regions which have a mild climate. (*See also* Hardy.)

Hardening Off

This is the method adopted to accustom plants to a cooler environment than the one in which they germinated. For example, plants that are germinated in a greenhouse are hardened off by being placed in a cold frame during late spring. The lights of the frame are raised further each day to allow more air in until they are completely removed. The plants can then be transferred to their permanent position. (*See also* Frame.)

Hardy

This refers to plants which are capable of surviving, indeed thriving, under the natural environment given to them. (*See also* Half-hardy.)

Heel-in

To make a rough trench in which plants can be laid and their roots covered with soil until the permanent planting place is ready.

Herbaceous

A plant which does not form a woody stem, remaining soft and green throughout its life. The term is used to refer to annuals, biennials and perennials. Such plants die down to the ground each winter.

Herbicides

A chemical used for killing weeds.

Humus

Decayed organic material: animal manure, compost, leaves, etc. are all sources of humus which is a vital element in a fertile soil.

Hybrid

A new plant which is the offspring of two different species. This is usually indicated by an × between the botanical names of the parent plants. For example; *Viola* × *wittrockiana* (pansy). (*See also* F_1; F_2.)

Inorganic

A chemical compound or fertilizer which does not contain carbon.

Insecticides

A chemical compound that destroys garden pests.

Lime

Lime is useful for increasing the fertility of soil generally and improving the texture of clay soil as it makes the tiny clay particles clump together.

Hydrated lime should be applied at a rate of 3 oz to the square yard (75g to the square metre). If ground limestone is used it should be applied at the rate of 6 oz to the square yard (150g to the square metre). Lime should be applied during the late autumn and winter, ie between October and February. It must never be applied at the same time as other fertilizers or manure as it reacts chemically with them or prevents them from acting by making them less soluble. NOTE: Lime should never be given to ericaceous plants such as heathers, azaleas or rhododendrons.

Manures

There are two types, green manure and organic manure, both of which add humus to the soil.

GREEN MANURE

This refers to any fast-growing crop which is planted specifically to be dug into the soil. Legumes, such as French beans or peas, are especially valuable for this purpose as they fix nitrogen in the soil and this is vital for plant development. Italian rye grass can also be used as a green manure. Any plant used for this purpose must be dug in as soon as flowering starts.

ORGANIC MANURE

These are animal manures and include most of the nutrients which are essential to healthy plant growth. Farmyard and stable manures are perhaps the best known. Manure from poultry farms is not suitable for use in small town gardens as it tends to develop an offensive smell as it breaks down. Vegetable wastes are also organic manures and include spent hops and mushroom compost, leaf-mould and, in coastal areas, seaweed. All of this material will have to be composted before use. Also under the heading of organic manure come the processed manures such as bonemeal and dried blood which are very concentrated and are not used to treat the whole garden. As they are in powder form they add no humus to the soil. They can, however, be added to the soil when it is dug over by being sprinkled into the trench.

Monocarpic

Such plants survive for many years, but die after flowering.

Monocotyledon

Plants in this group have one seed leaf (see Cotyledon).

Mulch

A soft layer of material such as compost, other plant material or manure which is placed on top of the soil to conserve the moisture in the soil and to prevent the growth of weeds. Non-organic materials such as black polythene and stones can also be used as a mulch.

Nutrients

Substances that provide the plant with nourishment including nitrogen, phosphorus, iron, potassium and magnesium. A soil deficient in these elements will produce poor plants. The three nutrients most essential to the health of the plant are nitrogen, potassium and phosphorus.

Organic

Refers to substances which are derived from the decay of living organisms and which therefore contain carbon.

Panicle

A large flower cluster made up of many individual flowers, each with its own stem. The flowers of buddleia and lilac are borne in panicles.

Perennial

A plant which lives for more than two years and produces flowers and seeds annually throughout its lifetime. Examples are *Aster novi-belgii* (Michaelmas daisy), *Campanula* spp (bellflower) and *Gentiana acaulis* (trumpet gentian).

Pinching out

To nip off, usually with finger and thumb, the growing point of a plant to encourage it to make more bushy growth.

Pollard

A tree cut back hard to the main stem so that new growths bush out in a mop-head arrangement. Willows are often treated in this way.

Potting On

The transference of a pot plant to a pot of a larger size than the one in which it is currently growing. It is time to pot on when the plant's roots begin to grow through the drainage hole.

This is done by watering the plant, removing it from the old pot together with the compost in which it is growing, and placing the plant and compost in the new pot which is then filled with compost to just above the original compost level. Firm down the compost and water the plant again. (*See also* Pots.)

Pricking Out

The transference of seedlings from the pots or boxes in which they germinated to larger pots or boxes in which they have more space to grow on before being planted out in their final position.

Ray Floret see Floret

Rhizome

A prostrate, fleshy stem with leaves above and roots below. Bearded irises grow from rhizomes.

Rootstock

A term for the tree on which another is grafted. Special dwarfing rootstocks have been developed so that fruit trees, especially, can be grown in a more confined space.

Runner

A rooting stem which will form a new plant where it touches the soil. Blackberry and strawberry plants can both be propagated by means of runners.

Seed-bed

A seed-bed is made during the spring on soil that was dug and manured during the previous autumn. First fork over the soil. When it is dry firm it down and rake it lightly. Make a shallow drill using the edge of a hoe. Make sure that the drill is straight by using a garden line. Sow the seeds spreading them thinly along the drill. Then gently draw the soil back to cover the seeds using the hoe. Firm down the earth without disturbing the seeds underneath. Label the row before removing the garden line.

Seed Chipping

The process of filing or cutting the outer skin of a very hard seed, eg sweet pea, in order to allow moisture to enter. This process hastens germination.

Seedling

A young plant after germination which has a single unbranched stem. This term is also sometimes applied to an older plant which has been raised from seed.

Shrub

A perennial plant which is smaller than a tree. It has branches and woody stems with little or no trunk.

Soil Testing

You can make a rough estimate of the type of soil in your garden by carrying out the following test. Take a handful of soil and put it in a jam jar which is half full of water. Shake the soil and water together and leave the jar to stand for an hour or two. Sand and gravel will sink to the bottom, loam and clay will be suspended in the middle and humus will be floating on top. The proportions of the various materials will give you some idea of the type of soil you have. You can also tell a great deal about your soil by observing what happens when it rains. If the water stays on the surface for a long time it is likely that you have a clay soil. On the other hand, if the rain drains away quickly you are likely to have a sandy soil.

Soil tends to fall into one of the following groups, although you may find that your garden contains patches of different types of soil.

CLAY SOIL

A dense heavy soil which tends to be wet, and is often water-logged during the winter. When you pick up a handful and roll it between your fingers it forms a solid ball. The tiny particles are tightly packed and plants can suffer badly during the summer as their roots are unable to penetrate the topsoil to obtain water from the subsoil. This type of soil can be improved by the addition of organic matter such as peat, leaves and garden compost. Lime can also be added (*see* Lime). In extreme cases land drains may have to be laid to carry off excess water.

LOAMY SOIL

A balanced blend of sand, clay and humus. When it is rolled in your hand it forms small crumbs. This is the ideal garden soil. The clay content prevents it drying out, the sand content ensures an open texture, and humus ensures a good supply of plant nutrients. Loams can be subdivided into sandy loams, which contain a high proportion of sand; heavy loams, which contain a high proportion of clay; and marls, which contain a high proportion of chalk.

SANDY SOIL

A type of soil found mainly in coastal areas. When you pick up a handful and run it between your fingers it trickles through them. It drains very rapidly and as a result nutrients are leached out of the soil. In order to prevent this happening bulky organic material such as farmyard manure, garden compost, or grass clippings should be added to the soil.

Soils can also be divided according to their acid or alkaline content. This is discovered by measuring their potential hydrogen (pH). Seedsmen can usually supply small kits for testing the pH of garden soil. These kits contain small bottles of chemicals which are mixed with samples of soil following the instructions given with the kit and matched to a colour chart which gives the pH. Alkaline soils have a pH of 7 and above, neutral soils have a pH of 6.6–7; and acidic soils have a pH of less than 6.6. Soils are described as very acid when their pH is 4.5 or less. Most plants grow best in soils which are slightly acidic or neutral, that is soils with a pH of 6.5–7.

Sowing

Fill a box or pot with compost, level it off and firm it down. Sow the seeds as thinly as possible; fine seed can be sprinkled from a piece of folded paper; sow large seeds individually in holes made with a pencil or a dibber.

Species

A sub-division of a genus, abbreviated to sp in the singular and spp in the plural. (*See also* Genus.)

Standard

A tree or shrub which has a tall, bare stem several feet long before the first branches. Standard fruit trees usually have a 6-foot (1.8m) trunk, standard roses rather less.

Stopping

The removal of the growing tip in order to

encourage the plant to branch out and become more bushy or to control the size or blooming of the flowers.

Stratification

A way of hastening the germination of hard-coated seeds by exposing them to frost. The seeds should be placed in layers in boxes of sand and left covered with wire netting in an exposed position outside. Peach stones respond well to this treatment as do the seeds of the Himalayan blue poppy (*Meconopsis betonicifolia*).

Subsoil

The soil below the fertile top layer.

Succulent

Any plant which has thick, fleshy leaves or stems in which water can be stored. These plants are adapted to survive in arid conditions.

Sucker

A shoot which comes up from below ground level, usually from the roots of a tree or shrub. Suckers are a particular problem on grafted plants and must be removed immediately, as they may swamp the plant which is grafted onto the rootstock.

Taproot

A thick fleshy root that descends for a considerable distance into the soil. Other roots branch off from it. Taproots can become very fleshy as with carrot and parsnip.

Tendril

A slender clinging stemlike organ which is sensitive enough to twine around anything that it touches.

Tilth

The fine crumbly surface layer of the soil.

Topsoil

The fertile top layer of the soil.

Transplanting

The process of moving young plants from one place to another to give them more space in which to develop. When plants are moved it is essential to ensure that they are firmly planted in their new position. Test this by pulling gently on a leaf; if the whole plant moves it is not planted firmly enough.

Tuber

A swollen underground root or stem used by the plant to store food. Potatoes are tubers. Dahlias and begonias are tuberous plants.

Variegated

A leaf which is marked by regular or irregular stripes in a colour different from that of the leaf or by patches of another colour, such as white, cream or yellow. Such plants are usually grown for their foliage as the flowers tend to be insignificant.

Variety

A group of plants which vary from the species type. It may also refer to a cultivar or a member of a hybrid group. (*See also* Cultivar; Hybrid.)

Vegetative Propagation

This refers to methods of propagation other than by seeds, for example by cuttings, layering, root division or grafting.

ACKNOWLEDGEMENTS

The authors and publishers are grateful to Sheila Ladner for her help in compiling the book and would also like to thank the following for supplying colour illustrations and artwork:

Ardea London 78 left, 111, 195 above/Ian Beames 43 above, left, 73, 74 above, 75 left/Eric Lindgren 74 below/John Mason 75 below, 79 above, 233 above/P. Morris 75 right/Wardene Weisser 74 centre; Pat Brindley 79 below, 177; Linda Burgess 8/9, 10, 15, 19, 28, 53 (Convolvulus, Dimorphotheca, Linum, Oenothera), 54 left, right, 62, 63 above, below, 65, 78, 81, 82 right, 83, 86, 90, 91, 92, 98, 100 above, below, 101, 108, 123, 138 left, 139 left, 193, 199 left, 207; Mike Burgess 82 below, 151 below; Bruce Coleman/Eric Crichton 180 above left/Colin Molyneux 41; Jenny de Gex 154; Peter Dodd 211 above, 212 below, 216, 217, 218; Brian Furner 18 below; Susan Griggs/Michael Boys 134 left/Julian Nieman 11; Robert Harding/British Library Department of Oriental Manuscripts 16; Arthur Hellyer 53 (Dianthus), 94; The Image Bank 103; Alain le Garsmeur 188/9, 204; Macdonald BPCC Archive/Rex Bamber 235; Tania Midgley 138 right; Natural History Photographic Agency 226; Harry Smith Collection 70 below, 71, 195 below, 197, 205, 231, 232 above, below, 233 below; Werner Strauli 82 above left; Pamla Toler 1, 14, 18 above, 23, 24, 26, 31, 51, 52, 53 (Limnanthes, Verbascum), 57, 59 above left, centre left, below left, above right, below right, 60 above, below, 61, 64 left, right, 66 above, below 68, 69, 70 above, 76, 77, 78 right, 80, 89, 97, 99, 102, 107, 109, 110, 112, 113, 114 above, below, 115, 116, 117, 118 above, below, 147 above, below, 149, 150 above, 151 above, 152 above, 120, 121 above, below, 122 above, below, 125, 126, 127 left, right, 129, 130 left, right, 131, 134 right, 139 right, 140, 141, 142, 143, 144, 145, 157, 159 left, 160, 161, 162 right, 163, 166 above, 174, 175, 176, 179 left, right, 180 below left, above right, below right, 183, 185 right, 187, 190, 191, 196, 201 left, right, 215, 224, 227, 229; Brian Tree 43 right, 44, 45 Vision International/Angelo Hornak 20/Tania Midgley 21, 132, 184/John Sims 104, 105, 106 left, right; Michael Warren 13, 93, 148 above, below, 153, 159 right, 162 left, 165, 166 left, right, 170, 178, 185 left, 199 right, 203 above, below left, 208, 211 left, below right, 212 above left, above right, 220/J. Matthews 146; Victor Watts 157; George Wright 3, 26/7, 29, 38, 119, 150 below, 151 centre, below, 152 centre, 128, 198, 203 below right, 234.

All line illustrations by Will Giles except for: Garden Studio/Rachel Birkett 39 above, 87/Patrick Cox 230/Josephine Martin 88; John Regnall 206.

INDEX